D0690056

FOR THE MOMENTS **WORTH CELEBRATING**

Did someone say *party*? Let us help! This year's ***Taste of Home Holiday & Celebrations*** cookbook is a collection of more than 250 recipes and 22 events designed to bring the people you love together. From family birthdays and slumber parties to formal holiday dinners and kicked-back potlucks, you'll find all the entertaining ideas you need to make the most of those special moments. Let never-before-published recipes and original craft ideas inspire you to try something new for your next special occasion. Your friends and family will not only thank you, they'll see—and taste—just how much you care.

WOULD YOU LIKE TO SEE ONE OF YOUR FAMILY RECIPES FEATURED IN A *TASTE OF HOME* COLLECTION?

Visit **tasteofhome.com/submit** to share your story and recipes.

ON THE **COVER**

ON THE FRONT COVER Creamy Vanilla-Chocolate Cheesecake (p. 15).

ON THE BACK COVER Creamy Turkey Gravy (p. 98), Herbed Corn Saute (p. 98), Spinach Gorgonzola Salad (p. 98), Cheddar-Broccoli Casserole (p. 101), Garden Herb Drop Biscuits (p. 101), Sage-Roasted Turkey & Corn Bread Stuffing (p. 100), Key-Lime Butter Cookies (p. 70), Star-Bright Cookies (p. 71), Sausage & Rice Stuffed Pumpkins (p. 104), Amaretto Cake with Buttercream Frosting (p. 224).

PAGE 58

PAGE 204

PAGE 175

PAGE 236

PAGE 235

PAGE 182

Taste of Home Holiday & Celebrations

EDITORIAL
Editor-in-Chief **Catherine Cassidy**

Creative Director **Howard Greenberg**
Editorial Operations Director **Kerri Balliet**

Managing Editor/Print & Digital Books **Mark Hagen**
Associate Creative Director **Edwin Robles Jr.**

Editor **Heather Ray**
Associate Editor **Molly Jasinski**
Art Director **Raeann Sundholm**
Contributing Art Director **Maggie Conners**
Associate Craft Editor **Vanessa Tsumura**
Layout Designer **Catherine Fletcher**
Contributing Layout Designer **Courtney Lovetere**
Editorial Production Manager **Dena Ahlers**
Copy Chief **Deb Warlaumont Mulvey**
Copy Editor **Mary C. Hanson**

Chief Food Editor **Karen Berner**
Food Editors **James Schend; Peggy Woodward, RD**
Associate Food Editor **Krista Lanphier**
Recipe Editors **Mary King; Annie Rundle; Jenni Sharp, RD; Irene Yeh**
Content Operations Manager **Colleen King**
Content Operations Assistant **Shannon Stroud**
Executive Assistant **Marie Brannon**

Test Kitchen & Food Styling Manager **Sarah Thompson**
Test Cooks **Nicholas Iverson (Lead), Matthew Hass, Lauren Knoelke**
Food Stylists **Kathryn Conrad (Senior), Shannon Roum, Leah Rekau**
Prep Cooks **Megumi Garcia, Melissa Hansen, Bethany Van Jacobson, Sara Wirtz**

Photography Director **Stephanie Marchese**
Photographers **Dan Roberts, Jim Wieland**
Photographer/Set Stylist **Grace Natoli Sheldon**
Set Stylists **Stacey Genaw, Melissa Haberman, Dee Dee Jacq**
Creative Contributors **Mark Derse (Photographer); Diane Armstrong, Sue Draheim (Food Stylists)**

Editorial Business Manager **Kristy Martin**

BUSINESS
Vice President, Chief Sales Officer **Mark S. Josephson**
Vice President, Business Development & Marketing **Alain Begun**
General Manager, Taste of Home Cooking School **Erin Puariea**
Vice President, Digital Experience & E-Commerce **Jennifer Smith**
Vice President, Marketing Operations **Dave Fiegel**

THE READER'S DIGEST ASSOCIATION, INC.
President and Chief Executive Officer **Bonnie Kintzer**

Vice President, Chief Operating Officer, North America **Howard Halligan**
Vice President, Enthusiast Brands, Books & Retail **Harold Clarke**
Vice President, North American Operations **Philippe Cloutier**
Vice President, Chief Marketing Officer **Leslie Doty**
Vice President, North American Human Resources **Phyllis E. Gebhardt, SPHR**
Vice President, Consumer Marketing Planning **Jim Woods**

FRONT COVER PHOTOGRAPHY
Photographer **Jim Wieland**
Set Stylist **Dee Dee Jacq**
Food Stylist **Kathryn Conrad**

1610 N. 2nd St., Suite 102, Milwaukee WI 53212-3906

International Standard Book Number: 978-1-61765-313-1
Library of Congress Control Number: 1535-2781
Component Number: 118000036H00

For other Taste of Home books and products, visit us at **tasteofhome.com.**

Printed in USA.
1 3 5 7 9 10 8 6 4 2

TABLE OF **CONTENTS**

tis*the*season

giving*thanks*

easter*gatherings*

special*celebrations*

tis*the*season

When you think of your best-loved Christmas traditions, what comes to mind? Trimming the tree? Baking cookies with friends? Hosting a spectacular party? From formal dinners to kicked-back potlucks, holiday get-togethers are meant to be savored. This section is filled with inspiring menus, ideas for entertaining and delicious gift-worthy recipes—the kind that loved ones will always remember.

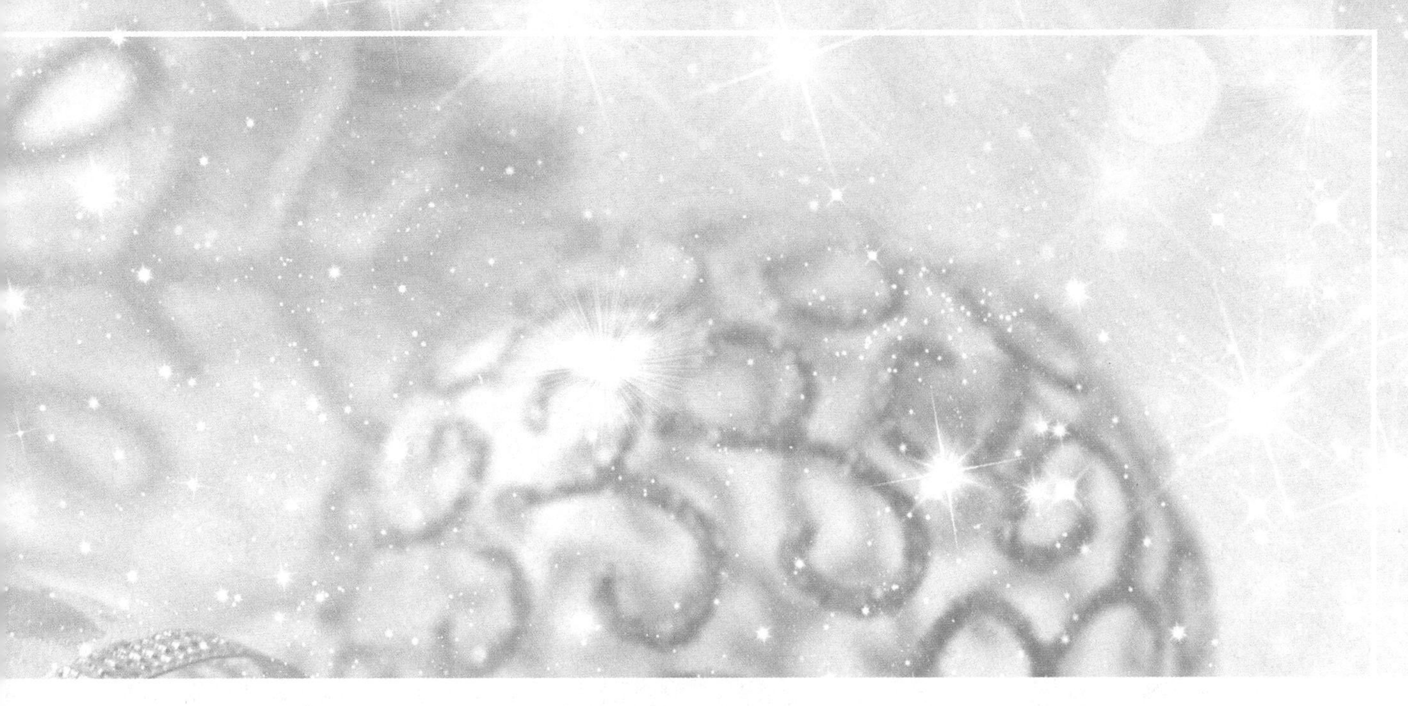

The dinnerware you have on display in the china cabinet is ready for showtime, the little black dress in the back of your closet is begging to be worn, and the bottle of wine you've been saving for a special occasion is calling your name. It's time for a formal affair.

On this evening, you want a menu that's as rich and inviting as it is upscale and elegant. You want a dessert that's worthy of a cover and a creamy cocktail that nods to your subtle black-and-white theme.

Heirloom crystal and accents of ruby linens add to the holiday flavor while suggesting that the Christmas spirit is near. Let the celebration begin!

Apple Fennel Salad (p. 13)
Simple Creamed Spinach (p. 14)
Garlic Mashed Cauliflower (p. 11)
Beef Tenderloin with Mushroom-Wine Sauce (p. 13)

A BLACK-TIE **AFFAIR**

tistheseason | BLACK-TIE MENU TIMELINE

Many of the dishes in this menu can be prepared in advance, while others are best to make the day of. Use this timeline as your guide to get a head start on the big day.

A FEW WEEKS BEFORE

- Prepare the Three-Cheese Souffles, but do not bake. Wrap souffles with foil and freeze.
- Prepare the Sweet Potato Tortellini with Hazelnut Sauce, but do not cook. Flash freeze the tortellini and store in a freezer bag according to directions on p. 10.

ONE DAY BEFORE

- Prepare, cover and store the White Chocolate Mousse Cups in the refrigerator overnight.
- Prepare, cover and store Creamy Vanilla–Chocolate Cheesecake in the refrigerator overnight. (Garnish just before serving.)
- Prepare the soup. After processing in batches (do not add cream), cool, cover and store in the refrigerator overnight.
- Set the table.

DAY OF

- 2 hours before dinnertime, make Beef Tenderloin with Mushroom-Wine Sauce.
- Prepare the salad, but wait until serving time to toss with dressing.
- While the tenderloin is in the oven, cook the tortellini and prepare the brown butter sauce.
- When the tenderloin is done, lower oven temperature to 325° and bake the frozen souffles according to freezer directions on p. 9.
- While the souffles are baking, prepare the Simple Creamed Spinach and Garlic Mashed Cauliflower.
- Reheat soup, gently stir in cream and heat through.
- The souffles should be served soon after they're done, so plan to have your soup and salad while they finish baking.

Three-Cheese Souffles

No matter when I've made these souffles, they have always been a success. Although I've never seen the centers start to fall, it's best to plan on serving them hot from the oven.

—JEAN FERENCE SHERWOOD PARK, AB

PREP: 40 MIN. + COOLING
BAKE: 40 MIN.
MAKES: 8 SERVINGS

⅓ cup butter, cubed
⅓ cup all-purpose flour
2 cups whole milk
1 teaspoon Dijon mustard
¼ teaspoon salt
Dash hot pepper sauce
1½ cups (6 ounces) shredded Swiss cheese
1 cup (4 ounces) shredded cheddar cheese
¼ cup shredded Parmesan cheese
6 eggs
½ teaspoon cream of tartar

1. In a small saucepan, melt butter over medium heat. Stir in flour until smooth; cook for 1 minute. Gradually whisk in milk, mustard, salt and pepper sauce. Bring to a boil, stirring constantly; cook and stir 1-2 minutes or until thickened. Reduce heat to medium-low; stir in cheeses until melted. Transfer to a large bowl.

2. Separate eggs. Place egg whites in a medium bowl; stand at room temperature for 30 minutes. Meanwhile, in a small bowl, beat egg yolks until thick and lemon-colored, about 4 minutes. Stir in ⅓ cup hot cheese mixture; return all to remaining cheese mixture, stirring constantly. Cool completely, about 30 minutes.

3. Preheat oven to 325°. Place eight ungreased 8-oz. ramekins in a baking pan.

4. With clean beaters, beat egg whites with cream of tartar on high speed until stiff but not dry. With a rubber spatula, gently stir a fourth of the egg whites into cheese mixture. Fold in remaining whites.

5. Transfer to prepared ramekins. Add 1 in. of hot water to baking pan. Bake 40-45 minutes or until tops are golden brown. Serve immediately.

NOTE *Souffles can be made ahead and frozen. Cover each dish or cup with foil and freeze. To bake, remove foil and place frozen souffles in a shallow pan; add warm water to a depth of 1 in. Bake at 325° for 60-65 minutes or until tops are golden brown.*

Sweet Potato Tortellini with Hazelnut Sauce

Using wonton wrappers instead of fresh pasta dough makes homemade tortellini easy to prepare. For more formal dinners, this makes an impressive vegetarian entree.
—CHARLENE CHAMBERS ORMOND BEACH, FL

PREP: 1 HOUR • **COOK:** 10 MIN./BATCH • **MAKES:** 8 SERVINGS

- **3 large sweet potatoes, peeled and cubed**
- **¼ cup olive oil, divided**
- **1½ teaspoons herbes de Provence**
- **¾ teaspoon salt, divided**
- **½ teaspoon pepper, divided**
- **2 shallots, chopped**
- **2 garlic cloves, minced**
- **1 cup whole-milk ricotta cheese**
- **1 tablespoon hazelnut liqueur**
- **¼ teaspoon ground nutmeg**
- **72 wonton wrappers**
- **3 quarts water**
- **¾ cup unsalted butter, cubed**
- **3 tablespoons minced fresh sage**
- **½ cup dried cherries, chopped**
- **¼ cup chopped hazelnuts, toasted**
- **1 cup shaved Asiago cheese**

1. Preheat oven to 400°. Place sweet potatoes on a greased 15x10x1-in. baking pan; toss with 2 tablespoons oil, herbes de Provence, 1/2 teaspoon salt and 1/4 teaspoon pepper. Roast 25-30 minutes or until tender, stirring once. Cool slightly.

2. In a small skillet, heat remaining oil over medium-high heat. Add shallots and garlic; cook and stir until tender. Transfer to a food processor. Add sweet potatoes, ricotta cheese, liqueur, nutmeg and the remaining salt and pepper; process until blended.

3. Place 1 tablespoon filling in center of each wonton wrapper. (Cover remaining wrappers with a damp paper towel until ready to use.) Moisten wrapper edges with water. Fold one corner diagonally over filling to form a triangle; press edges to seal. Bring opposite corners up over filling; moisten with water and press to attach.

4. In a Dutch oven, bring water to a boil. Reduce heat to a gentle boil. Cook tortellini in batches 30-60 seconds or until they float. Remove with a slotted spoon; keep warm.

5. In a small heavy saucepan, melt butter over medium heat. Add sage; heat 5-7 minutes or until butter is golden brown, stirring constantly. Remove from heat; stir in cherries and hazelnuts. Serve with tortellini. Top with cheese.

TO MAKE AHEAD *The sweet potato puree can be made and refrigerated the day before the wontons are filled. Freeze option: Freeze uncooked tortellini on waxed paper-lined baking sheets until firm. Transfer to resealable plastic freezer bags; return to freezer. To use, cook tortellini as directed, increasing time to 1½ to 2 minutes or until they float. Serve as directed.*

NOTE *Look for herbes de Provence in the spice aisle.*

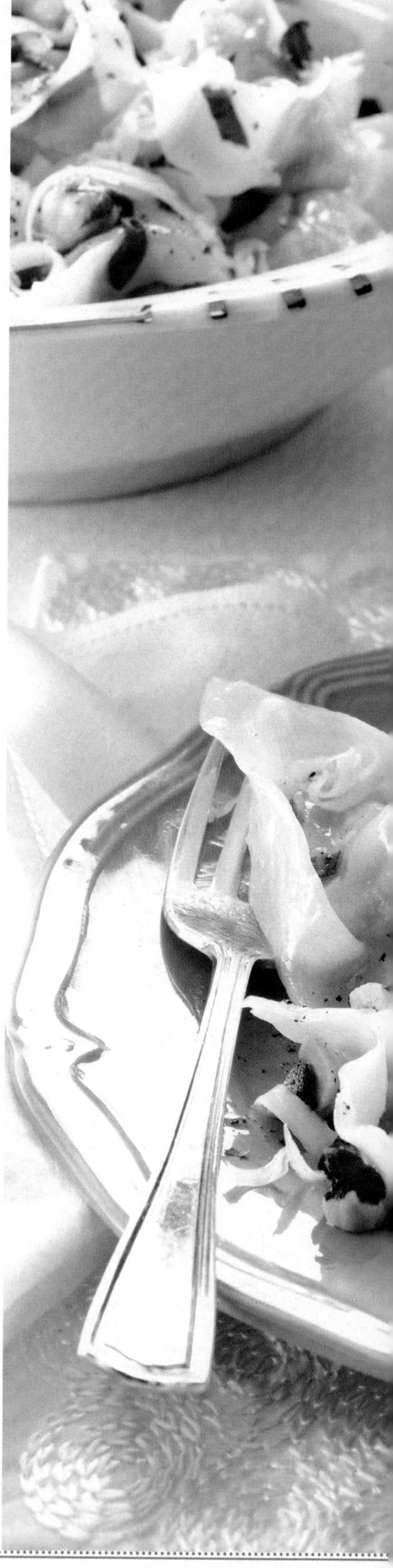

Garlic Mashed Cauliflower

PICTURED ON PAGE 7

I've always enjoyed mashed cauliflower at my favorite restaurant. So I came up with this easy recipe we can make at home. Because it only takes a few minutes to prepare, you can make two batches for larger dinner parties.
—JEAN KEISER WEST CHESTER, PA

START TO FINISH: 25 MIN.
MAKES: 4 SERVINGS

- **5 cups fresh cauliflowerets**
- **1 garlic clove, minced**
- **3 tablespoons fat-free milk**
- **3 tablespoons reduced-fat mayonnaise**
- **½ teaspoon salt**
- **⅛ teaspoon white pepper**
- **Coarsely ground pepper and minced fresh chives, optional**

1. Place 1 in. of water in a large saucepan; add cauliflower and garlic. Bring to a boil. Reduce heat; simmer, covered, 5-10 minutes or until tender, stirring occasionally. Drain.

2. In a bowl, combine milk, mayonnaise, salt and pepper. Add cauliflower; beat until blended and creamy. If desired, shape into rounds by pressing ½-cup portions into a 2-in. biscuit cutter and sprinkle with black pepper and chives.

Roasted Parsnip and Pear Soup

I like to add a finishing touch to this lovely winter soup by sauteeing sliced pears in butter and brown sugar and floating a couple slices in each bowl.
—SARA PETRIE GRASSIE, ON

PREP: 1¼ HOURS • **COOK:** 45 MIN.
MAKES: 8 SERVINGS (2¼ QUARTS)

- **1½ pounds parsnips, peeled and coarsely chopped (about 4 cups)**
- **2 tablespoons olive oil**
- **¾ teaspoon ground nutmeg**
- **¼ teaspoon salt**
- **⅛ teaspoon pepper**
- **3 medium pears, peeled and chopped**
- **¼ cup butter, cubed**
- **3 medium leeks (white portion only), thinly sliced**
- **2 celery ribs, chopped**
- **3 shallots, chopped**
- **6 cups chicken broth**
- **¼ cup maple syrup**
- **1 bay leaf**
- **1 teaspoon minced fresh thyme**
- **½ cup heavy whipping cream**

TOPPING

- **2 tablespoons butter**
- **2 medium pears, thinly sliced**
- **2 teaspoons brown sugar**
- **⅛ teaspoon ground cumin**
- **⅛ teaspoon ground coriander**

1. Preheat oven to 425°. Place parsnips in a greased 15x10x1-in. baking pan; toss with oil, nutmeg, salt and pepper. Roast for 25 minutes. Stir in pears; roast 15-20 minutes longer or until tender, stirring occasionally.

2. In a Dutch oven, heat butter over medium-high heat. Add leeks, celery and shallots; cook and stir 4-6 minutes or until tender. Stir in parsnip mixture, broth, maple syrup, bay leaf and thyme. Bring to a boil. Reduce heat; simmer, uncovered, for 30 minutes. Remove from heat; cool slightly.

3. For topping, in a large skillet, heat butter over medium-high heat. Add remaining ingredients; cook and stir 2-4 minutes or until pears are crisp-tender.

4. Remove bay leaf from soup. Process soup in batches in a blender until smooth; return to pan. Stir in cream; heat through. Top servings with sliced pears.

Beef Tenderloin with Mushroom-Wine Sauce

PICTURED ON PAGE 7

This succulent roast takes a little more time to prepare than a usual weeknight meal, but it's worth it for a special occasion. It's one of my top dinner requests from friends.

—**TONYA BURKHARD** DAVIS, IL

PREP: 15 MIN. • **BAKE:** 50 MIN. + STANDING • **MAKES:** 12 SERVINGS (ABOUT 3½ CUPS SAUCE)

- **2 teaspoons dried thyme**
- **2 teaspoons seasoned salt**
- **1 beef tenderloin roast (5 pounds)**
- **9 bacon strips, finely chopped**
- **3 cups sliced fresh mushrooms**
- **4 tablespoons butter, divided**
- **4 medium onions, chopped (about 3 cups)**
- **9 garlic cloves, minced**
- **⅓ cup tomato paste**
- **6 cups beef stock**
- **2¼ cups dry red wine**
- **3 tablespoons all-purpose flour**
- **¼ teaspoon salt**
- **¼ teaspoon pepper**

1. Preheat oven to 425°. Rub thyme and seasoned salt onto all sides of roast. Place tenderloin on a rack in a shallow roasting pan. Roast 50-60 minutes or until meat reaches desired doneness (for medium-rare, a thermometer should read 145°; medium, 160°; well-done, 170°).

2. Meanwhile, in a Dutch oven, cook bacon over medium heat until crisp, stirring occasionally. Remove with a slotted spoon; drain on paper towels. Discard the drippings, reserving 2 tablespoons in pan. Add mushrooms to drippings; cook and stir 4-5 minutes or until tender. Remove from pan.

3. Place 1 tablespoon butter in pan. Add onions; cook and stir over medium heat 6-8 minutes or until tender. Stir in garlic; cook 1 minute longer. Add tomato paste, stock and wine, stirring to loosen browned bits from pan. Bring to a boil; cook 20-25 minutes or until liquid is reduced almost by half.

4. In a microwave, melt the remaining butter. Mix flour with butter until smooth; gradually whisk into sauce. Return to a boil, stirring constantly; cook and stir 1-2 minutes or until thickened. Stir in bacon, mushrooms, salt and pepper; heat through.

5. Remove roast from oven; tent with foil. Let stand 15 minutes before slicing. Serve with sauce.

Apple Fennel Salad

PICTURED ON PAGE 6

My wife has never been a big fan of fennel, but it's always been a favorite of mine. I was able to successfully sneak it into this salad, and ever since, she has given me the green light on dishes with fennel. This particular recipe is especially delicious with little pieces of vanilla bean added to the balsamic vinegar.

—**JASON PURKEY** OCEAN CITY, MD

START TO FINISH: 25 MIN. • **MAKES:** 8 SERVINGS

- **½ cup balsamic vinegar**
- **8 cups fresh arugula or baby spinach**
- **1 large fennel bulb, thinly sliced**
- **1 large tart apple, julienned**
- **3 tablespoons lemon juice**
- **3 tablespoons olive oil**
- **1 teaspoon coarsely ground pepper**
- **½ teaspoon salt**
- **4 ounces crumbled goat cheese**
- **1 cup glazed walnuts**

1. In a small bowl, bring vinegar to a boil; cook 4-5 minutes or until thickened to a glaze consistency. Cool slightly.

2. In a large bowl, combine arugula, fennel and apple. In a small bowl, whisk lemon juice, oil, pepper and salt until blended. Pour over salad and toss to coat. Add cheese and walnuts.

3. Drizzle eight plates with balsamic glaze. Top with salad.

Simple Creamed Spinach

PICTURED ON PAGE 7

Whipping cream and a touch of nutmeg and cayenne add richness and spice to this classic side dish. Make it your easy go-to for special-occasion dinner parties.

—KRISTIN REYNOLDS VAN BUREN, AR

START TO FINISH: 25 MIN. • **MAKES:** 4 SERVINGS

- **1 package (10 ounces) frozen chopped spinach**
- **2 tablespoons butter**
- **2 teaspoons all-purpose flour**
- **¾ cup heavy whipping cream**
- **¼ teaspoon salt**
- **⅛ teaspoon pepper**
- **Dash each ground nutmeg and cayenne pepper**

1. Cook spinach according to package directions; drain and squeeze dry.

2. Meanwhile, in a small saucepan, melt butter. Stir in flour until smooth; gradually add cream. Bring the mixture to a boil; cook and stir 2 minutes or until thickened.

3. Add seasonings and spinach; heat through, stirring occasionally. Serve warm.

White Chocolate Mousse Cups

PICTURED AT RIGHT

If you want to pull out all the stops for dessert, a batch of these stunning black-and-white mousse cups will have all your guests talking. For an extra-special touch, drizzle the dessert plates with warmed raspberry jam and garnish with fresh mint.

—MICHELE FIELD SYKESVILLE, MD

PREP: 1 HOUR + CHILLING • **MAKES:** 6 SERVINGS

- **6 ounces semisweet chocolate, chopped**
- **1 tablespoon shortening**
- **1½ cups heavy whipping cream, divided**
- **6 ounces white baking chocolate. chopped**
- **⅓ cup confectioners' sugar**
- **2 teaspoons vanilla extract**
- **Seedless raspberry jam, optional**
- **Fresh raspberries and mint, optional**

1. In a microwave, melt semisweet chocolate and shortening; stir until smooth. Using a narrow pastry brush, evenly coat the inside of six paper or foil muffin cup liners with chocolate. Refrigerate until firm, about 25 minutes. Repeat once to add a second coat.

2. For mousse, in a small saucepan, combine ½ cup cream and white baking chocolate; cook and stir over low heat until melted. Cool completely.

3. Carefully remove chocolate cups from liners. In a small bowl, beat remaining cream until it begins to thicken. Add confectioners' sugar and vanilla; beat until stiff peaks form. Fold into cooled chocolate mixture. Spoon into chocolate cups. Refrigerate until cold.

4. If desired, in a microwave, warm the raspberry jam; transfer to a resealable plastic bag. Cut a small hole in a corner of bag; pipe designs onto plates. Top with mousse cups. If desired, decorate with raspberries and mint.

HOW TO MAKE A WHITE RUSSIAN

Chocolate desserts go great with coffee, it's true. But if you're in the mood for a really delicious rich and creamy cocktail, whip up a simple White Russian instead. Here's how: In a rocks glass, place ½ cup ice cubes. Stir in 1½ ounces vodka and 1½ ounces Kahlua. Then add 3 ounces heavy whipping cream or milk and serve.

Creamy Vanilla-Chocolate Cheesecake

This recipe is the most recent cheesecake I gave to my mother for her birthday, and we all just loved it...too much! There's a hint of orange in the chocolate crust that makes every bite worth savoring.

—JENN TIDWELL FAIR OAKS, CA

PREP: 50 MIN.
BAKE: 1 HOUR + CHILLING
MAKES: 16 SERVINGS

- **2 cups chocolate graham crackers crumbs (about 16 graham crackers)**
- **4 teaspoons grated orange peel**
- **⅓ cup butter, melted**

FILLING

- **3 packages (8 ounces each) cream cheese, softened**
- **1 cup sugar**
- **1 cup (8 ounces) sour cream**
- **1 vanilla bean or 1 teaspoon vanilla extract**
- **3 eggs, lightly beaten**

TOPPING

- **1 cup (6 ounces) semisweet chocolate chips**
- **⅔ cup heavy whipping cream**
- **2 cups fresh raspberries**

1. Preheat oven to 325°. Place a greased 9-in. springform pan on a double thickness of heavy-duty foil (about 18 in. square). Wrap foil securely around pan.

2. In a small bowl, mix cracker crumbs and orange peel; stir in butter. Press onto bottom and 2 in. up sides of prepared pan. Refrigerate 5 minutes.

3. In a large bowl, beat cream cheese and sugar until smooth. Beat in sour cream. Split vanilla bean lengthwise; using the tip of a sharp knife, scrape seeds from the center into cream cheese mixture. Add eggs; beat on low speed just until blended. Pour into crust. Place springform pan in a larger baking pan; add 1 in. of hot water to larger pan.

4. Bake 60-70 minutes or until center is just set and top appears dull. Remove springform pan from water bath. Cool cheesecake on a wire rack 10 minutes. Loosen sides from pan with a knife; remove foil. Cool 1 hour longer. Refrigerate overnight, covering when completely cooled.

5. For topping, place chocolate chips in a small bowl. In a small saucepan, bring cream just to a boil. Pour over chocolate chips; stir with a whisk until smooth. Cool to room temperature and until the mixture thickens to spreading consistency, about 10 minutes.

6. Remove rim from springform pan. Spread chocolate mixture over cheesecake. Refrigerate for 1 hour longer or until set. Top cheesecake with raspberries before serving.

The trimming of the holiday tree is a revered tradition. It lends an opportunity to share the origins of heirloom keepsakes with your children and friends. From the ornament your grandmother made for you to your child's first snowflake craft, each decoration has a story to tell.

Hosting an informal potluck sets a comfortable backdrop for reminiscing and trading cherished anecdotes. Here you'll find a collection of Italian-inspired recipes meant to be served family-style while admiring your newly adorned tree. After all, it's more than the main attraction of your home's holiday decor, it's the keeper of sacred evergreen memories.

Lasagna Dip (p. 18)
Pink Sparkling Wine Punch (p. 20)
Fresh Antipasto Salad (p. 23)
Mom's White Lasagna (p. 24)

TREE-TRIMMING **POTLUCK**

Lasagna Dip

PICTURED ON PAGE 16

My lasagna noodle chips turned out great and are out-of-this-world crispy. And the dip truly tastes like rich, cheesy Italian-American lasagna.
—**LINDA CIFUENTES** MAHOMET, IL

PREP: 25 MIN. • **COOK:** 15 MIN. • **MAKES:** 3 CUPS DIP (36 CHIPS)

- **6 uncooked lasagna noodles**
- **2 tablespoons grated Parmesan cheese**
- **2 tablespoons Italian seasoning**
- **½ teaspoon garlic powder**
- **Oil for deep-fat frying**

DIP

- **½ pound bulk Italian sausage**
- **2 cups whole-milk ricotta cheese**
- **1 cup spaghetti sauce**
- **2 garlic cloves, minced**
- **1 teaspoon dried basil**
- **1 teaspoon dried oregano**
- **½ teaspoon salt**
- **½ teaspoon pepper**
- **½ cup shredded Italian cheese blend**

1. Cook lasagna noodles according to package directions; drain. Cut noodles into 2-in. pieces; prick each piece several times with a fork. Mix Parmesan cheese, Italian seasoning and garlic powder.

2. In an electric skillet or deep fryer, heat oil to 375°. Fry the noodles in batches 1-2 minutes or until golden brown, turning once. Drain on paper towels. Immediately sprinkle with the cheese mixture.

3. For dip, in a large skillet, cook sausage over medium heat 4-6 minutes or until no longer pink, breaking into fine crumbles. Stir in ricotta, spaghetti sauce, garlic and seasonings; bring to a boil. Reduce heat; simmer, uncovered, 5 minutes or until slightly thickened, stirring occasionally.

4. Transfer to a 1-qt. microwave-safe dish. Sprinkle with Italian cheese. Microwave, covered, on high for 45-60 seconds or until cheese is melted. Serve with lasagna chips.

NAME THAT DISH!

When hosting a potluck, consider putting out a stack of blank store-bought or hand-crafted labels, along with a pen or marker. Encourage guests to write the name of their dish as well as their own name. Not only will people know what they're digging into, but they'll know just who to thank and ask for the recipe.

Easy Minestrone

Here's a wonderful recipe to put together in the morning and forget about the rest of the day. I have three small boys who are not big fans of vegetables, but they especially enjoy this hearty, comforting soup.
—**YVONNE ANDRUS** HIGHLAND, UT

PREP: 20 MIN. • **COOK:** 6 HOURS • **MAKES:** 10 SERVINGS (ABOUT 3¼ QUARTS)

- **4 medium tomatoes, chopped**
- **2 medium carrots, chopped**
- **2 celery ribs, chopped**
- **1 medium zucchini, halved and sliced**
- **1½ cups shredded cabbage**
- **1 can (16 ounces) kidney beans, rinsed and drained**
- **1 can (15 ounces) garbanzo beans or chickpeas, rinsed and drained**
- **6 cups reduced-sodium chicken broth or vegetable broth**
- **1¼ teaspoons Italian seasoning**
- **1 teaspoon salt**
- **¼ teaspoon pepper**
- **2 cups cooked elbow macaroni**
- **5 tablespoons shredded Parmesan cheese**

1. In a 5- or 6-qt. slow cooker, combine the first 11 ingredients. Cook, covered, on low 6-8 hours or until vegetables are tender.

2. Just before serving, stir in macaroni; heat through. Serve with cheese.

Festive Tortellini Toss

Fall is my favorite season, and I love the foods of autumn, such as mushrooms, squash, apples and walnuts. I combined all these with pasta to make a delicious side dish perfect for sharing at a potluck; the recipe can easily be doubled and can be served warm or at room temperature.

—ROXANNE CHAN ALBANY, CA

PREP: 25 MIN. • **COOK:** 10 MIN.
MAKES: 12 SERVINGS (⅔ CUP EACH)

1 package (9 ounces) refrigerated cheese tortellini
2 tablespoons olive oil
½ pound sliced baby portobello mushrooms
1¾ cups cubed peeled butternut squash (about ¼-inch cubes)
½ teaspoon poultry seasoning
1 medium tart apple, chopped
3 tablespoons thawed apple juice concentrate
3 tablespoons cider vinegar
1 green onion, thinly sliced
⅓ cup chopped walnuts, toasted
⅓ cup cubed smoked Gouda cheese (about ¼-inch cubes)
2 tablespoons minced fresh parsley

1. Cook tortellini according to package directions. In a large skillet, heat oil over medium-high heat. Add mushrooms, squash and poultry seasoning; cook and stir 6-8 minutes or until the mushrooms are tender. Add apple, apple juice concentrate, vinegar and onion; cook 2-3 minutes longer or until the squash is tender.

2. Drain tortellini; rinse with cold water and place in a large bowl. Add squash mixture, walnuts, cheese and parsley; toss gently to coat.

Coconut Raspberry Trifle

Raspberry Zingers or cream-filled cakes cut into quarters and layered with instant French vanilla pudding and fresh raspberries make a tasty and unexpected trifle—perfect for potlucks.
—TASTE OF HOME TEST KITCHEN

START TO FINISH: 15 MIN. • **MAKES:** 12 SERVINGS

- **4 cups cold milk**
- **2 packages (3.4 ounces each) instant French vanilla pudding mix**
- **1 package (18 ounces) individual raspberry cream-filled cakes**
- **3 cups fresh raspberries**
- **2 cups whipped topping**

1. In a large bowl, whisk milk and pudding mixes for 2 minutes. Let stand for 2 minutes or until soft-set. Cut each cake into quarters.
2. Line bottom of a 3½-qt. glass bowl with half of the cake pieces. Top with half of the pudding and 1 cup raspberries; repeat layers. Refrigerate until serving.
3. Just before serving, spread with whipped topping; sprinkle with remaining raspberries.
NOTE *This recipe was tested with Dolly Madison brand Zingers.*

Pink Sparkling Wine Punch

PICTURED ON PAGE 16

A long-standing tradition in our home, this sparkling punch makes spirits bright. Garnished with fresh strawberries and lime, it's a colorful Christmas cocktail.
—KAREN KUEBLER DALLAS, TX

PREP: 20 MIN. + CHILLING • **MAKES:** 18 SERVINGS (¾ CUP EACH)

- **2 cups fresh strawberries, hulled**
- **3 tablespoons lemon juice**
- **3 tablespoons honey**
- **2 bottles (32 ounces each) cranberry juice, chilled**
- **1 cup cold water**
- **¾ cup thawed pink lemonade concentrate**
- **1 bottle (750 milliliters) sparkling rose wine, chilled**
- **Thinly sliced strawberries, lemons and limes**

1. Place strawberries, lemon juice and honey in a food processor; process until pureed. If desired, press through a fine-mesh strainer into a punch bowl; discard seeds. Stir in cranberry juice, water and lemonade concentrate.
2. Just before serving, stir in the wine. Serve with sliced fruit.

Tomato & Artichoke Bruschetta

A healthy and refreshing appetizer, bruschetta is one I enjoy anytime of year. When serving guests, I like to slice the garlic instead of chopping it for both beauty and flavor infusion. This is also a simple make-ahead dish: You can mix it up, cover and refrigerate for a few hours before serving.

—GINA BERGAMINO
CHANHASSEN, MN

START TO FINISH: 30 MIN.
MAKES: ABOUT 6½ DOZEN

- **4 cups grape tomatoes, chopped**
- **1 cup (4 ounces) shredded part-skim mozzarella cheese**
- **¾ cup water-packed artichoke hearts, rinsed, drained and chopped**
- **3 green onions, chopped**
- **3 tablespoons pine nuts, toasted**
- **¼ cup olive oil**
- **3 tablespoons red wine vinegar**
- **3 garlic cloves, minced**
- **¾ teaspoon pepper**
- **¼ teaspoon salt**
- **1 French bread baguette (10½ ounces), cut into ¼-inch slices**

1. Preheat oven to 425°. In a large bowl, combine tomatoes, cheese, artichokes, green onions and pine nuts. In a small bowl, whisk oil, vinegar, garlic, pepper and salt. Pour over tomato mixture; toss to coat.

2. Place bread on ungreased baking sheets. Bake 4-5 minutes on each side or until golden brown. Top with tomato mixture.

Raspberry & Chocolate Shortbread Bars

A very long time ago, when I was a child, I decided that chocolate and raspberries was a combination made in heaven, and that any treat made with these two delicious ingredients would be at the top of my holiday list. Use any seedless jam or preserves in these bars—raspberry is our favorite.

—LILY JULOW LAWRENCEVILLE, GA

PREP: 25 MIN.
BAKE: 30 MIN. + COOLING
MAKES: 2 DOZEN

- **1 cup unsalted butter, softened**
- **1 cup sugar**
- **2 egg yolks**
- **½ teaspoon vanilla extract**
- **2 cups all-purpose flour**
- **1 teaspoon baking powder**
- **¼ teaspoon salt**
- **1 jar (10 ounces) seedless raspberry spreadable fruit**
- **4 ounces bittersweet chocolate, finely chopped**
- **⅓ cup heavy whipping cream**

1. Preheat oven to 350°. In a large bowl, cream butter and sugar until light and fluffy. Beat in egg yolks and vanilla. In a small bowl, mix flour, baking powder and salt; gradually add to creamed mixture, mixing well.

2. Press half of the dough onto bottom of a greased 11x7-in. baking dish. Top with spreadable fruit. Crumble remaining dough over fruit. Bake on lowest oven rack 30-40 minutes or until golden brown. Cool completely on a wire rack.

3. Place chocolate in a small bowl. In a small saucepan, bring cream just to a boil. Pour over chocolate; stir with a whisk until smooth. Drizzle over top; let stand until set. Cut into bars.

Fresh Antipasto Salad

PICTURED ON PAGE 17

Take an exquisite blend of vegetables, such as asparagus, artichokes, broccoli, cauliflower and mushrooms, and marinate in a homemade vinaigrette seasoned with garlic and fresh herbs.

—**LYNDA BARRON** MCFARLAND, WI

PREP: 40 MIN. + CHILLING • **MAKES:** 16 SERVINGS (¾ CUP EACH)

- **3 cups cut fresh asparagus (2-inch pieces)**
- **3 cups quartered fresh mushrooms**
- **2 cans (14 ounces each) water-packed artichoke hearts, rinsed, drained and quartered**
- **1½ cups chopped fresh broccoli**
- **5 ounces fresh mozzarella cheese pearls**
- **1 cup chopped fresh cauliflower**
- **1 cup julienned sweet red pepper**
- **1 cup pitted Greek olives**
- **8 pepperoncini, sliced**

VINAIGRETTE

- **⅔ cup cider vinegar**
- **¼ cup olive oil**
- **¼ cup minced fresh parsley**
- **4 garlic cloves, minced**
- **1 tablespoon sugar**
- **2 teaspoons minced fresh oregano or ¾ teaspoon dried oregano**
- **1 teaspoon honey**
- **¼ teaspoon salt**
- **¼ teaspoon pepper**

1. In large saucepan, bring 5 cups of water to a boil. Add asparagus; cook, uncovered, 2-4 minutes or just until crisp-tender. Drain and immediately drop into ice water. Drain and pat dry.

2. In a large bowl, combine the mushrooms, artichokes, broccoli, cheese, cauliflower, red pepper, olives, pepperoncini and the cooked asparagus.

3. In a small bowl, whisk the vinaigrette ingredients. Pour over salad; toss to coat. Refrigerate, covered, 2 hours before serving.

NOTE *Look for pepperoncinis (pickled peppers) in the pickle and olive section of your grocery store.*

Cranberry-Maple Chicken Meatballs

When you need a festive appetizer to bring to a party, these saucy chicken meatballs made with maple syrup, Dijon and orange zest taste like the holidays.

—**SALLY SIBTHORPE** SHELBY TOWNSHIP, MI

PREP: 25 MIN. • **BAKE:** 15 MIN. • **MAKES:** ABOUT 1½ DOZEN

- **2 eggs, lightly beaten**
- **⅓ cup soft bread crumbs**
- **¼ cup finely chopped onion**
- **¼ cup finely chopped celery**
- **¼ cup ground walnuts**
- **¼ cup minced fresh parsley**
- **1 teaspoon salt**
- **1 pound lean ground chicken**

SAUCE

- **1 cup whole-berry cranberry sauce**
- **1 cup maple syrup**
- **3 tablespoons Dijon mustard**
- **½ teaspoon salt**
- **½ teaspoon grated orange peel**
- **Minced fresh parsley, optional**

1. Preheat oven to 400°. In a large bowl, combine the first seven ingredients. Add chicken; mix lightly but thoroughly (mixture will be soft). Shape into 1½-in. balls.

2. Place meatballs on a greased rack in a shallow baking pan. Bake 15-20 minutes or until cooked through.

3. For sauce, in a large saucepan, combine the first five sauce ingredients; bring just to a boil, stirring occasionally. Gently stir in meatballs. If desired, sprinkle with parsley just before serving.

SCOOP THEM UP

For meatballs to cook evenly, it's important for them to be the same size. The easiest way to do this is by using a 1- or 1½-inch cookie scoop. Scoop the meat mixture and level off the top. Gently roll into a ball and place on rack.

Mom's White Lasagna

PICTURED ON PAGE 17

My mother made this lasagna for special occasions such as birthdays. When she passed, I inherited her cookbooks—tucked inside one of them, I found this recipe folded into a letter she wrote to me while I was stationed overseas. It's a hearty, rich dish that always reminds me of home.

—**JANET WING** MINOT, ND

PREP: 30 MIN. • **BAKE:** 40 MIN. + STANDING • **MAKES:** 12 SERVINGS

- **9 lasagna noodles**
- **1 pound bulk Italian sausage**
- **2 celery ribs, chopped**
- **1 medium onion, chopped**
- **3 garlic cloves, minced**
- **½ cup white wine**
- **1 cup half-and-half cream**
- **3 ounces cream cheese, cubed**
- **¼ cup minced fresh basil**
- **2 teaspoons minced fresh oregano or ½ teaspoon dried oregano**
- **1 teaspoon pepper**
- **¾ teaspoon salt**
- **1 egg, lightly beaten**
- **2 cups (8 ounces) shredded white cheddar cheese**
- **1½ cups (12 ounces) 2% cottage cheese**
- **¾ pound fresh mozzarella cheese, sliced**
- **1½ cups (6 ounces) shredded Gouda cheese**
- **Additional minced fresh basil and oregano, optional**

1. Preheat oven to 375°. Cook noodles according to package directions for al dente. In a large skillet, cook sausage, celery, onion and garlic over medium heat 6-8 minutes or until sausage is no longer pink, breaking up sausage into crumbles; drain.

2. Stir in wine. Bring to a boil; cook 3-4 minutes or until liquid is reduced by half. Add cream, cream cheese, herbs, pepper and salt; stir until cream cheese is melted. Drain noodles.

3. In a small bowl, combine egg, cheddar and cottage cheeses. In a greased 13x9-in. baking dish, layer three noodles, half of the sausage mixture, half of the cheddar cheese mixture and half of the mozzarella slices. Repeat layers. Top with the remaining noodles; sprinkle with the Gouda cheese.

4. Bake, covered, 40-50 minutes or until bubbly and cheese is melted. Let stand 15 minutes before serving. If desired, sprinkle with additional basil and oregano.

Rich & Creamy Eggnog

Mom is a huge eggnog fan around the holidays, but I've never been crazy about the store-bought kind. However, when I whip up this homemade festive treat, nobody can resist!

—**JENNA FLEMING** LOWVILLE, NY

PREP: 15 MIN. • **COOK:** 20 MIN. + CHILLING • **MAKES:** 12 SERVINGS (¾ CUP EACH)

- **8 eggs**
- **⅓ cup sugar**
- **2 tablespoons confectioners' sugar**
- **2 cups whole milk**
- **4 cups heavy whipping cream**
- **1 cup amaretto**
- **1 teaspoon ground cinnamon**
- **1 teaspoon ground nutmeg**
- **Additional ground nutmeg**

1. In a large heavy saucepan, whisk eggs, sugar and confectioners' sugar until blended. Stir in milk.

2. Cook over low heat 20 minutes or until the mixture is just thick enough to coat a metal spoon and a thermometer reads at least 160°, stirring constantly. Do not allow to boil. Remove from the heat immediately.

3. Stir in cream, amaretto, cinnamon and nutmeg. Refrigerate, covered, several hours or until cold. Sprinkle servings with additional nutmeg.

Helping Hands Christmas Tree

Is that a Christmas tree or a "palm" tree? Whatever you call it, make sure everyone in the family has a hand in this fun project—it's the perfect activity for your tree-trimming potluck.

MATERIALS

Pencil
25 to 30 sheets green construction paper
Scissors
1 sheet yellow construction paper
1 sheet brown construction paper
Glue
24x36-in. frame, bulletin board, poster board or background of your choice (we used a 24x36-in. frame)
Measuring tape or ruler (optional)

DIRECTIONS

1. Use a pencil to gently trace two hands on 1 piece of green construction paper. Cut out the hands and repeat to make 50 to 60 paper hands.
2. Use a pencil to draw a star on the yellow construction paper and cut out.
3. Cut the piece of brown construction paper in half to make a tree trunk.
4. Optional: Trace an 18x18x18-in. triangle on the surface of your selected background.
5. Assemble your tree by gluing a row of paper hands along the base, with fingers pointing down. Continue making rows to fill in your triangle.
6. Glue on the star and trunk.
7. If desired, decorate with paper ornaments, photos and glitter.

For too long, entrees have been getting all the love—while dinner rolls and Brussels sprouts get pushed aside. What a shame. With tender slices of homemade Bacon Date Bread (p. 28) and heaping servings of Eggnog Sweet Potato Bake (p. 33) gracing the holiday table, it's time to put an end to this menu inequality and start singing the praises of those unsung heroes—the side dishes.

We're counting down 12 days of dressed-up vegetables and grains worth celebrating. Watch as we shift the spotlight from ham and turkey to the colorful companions that no holiday feast would be complete without.

Minted Beet Salad (p. 29)
Parmesan-Walnut Bubble Bread (p. 30)

12 DAYS OF SIDES

Bacon Date Bread

There is a standing joke among my friends that whenever I'm asked to bring a dish to a party, it always contains bacon. My partner loves bacon-wrapped dates and my grandmother got me hooked on date-nut bread, so I made a sweet and salty combination of both recipes.

—**TERRIE GAMMON** EDEN PRAIRIE, MN

PREP: 25 MIN.
BAKE: 45 MIN. + COOLING
MAKES: 1 LOAF (16 SLICES)

8 bacon strips, chopped
8 green onions, thinly sliced
2 cups all-purpose flour
3 teaspoons baking powder
1 teaspoon sugar
¼ teaspoon salt
⅛ teaspoon cayenne pepper
2 eggs
1 cup (8 ounces) sour cream
¼ cup butter, melted
1½ cups (6 ounces) shredded Asiago cheese, divided
⅔ cup pitted dates, chopped

1. Preheat oven to 350°. In a large skillet, cook bacon over medium heat until crisp, stirring occasionally. Remove with a slotted spoon; drain on paper towels. Discard drippings, reserving 2 tablespoons in pan.

2. Add green onions to drippings; cook and stir over medium-high heat 1-2 minutes or until tender. Cool slightly.

3. In a large bowl, whisk flour, baking powder, sugar, salt and cayenne. In another bowl, whisk eggs, sour cream and melted butter until blended. Add to flour mixture; stir just until moistened. Fold in 1 cup of cheese, the dates, bacon and green onions (batter will be thick).

4. Transfer to a greased 9x5-in. loaf pan; sprinkle with remaining cheese. Bake 45-50 minutes or until a toothpick inserted in center comes out clean. Cool in pan 10 minutes before removing to a wire rack. Serve warm.

Minted Beet Salad

PICTURED ON PAGE 27

We have neighbors who share vegetables from their garden, and every year my husband and I look forward to their beets. My interest in Mediterranean food inspired this beet salad recipe—the vinegar and oil dressing with fresh mint is excellent with the beets, and the kalamata olives add a salty touch.

—BARBARA ESTABROOK RHINELANDER, WI

PREP: 20 MIN. • **COOK:** 15 MIN. + CHILLING • **MAKES:** 6 SERVINGS

- **5 medium fresh beets (about 2 pounds)**
- **2 tablespoons water**
- **2 tablespoons champagne vinegar or rice vinegar**
- **2 tablespoons olive oil**
- **½ teaspoon salt**
- **¼ teaspoon coarsely ground pepper**
- **¼ cup pitted kalamata olives, quartered**
- **2 tablespoons thinly sliced fresh mint, divided**

1. Scrub beets; trim tops to 1 in. Place in a single layer in a large microwave-safe dish. Drizzle with water. Microwave, covered, on high 14-15 minutes or until easily pierced with a fork, turning once; let stand 5 minutes.

2. When cool enough to handle, peel and cut beets into ¾-in. pieces. In a bowl, whisk the vinegar, oil, salt and pepper until blended. Add the olives, beets and 1 tablespoon mint; toss to coat. Refrigerate, covered, at least 1 hour or until cold. Top with remaining mint.

NOTE *This recipe was tested in a 1,100-watt microwave.*

Maple-Pumpkin Dinner Rolls

Every year after my family and I visit our local pumpkin patch, we come home and enjoy our first autumn meal. These dinner rolls always show up—along with corn chowder and apple pie.

—SABRINA FRALEY GEORGETOWN, KY

PREP: 30 MIN. + RISING • **BAKE:** 15 MIN. • **MAKES:** 16 ROLLS

- **½ cup cornmeal**
- **¼ cup packed brown sugar**
- **1 package (¼ ounce) quick-rise yeast**
- **½ teaspoon salt**
- **¼ teaspoon pumpkin pie spice**
- **2½ to 3 cups all-purpose flour**
- **¾ cup plus 2 tablespoons milk, divided**
- **¼ cup maple syrup**
- **4 tablespoons butter, divided**
- **¾ cup canned pumpkin**

1. In a large bowl, mix cornmeal, brown sugar, yeast, salt, pie spice and 2 cups flour. In a small saucepan, heat ¾ cup milk, syrup and 2 tablespoons butter to 120°-130°; stir into dry ingredients. Stir in pumpkin and enough remaining flour to form a soft dough (dough will be sticky).

2. Turn dough onto a floured surface; knead until smooth and elastic, about 6-8 minutes. Cover with plastic wrap and let rest for 10 minutes.

3. Divide and shape dough into 16 balls. Place in two greased 9-in. round baking pans. Cover with kitchen towels; let rise until doubled, about 1 hour. Preheat oven to 375°.

4. Brush remaining milk over dough. Bake 12-15 minutes or until golden brown.

5. Melt remaining butter; brush over hot rolls. Remove from pans to wire racks; serve warm.

Brussels Sprouts Saute

Salty, savory and sprinkled with Parmesan, this dish appeals even to people who don't like Brussels sprouts.
—DEIRDRE DEE COX KANSAS CITY, KS

START TO FINISH: 30 MIN. • **MAKES:** 8 SERVINGS

- **2 pounds fresh Brussels sprouts, thinly sliced**
- **3 tablespoons canola oil**
- **1 large onion, finely chopped**
- **7 thin slices prosciutto or deli ham (about 5 ounces), cut into strips**
- **4 garlic cloves, minced**
- **½ teaspoon pepper**
- **¼ teaspoon salt**
- **⅔ cup plus 3 tablespoons grated Parmesan cheese, divided**

1. In a Dutch oven, bring 8 cups water to a boil. Add Brussels sprouts; cook, uncovered, for 3-4 minutes or until tender. Drain.

2. In a large skillet, heat oil over medium-high heat. Add onion and prosciutto; cook and stir 5-6 minutes or until onion is tender. Add garlic; cook 1 minute longer. Add Brussels sprouts, pepper and salt; heat through. Stir in ⅔ cup cheese. Sprinkle with the remaining cheese.

Parmesan-Walnut Bubble Bread

PICTURED ON PAGE 27

The ladies in my home state of Indiana used to make all kinds of lovely bubble breads because they're easy and look great. I created my own recipe, and when I make a loaf, it always reminds me of home.
—LORI MCLAIN DENTON, TX

PREP: 20 MIN. • **BAKE:** 45 MIN. • **MAKES:** 12 SERVINGS

- **3 tubes (16.3 ounces each) large refrigerated flaky biscuits**
- **½ cup butter, melted**
- **1¾ cups shredded Parmesan cheese**
- **⅔ cup chopped walnuts**
- **4 green onions, finely chopped**
- **¼ cup minced fresh chives**
- **3 tablespoons minced fresh basil**

1. Preheat oven to 350°. Cut biscuits into quarters; place in a large bowl. Drizzle with butter and toss to coat. In a small bowl, mix remaining ingredients; sprinkle over biscuits and toss to coat. Transfer to a greased 10-in. fluted tube pan.

2. Bake 40-45 minutes or until golden brown. Cool 5 minutes before inverting onto a serving plate. Serve warm.

Harvest Salad with Lime-Curry Dressing

A friend gave me this salad recipe to help me impress my new husband, who loves citrus. We serve the dressing over greens we harvest from our garden—the lime and curry make a fantastic pairing.

—RACHEL MUILENBURG
PRINEVILLE, OR

PREP: 25 MIN. + CHILLING
MAKES: 12 SERVINGS (1⅓ CUPS EACH)

- **½ cup plain yogurt**
- **½ cup mayonnaise**
- **3 tablespoons lime juice**
- **2 tablespoons honey**
- **1½ teaspoons grated lime peel**
- **1½ teaspoons curry powder**
- **1 bunch romaine lettuce, torn (about 15 cups)**
- **1 bunch red leaf lettuce, torn (about 12 cups)**
- **2 celery ribs, diagonally sliced**
- **1 large apple, cut into ½-inch pieces**
- **1 medium pear, cut into ½-inch pieces**
- **¾ cup raisins**
- **½ cup chopped pecans, toasted**

1. In a small bowl, whisk the first six ingredients until blended. Refrigerate, covered, for at least 1 hour to allow flavors to blend.

2. In a large bowl, combine remaining ingredients. Pour dressing over salad and toss to coat; serve immediately.

Winter Squash with Maple Glaze

You can use any type of winter squash in this simple vegetable bake, but I like to use at least two varieties. It can be assembled a day ahead, then baked just before serving.
—**TERI KREYCHE** TUSTIN, CA

PREP: 20 MIN. • **BAKE:** 50 MIN. • **MAKES:** 6 SERVINGS

- **2 cups chopped peeled parsnips**
- **2 cups cubed peeled kabocha squash**
- **2 cups cubed peeled butternut squash**
- **⅓ cup butter, cubed**
- **½ cup maple syrup**
- **1 tablespoon minced fresh rosemary or 1 teaspoon dried rosemary, crushed**
- **1 garlic clove, minced**
- **½ teaspoon salt**
- **¼ teaspoon pepper**
- **¾ cup coarsely chopped almonds**

1. Preheat oven to 375°. In a large bowl, combine parsnips and squashes. In a small saucepan, melt butter over medium heat; whisk in maple syrup, rosemary, garlic, salt and pepper. Pour over vegetables and toss to coat.

2. Transfer to a greased 11x7-in. baking dish. Bake, covered, 40 minutes. Uncover; sprinkle with almonds. Bake 10-15 minutes longer or until vegetables are tender.

NO KABOCHA? TRY BUTTERCUP

Kabocha squash is an Asian variety sometimes referred to as Japanese pumpkin. It's very similar in taste and texture to buttercup squash.

Savory Stuffing Bread

Poultry seasoning and celery salt make this hearty loaf taste just like stuffing! It's the perfect bread to serve with turkey during the holidays, and it's nice for making sandwiches with the leftovers.
—**BETSY KING** DULUTH, MN

PREP: 30 MIN. + RISING • **BAKE:** 20 MIN. + COOLING • **MAKES:** 2 LOAVES (16 SLICES EACH)

- **2 tablespoons sugar**
- **2 packages (¼ ounce each) active dry yeast**
- **1½ teaspoons poultry seasoning**
- **½ teaspoon salt**
- **½ teaspoon celery salt**
- **½ teaspoon pepper**
- **5½ to 6 cups all-purpose flour**
- **¼ cup butter, cubed**
- **1 small onion, finely chopped**
- **1 can (14½ ounces) chicken broth**
- **2 eggs**

1. In a large bowl, mix sugar, yeast, seasonings and 2 cups flour. In a small saucepan, heat butter over medium-high heat. Add onion; cook and stir for 2-3 minutes or until tender. Stir in broth; heat to 120°-130°. Add to dry ingredients; beat on medium speed 2 minutes. Add eggs; beat 2 minutes longer. Stir in enough remaining flour to form a soft dough (dough will be sticky).

2. Turn dough onto a floured surface; knead until smooth and elastic, about 6-8 minutes. Place in a greased bowl, turning once to grease the top. Cover with plastic wrap and let rise in a warm place until doubled, about 1 hour.

3. Punch down dough. Turn onto a lightly floured surface; divide in half. Shape into loaves. Place in two greased 9x5-in. loaf pans, seam side down.

4. Cover with kitchen towels; let rise in a warm place until doubled, about 30 minutes.

5. Preheat oven to 375°. Bake 18-22 minutes or until golden brown. Remove from pans to wire racks to cool completely.

Eggnog Sweet Potato Bake

I love eggnog, so I'm always looking for new ways to use it. When I added it to mashed sweet potatoes, I knew I had a winner. You can make this the night before and refrigerate it unbaked. The next day, let it stand at room temperature for 30 minutes before baking.

—KATIE WOLLGAST FLORISSANT, MO

PREP: 1¼ HOURS + COOLING
BAKE: 30 MIN.
MAKES: 8 SERVINGS

- **3½ pounds sweet potatoes (about 5 large)**
- **⅔ cup eggnog**
- **½ cup golden raisins**
- **2 tablespoons sugar**
- **1 teaspoon salt**

TOPPING

- **¼ cup all-purpose flour**
- **¼ cup quick-cooking oats**
- **¼ cup packed brown sugar**
- **¼ cup chopped pecans**
- **½ teaspoon ground cinnamon**
- **¼ teaspoon ground nutmeg**
- **2 tablespoons butter, melted**

1. Preheat oven to 400°. Scrub sweet potatoes; pierce several times with a fork. Place on a foil-lined 15x10x1-in. baking pan; bake 1 hour or until tender. Remove from oven. Reduce oven setting to 350°.

2. When potatoes are cool enough to handle, remove and discard peel. Mash potatoes in a large bowl (you should have about 6 cups mashed). Stir in eggnog, raisins, sugar and salt. Transfer to a greased 11x7-in. baking dish.

3. For topping, in a small bowl, mix flour, oats, brown sugar, pecans and spices; stir in butter. Sprinkle over sweet potatoes. Bake, uncovered, 30-35 minutes or until heated through and topping is lightly browned.

NOTE *This recipe was tested with commercially prepared eggnog.*

Braided Multigrain Loaf

Here's a hearty, chewy loaf made with oats, rye flour, rice and sunflower seeds. It's so robust, you could almost make a meal out of a piece of this bread and a little butter.

—JANE THOMAS BURNSVILLE, MN

PREP: 40 MIN. + RISING
BAKE: 30 MIN. + COOLING
MAKES: 1 LOAF (24 SLICES)

- **2 cups whole wheat flour**
- **1 cup quick-cooking oats**
- **½ cup rye flour**
- **2 packages (¼ ounce each) active dry yeast**
- **2 teaspoons salt**
- **3 cups all-purpose flour**
- **2 cups milk**
- **½ cup honey**
- **⅓ cup water**
- **2 tablespoons butter**
- **1 cup cooked long grain rice, cooled**

TOPPING

- **1 egg**
- **1 tablespoon water**
- **⅓ cup sunflower kernels**

1. In a large bowl, mix whole wheat flour, oats, rye flour, yeast, salt and 1 cup all-purpose flour. In a small saucepan, heat milk, honey, water and butter to 120°-130°. Add to dry ingredients; beat on medium speed 2 minutes. Add 1 cup all-purpose flour; beat 2 minutes longer. Stir in rice and enough of the remaining flour to form a stiff dough.

2. Turn dough onto a floured surface; knead until smooth and elastic, about 6-8 minutes. Place in a greased bowl, turning once to grease the top. Cover with plastic wrap and let rise in a warm place until doubled, about 1 hour.

3. Punch down dough. Turn onto a lightly floured surface; divide into thirds. Cover and let rest 5 minutes. Roll each portion into an 18-in. rope. Place ropes on a greased baking sheet and braid. Shape into a ring. Pinch ends to seal; tuck under.

4. Cover with a kitchen towel; let rise in a warm place until doubled, about 30 minutes. Preheat oven to 375°.

5. For topping, in a small bowl, whisk egg and water; brush over dough. Sprinkle with sunflower kernels. Bake 30-40 minutes or until golden brown. Remove to a wire rack to cool.

Tuscan Corn Bread with Asiago Butter

I had some fresh basil on hand and needed to find a use for it. Peering into my pantry, I saw a bag of cornmeal and figured that corn bread with a Tuscan twist would be delicious.
—MICHELLE ANDERSON EAGLE, ID

PREP: 25 MIN. • **BAKE:** 20 MIN. • **MAKES:** 8 SERVINGS (1¼ CUPS BUTTER)

- **2 ounces sliced pancetta or bacon strips, finely chopped**
- **1 to 2 tablespoons olive oil, as needed**
- **1½ cups white cornmeal**
- **½ cup all-purpose flour**
- **2 teaspoons baking powder**
- **½ teaspoon salt**
- **2 eggs**
- **1 cup buttermilk**
- **¼ cup minced fresh basil**
- **1 garlic clove, minced**
- **1 can (14½ ounces) diced tomatoes, drained**
- **1 can (2¼ ounces) sliced ripe olives, drained**

BUTTER

- **1 cup butter, softened**
- **2 tablespoons olive oil**
- **⅓ cup shredded Asiago cheese**
- **2 tablespoons thinly sliced green onion**
- **1½ teaspoons minced fresh basil**
- **½ teaspoon minced fresh oregano**
- **1 garlic clove, minced, optional**

1. Preheat oven to 400°. In a 10-in. ovenproof skillet, cook pancetta over medium heat until crisp, stirring occasionally. Remove with a slotted spoon; drain on paper towels. Reserve drippings in skillet. If necessary, add enough oil to measure 2 tablespoons drippings.

2. In a large bowl, whisk cornmeal, flour, baking powder and salt. In another bowl, whisk eggs, buttermilk, basil and garlic until blended; stir in tomatoes. Add to flour mixture; stir just until moistened. Fold in olives and pancetta.

3. Place skillet with drippings in oven; heat 2 minutes. Tilt pan to coat bottom and sides with drippings. Add batter to hot pan. Bake 20-25 minutes or until a toothpick inserted in center comes out clean. Cool in pan on a wire rack.

4. Meanwhile, in a small bowl, beat butter until light and fluffy. Beat in oil until blended; stir in cheese, green onion, basil, oregano and, if desired, garlic. Serve 1/2 cup butter mixture with warm corn bread (save remaining butter for another use).

NOTE *If desired, remaining butter may be shaped into a log. Wrap in plastic wrap; refrigerate for a week or freeze for several months. To use, unwrap and slice; serve with bread, pasta, vegetables, seafood or poultry.*

Garlic Roasted Green Beans with Lemon Zest and Walnuts

I first tasted roasted green beans in a Chinese restaurant and fell in love with the texture and flavor. This is my Americanized version, and it's always a big hit at our holiday table.
—LILY JULOW LAWRENCEVILLE, GA

START TO FINISH: 25 MIN. • **MAKES:** 8 SERVINGS

- **2 pounds fresh green beans, trimmed**
- **2 shallots, thinly sliced**
- **6 garlic cloves, crushed**
- **2 tablespoons olive oil**
- **¾ teaspoon salt**
- **¼ teaspoon pepper**
- **2 teaspoons grated lemon peel**
- **½ cup chopped walnuts, toasted**

1. Preheat oven to 425°. In a large bowl, combine green beans, shallots and garlic; drizzle with oil and sprinkle with salt and pepper. Transfer to two 15x10x1-in. baking pans coated with cooking spray.

2. Roast 15-20 minutes or until tender and lightly browned, stirring occasionally. Remove from oven; stir in 1 teaspoon lemon peel. Sprinkle with walnuts and the remaining lemon peel.

It's not always easy to extend a warm welcome to winter. After all, the transition from cozy autumn nights to the first winter advisory warning is not without an unsought chill. But here's an inviting thought: Why not host a hot and spicy warm-up after the first snowfall of the season?

Friends and neighbors will look forward to toasting a mug of rum-spiked cider and feeling the heat of a few fiery foods. If there's one spread of appetizers and drinks that's sure to raise the temperature, it's this one.

Hot Spiced Apple Cider (p. 43)
Spicy-Good Chicken Wings (p. 39)
Bloody Mary Soup with Beans (p. 38)
Chicken Skewers with Sweet & Spicy Marmalade (p. 42)
Hoisin Meatball Lettuce Wraps (p. 41)

HOT & SPICY WINTER WARM-UP

Bloody Mary Soup with Beans

I love a good Bloody Mary, which inspired this recipe. The soup packs a spicy punch, and it'll warm you right up on a chilly day.

—AMBER MASSEY ARGYLE, TX

PREP: 20 MIN. • **COOK:** 55 MIN.
MAKES: 16 SERVINGS (4 QUARTS)

1 tablespoon olive oil
1 large onion, chopped
2 celery ribs, chopped
1 large carrot, finely chopped
1 poblano pepper, seeded and chopped
3 garlic cloves, minced
1 carton (32 ounces) reduced-sodium chicken broth
1 can (28 ounces) crushed tomatoes
1 can (14½ ounces) fire-roasted diced tomatoes, undrained
¼ cup tomato paste
2 cans (15 ounces each) white kidney or cannellini beans, rinsed and drained
¼ cup vodka
2 tablespoons Worcestershire sauce
½ teaspoon sugar
2 tablespoons lemon juice
1 tablespoon prepared horseradish
½ teaspoon pepper
Minced fresh parsley, celery ribs, lemon wedges and hot pepper sauce, optional

1. In a Dutch oven, heat oil over medium-high heat. Add onion, celery, carrot and poblano pepper; cook and stir 4-5 minutes or until crisp-tender. Add garlic; cook 1 minute longer.

2. Stir in broth, tomatoes and tomato paste. Bring to a boil. Reduce heat; simmer, covered, 15 minutes. Add beans, vodka, Worcestershire sauce and sugar; return to a boil. Reduce heat; simmer, uncovered, 25-30 minutes or until vegetables are tender, stirring occasionally.

3. Stir in the lemon juice, horseradish and pepper. If desired, sprinkle servings with parsley and serve with celery ribs, lemon wedges and pepper sauce.

NOTE *Wear disposable gloves when cutting hot peppers; the oils can burn skin. Avoid touching your face.*

Moroccan Spice Fruit-Nut Bread

Red pepper flakes combined with the cinnamon and allspice give each slice of this bread a subtle hint of warmth.

—DONNA MARIE RYAN TOPSFIELD, MA

PREP: 30 MIN. • **BAKE:** 50 MIN. + COOLING • **MAKES:** 1 LOAF (16 SLICES) AND ½ CUP BUTTER

- **½ cup chopped dried apricots**
- **½ cup chopped dates**
- **¼ cup orange juice**
- **2 cups all-purpose flour**
- **½ cup sugar**
- **¼ cup packed brown sugar**
- **2 teaspoons baking powder**
- **¾ teaspoon salt**
- **½ teaspoon ground cinnamon**
- **¼ teaspoon ground allspice**
- **¼ teaspoon crushed red pepper flakes**
- **2 eggs**
- **¾ cup 2% milk**
- **¼ cup unsalted butter, melted**
- **1 tablespoon grated orange peel**
- **⅓ cup flaked coconut**
- **¼ cup chopped pecans**

ORANGE BUTTER

- **½ cup unsalted butter, softened**
- **4 teaspoons confectioners' sugar**
- **2 teaspoons grated orange peel**
- **4 teaspoons orange juice**

1. Preheat oven to 350°. In a small saucepan, combine apricot, dates and orange juice; bring to a boil. Cook, uncovered, 1 minute. Remove from heat; let stand, covered, 10 minutes.

2. In a large bowl, whisk flour, sugars, baking powder, salt and spices. In another bowl, whisk eggs, milk, melted butter and orange peel until blended. Add to flour mixture; stir just until moistened. Fold in coconut, pecans and apricot mixture.

3. Transfer to a greased 9x5-in. loaf pan. Bake 50-55 minutes or until a toothpick inserted in center comes out clean. Cool in pan 10 minutes before removing to a wire rack to cool.

4. In a small bowl, beat remaining ingredients until blended. Serve bread with orange butter.

Spicy-Good Chicken Wings

PICTURED ON PAGE 37

We enjoy eating these chicken wings while watching football on TV, but make them on any occasion for a crowd favorite! The hot pepper sauce gives just the right amount of spice.

—DELLA CLUTTS NEW TAZEWELL, TN

PREP: 30 MIN. • **BAKE:** 20 MIN. • **MAKES:** ABOUT 1½ DOZEN

- **1 cup self-rising flour**
- **1 teaspoon celery salt**
- **1 teaspoon garlic powder**
- **1 teaspoon onion salt**
- **1 teaspoon barbecue seasoning**
- **½ teaspoon salt**
- **2 pounds chicken wingettes**
- **Oil for frying**
- **½ cup butter, melted**
- **1 bottle (2 ounces) hot pepper sauce**
- **Blue cheese salad dressing**

1. In a large resealable plastic bag, mix the first six ingredients. Add chicken, a few pieces at a time; close bag and shake to coat.

2. In an electric skillet, heat 1 in. of oil to 375°. Fry wingettes, a few at a time, for 4-5 minutes on each side or until browned. Drain on paper towels. Preheat the oven to 350°.

3. In a 13x9-in. baking dish, mix melted butter and pepper sauce. Add wings and turn to coat. Bake, uncovered, 10 minutes. Turn; bake 10-15 minutes longer or until chicken juices run clear. Serve with dressing.

NOTE *As a substitute for 1 cup of self-rising flour, place 1½ teaspoons baking powder and ½ teaspoon salt in a measuring cup. Add all-purpose flour to measure 1 cup.*

Spiced Pumpkin Warm-Up

Make this drink your own! You can add coffee—or even alcohol if you want an extra kick. I've also chilled the beverage and blended it with vanilla ice cream to create a pumpkin shake.

—ANDREA HEYART AUBREY, TX

START TO FINISH: 10 MIN. • **MAKES:** 2 SERVINGS

- **2 cups half-and-half cream**
- **3 tablespoons sugar**
- **2 tablespoons canned pumpkin**
- **1 teaspoon pumpkin pie spice**
- **¼ teaspoon vanilla extract**
- **Whipped cream and additional pumpkin pie spice**

In a small saucepan, combine cream, sugar, pumpkin and pie spice; cook and stir over medium heat until blended and heated through. Remove from heat; stir in vanilla. Top with whipped cream and additional pie spice.

GOT LEFTOVER PUMPKIN?

Many recipes that call for canned pumpkin do not require you to use the whole can. Use the leftovers to make these creamy and delicious drinks for dessert.

Pot Stickers With Spicy Sauce

This recipe makes a lot of pot sticker filling, so if you're hosting a small gathering, you can freeze the extras for later.

—ALISON BARNETT NEW YORK, NY

PREP: 45 MIN. • **COOK:** 5 MIN./BATCH • **MAKES:** 4 DOZEN (1 CUP SAUCE)

- **½ cup reduced-sodium soy sauce**
- **½ cup rice vinegar**
- **2 tablespoons sesame oil**
- **2 teaspoons sugar**
- **2 teaspoons Sriracha Asian hot chili sauce**
- **2 garlic cloves, minced**

POT STICKERS

- **1 egg, lightly beaten**
- **1 small onion, finely chopped**
- **1 medium carrot, shredded**
- **¼ cup sliced water chestnuts, finely chopped**
- **1 green onion, thinly sliced**
- **2 tablespoons sesame oil**
- **2 garlic cloves, minced**
- **⅛ teaspoon salt**
- **⅛ teaspoon pepper**
- **1 pound ground chicken**
- **48 pot sticker or gyoza wrappers**
- **3 tablespoons canola oil, divided**
- **1 cup water, divided**

TOPPINGS

- **2 green onions, sliced diagonally**
- **Sesame seeds**

1. In a small bowl, mix the first six ingredients. In a large bowl, combine the first nine pot sticker ingredients. Add chicken; mix lightly but thoroughly. Place 1 tablespoon filling in center of each wrapper. (Cover remaining wrappers with a damp paper towel until ready to use.)

2. Moisten wrapper edges with water. Fold wrapper over filling; seal edges, pleating the front side several times to form a pleated pouch. Stand pot stickers on a work surface to flatten bottoms; curve slightly to form crescent shapes, if desired.

3. In a large nonstick skillet, heat 1 tablespoon canola oil over medium-high heat. Arrange a third of the pot stickers in concentric circles in pan, flat side down; cook 1-2 minutes or until bottoms are golden brown.

4. Carefully add ⅓ cup water (water may splatter); reduce heat to medium-low. Cook, covered, 4-5 minutes or until water is almost absorbed and filling is cooked through.

5. Cook, uncovered, until bottoms are crisp and water is completely evaporated, about 1 minute. Repeat with remaining pot stickers. Sprinkle with green onions and sesame seeds before serving. Serve with sauce.

NOTE *Wonton wrappers may be substituted for pot sticker or gyoza wrappers. Stack two or three wonton wrappers on a work surface; cut into circles with a 3½-in. biscuit or round cookie cutter. Fill and wrap as directed.*

Hoisin Meatball Lettuce Wraps

The dipping sauce for these wraps packs in just enough heat to warm your taste buds. I make these tangy appetizers every year during the holidays, and they disappear fast.
—ELAINE SWEET DALLAS, TX

PREP: 35 MIN. • **COOK:** 35 MIN.
MAKES: 3 DOZEN

- **2 tablespoons cornstarch**
- **2 eggs, lightly beaten**
- **¼ cup minced fresh chives**
- **3 tablespoons dry bread crumbs**
- **3 tablespoons hoisin sauce**
- **4 teaspoons minced fresh gingerroot**
- **3 garlic cloves, minced**
- **½ teaspoon crushed red pepper flakes**
- **¾ pound lean ground beef (90% lean)**
- **½ pound ground pork**
- **2 to 3 tablespoons canola oil, divided**

SAUCE

- **½ cup red currant jelly**
- **½ cup hoisin sauce**
- **2 tablespoons mirin (sweet rice wine)**
- **3 garlic cloves, minced**
- **1½ teaspoons Thai red chili paste**

WRAPS

- **36 small Bibb or Boston lettuce leaves**
- **¼ cup minced fresh cilantro**

1. Place the cornstarch in a shallow bowl. In a large bowl, combine the next seven ingredients. Add the beef and pork; mix lightly but thoroughly. Shape into 1-in. balls; coat with cornstarch.

2. In a large skillet, heat 2 tablespoons oil over medium heat. Brown meatballs in batches, adding additional oil as needed. Remove with a slotted spoon; drain on paper towels.

3. Add sauce ingredients to skillet; cook and stir over medium heat until blended. Return meatballs to pan; bring to a boil. Reduce heat; simmer, uncovered, 5-8 minutes or until meatballs are glazed and cooked through, stirring occasionally. Serve meatballs in lettuce leaves; sprinkle with cilantro.

NOTE *Look for mirin in the Asian condiments section.*

Chicken Skewers with Sweet & Spicy Marmalade

My father-in-law loved this chicken dish and said that it reminded him of growing up in southern California. What a great way to bring a dose of summer sunshine to cold winter days!
—LAUREL DALZELL MANTECA, CA

PREP: 25 MIN. + MARINATING
BROIL: 5 MIN.
MAKES: 8 SERVINGS (1 CUP SAUCE)

- **1 pound boneless skinless chicken breasts**
- **¼ cup olive oil**
- **¼ cup reduced-sodium soy sauce**
- **2 garlic cloves, minced**
- **⅛ teaspoon pepper**

SAUCE

- **2 teaspoons butter**
- **2 tablespoons chopped seeded jalapeno pepper**
- **1 teaspoon minced fresh gingerroot**
- **¾ cup orange marmalade**
- **1 tablespoon lime juice**
- **1 tablespoon thawed orange juice concentrate**
- **¼ teaspoon salt**

1. Preheat broiler. Pound chicken breasts with a meat mallet to ¼-in. thickness; cut lengthwise into 1-in.-wide strips. In a large resealable plastic bag, combine oil, soy sauce, garlic and pepper. Add chicken; seal bag and turn to coat. Refrigerate 4 hours or overnight.

2. In a small saucepan, heat butter over medium-high heat. Add jalapeno; cook and stir until tender. Add ginger; cook 1 minute longer. Reduce heat; stir in marmalade, lime juice, orange juice concentrate and salt.

3. Drain chicken, discarding marinade. Thread chicken strips, weaving back and forth, onto eight metal or soaked wooden skewers. Place in a greased 15x10x1-in. baking pan. Broil 6 in. from heat for 2-4 minutes on each side or until chicken is no longer pink. Serve with sauce.

NOTE *Wear disposable gloves when cutting hot peppers; the oils can burn skin. Avoid touching your face.*

Jalapeno Crab Dip

Set this appetizer dip out for a football game, birthday party or even for an elegant holiday get-together. It's always a welcome spread.

—ERIN CONNER RIVERSIDE, CA

PREP: 30 MIN. • **BAKE:** 30 MIN. • **MAKES:** 16 SERVINGS (¼ CUP EACH)

- **2 tablespoons butter, divided**
- **1½ cups frozen corn**
- **½ teaspoon salt**
- **½ teaspoon pepper**
- **1 large onion, chopped**
- **1 small sweet red pepper, chopped**
- **2 green onions, chopped**
- **1 to 2 tablespoons chopped seeded jalapeno pepper**
- **1 garlic clove, minced**
- **2 cans (6 ounces each) lump crabmeat, drained**
- **1½ cups (6 ounces) shredded pepper jack cheese**
- **1½ cups (6 ounces) shredded cheddar cheese**
- **1 cup mayonnaise**
- **¼ cup chopped pickled jalapeno slices**
- **1 teaspoon Louisiana-style hot sauce**
- **1 teaspoon Worcestershire sauce**
- **⅔ cup grated Parmesan cheese**
- **Tortilla chips**

1. Preheat oven to 350°. In a large skillet, heat 1 tablespoon butter over medium-high heat. Add corn, salt and pepper; cook and stir until corn is golden brown. Remove from pan.

2. In same skillet, heat remaining butter over medium-high heat. Add onion and red pepper; cook and stir until onion is tender. Add green onions, fresh jalapeno and garlic; cook 1-2 minutes longer. Remove from heat.

3. In a large bowl, combine crab, pepper jack cheese, cheddar cheese, mayonnaise, pickled jalapenos, hot sauce and Worcestershire sauce; stir in corn and onion mixture. Transfer to a greased 8-in.-square baking dish; sprinkle with Parmesan cheese.

4. Bake, uncovered, 30-35 minutes or until edges are golden brown. Serve with chips.

NOTE *Wear disposable gloves when cutting hot peppers; the oils can burn skin. Avoid touching your face.*

Hot Spiced Apple Cider

PICTURED ON PAGE 36

My husband and I enjoy this adult drink by our fire pit during the cooler months of the year. Our house is filled with an amazing aroma while the cider is simmering!

—LISA BYNUM BRANDON, MS

PREP: 10 MIN. • **COOK:** 2 HOURS • **MAKES:** 10 SERVINGS (¾ CUP EACH)

- **2 cinnamon sticks (3 inches)**
- **1 piece fresh gingerroot (about 1 inch), peeled and thinly sliced**
- **1 teaspoon whole allspice**
- **1 teaspoon whole cloves**
- **½ teaspoon cardamom pods, crushed**
- **2 quarts apple cider or juice**
- **Rum, optional**

1. Place the first five ingredients on a double thickness of cheesecloth. Gather corners of cloth to enclose spices; tie securely with string.

2. Place apple cider and spice bag in a 3-qt. slow cooker. Cook, covered, on low 2-3 hours or until heated through. Discard spice bag. If desired, stir in rum.

CINNAMON STICKS

These make great stirrers for cider, tea and coffee, but you can cook with them, too. Try adding a cinnamon stick to rice as you boil it.

Salt & Pepper Caramel Cups

With sea salt and pink peppercorns, these sophisticated treats will wow your guests. The festive little cups look and taste like they came from a pricey confectionery, but you'll be proud to say you made them yourself!
—TASTE OF HOME TEST KITCHEN

PREP: 25 MIN. + CHILLING • **COOK:** 25 MIN. + COOLING • **MAKES:** 2½ DOZEN

1 cup sugar
1 cup dark corn syrup
1 cup butter, cubed
1 can (14 ounces) sweetened condensed milk
2 cups chopped pecans
1 teaspoon vanilla extract

CHOCOLATE CUPS
1 package (12 ounces) dark chocolate chips
4 teaspoons shortening

TOPPINGS
¼ cup dark chocolate chips, melted
Coarse sea salt and whole pink peppercorns

CHOCOLATE CUPS

1. With a clean paintbrush, evenly brush the melted chocolate inside the foil muffin cup liner. Chill until set. Repeat.
2. When set, gently peel off the foil liner. Avoid handling the cups too much or they may begin to melt.

1. In a large heavy saucepan, combine sugar, corn syrup and butter; bring to a boil over medium heat, stirring constantly. Cook 4 minutes longer without stirring.

2. Remove from heat; gradually stir in milk. Cook and stir over medium-low heat until a candy thermometer reads 238° (soft-ball stage). Remove from heat; stir in pecans and vanilla. Transfer to a large bowl; cool completely, about 1½ hours (mixture will thicken upon cooling).

3. For cups, in a microwave, melt chocolate chips and shortening; stir until smooth. Using a narrow pastry brush, evenly coat the inside of thirty 2-in. foil liners with chocolate. Refrigerate until firm, about 15 minutes. Repeat twice to coat three times, reheating melted chocolate as necessary.

4. Remove chocolate cups from liners; fill each with 2 tablespoons caramel. Drizzle tops with melted chocolate; sprinkle with the salt and peppercorns.

NOTE *We recommend that you test your candy thermometer before each use by bringing water to a boil; the thermometer should read 212°. Adjust your recipe temperature up or down based on your test.*

Dijon-Marinated Cocktail Shrimp

I like this spicy appetizer because it's an easy make-ahead dish and unlike any other shrimp cocktail you've ever had.

—SARAH CONAWAY
LYNCHBURG, VA

PREP: 15 MIN. + MARINATING
MAKES: 3½ DOZEN

- **½ cup olive oil**
- **¼ cup tarragon vinegar**
- **¼ cup Dijon mustard**
- **1 teaspoon salt**
- **1 teaspoon crushed red pepper flakes**
- **¼ teaspoon pepper**
- **1½ pounds peeled and deveined cooked large shrimp**
- **2 green onions, chopped**
- **¼ cup minced fresh parsley**

In a small bowl, whisk the first six ingredients until blended. In a large resealable plastic bag, combine shrimp, green onions, parsley and marinade; seal bag and turn to coat. Refrigerate for 2 hours or overnight. To serve, remove shrimp from marinade; discard marinade.

Bacon-Pecan Chocolate Truffles

PICTURED AT RIGHT

The secret ingredient in these sweets adds a hint of smoky flavor that brings out the taste of the chocolate. I love eating these truffles the day after I make them—the bacon comes through more.

—SYLVIA SHANKLE MUNHALL, PA

PREP: 40 MIN. + CHILLING • **COOK:** 5 MIN. + CHILLING • **MAKES:** 3½ DOZEN

- **1 package (12 ounces) dark chocolate chips**
- **6 tablespoons butter, cubed**
- **⅓ cup heavy whipping cream**
- **8 bacon strips, cooked and finely chopped**

COATING

- **1 cup white baking chips**
- **½ cup heavy whipping cream**
- **½ teaspoon maple flavoring**
- **1¾ cups chopped pecans, toasted**

1. Place dark chocolate chips in a small bowl. In a small saucepan, heat butter and cream just to simmering. Pour over chocolate; stir until smooth. Stir in bacon. Cool to room temperature, stirring occasionally. Refrigerate, covered, 1½ hours or until firm enough to shape.
2. For coating, place baking chips in a small bowl. In a small saucepan, bring cream just to a boil. Pour over baking chips; stir with a whisk until smooth. Stir in maple flavoring. Cool completely, stirring occasionally, for about 1½ hours.
3. Shape dark chocolate mixture into 1-in. balls. Dip truffles in maple mixture; allow excess to drip off. Roll in pecans; place on a waxed paper-lined 15x10x1-in. baking pan. Refrigerate until set. Store between layers of waxed paper in an airtight container in the refrigerator.

NOTE *To toast nuts, spread in a 15x10x1-in. baking pan. Bake at 350° for 5-10 minutes or until lightly browned, stirring occasionally. Or, spread in a dry nonstick skillet and heat over low heat until lightly browned, stirring occasionally.*

Spiced Coffee

Even people who don't usually drink coffee will find this special chocolaty blend appealing.

—JOANNE HOLT BOWLING GREEN, OH

PREP: 10 MIN. • **COOK:** 2 HOURS • **MAKES:** 8 SERVINGS

- **8 cups brewed coffee**
- **⅓ cup sugar**
- **¼ cup chocolate syrup**
- **½ teaspoon anise extract**
- **4 cinnamon sticks (3 inches)**
- **1½ teaspoons whole cloves**
- **Additional cinnamon sticks, optional**

1. In a 3-qt. slow cooker, combine coffee, sugar, chocolate syrup and extract. Place cinnamon sticks and cloves on a double thickness of cheesecloth. Gather corners of cloth to enclose spices; tie securely with string. Add to slow cooker. Cook, covered, on low 2-3 hours.
2. Discard the spice bag. If desired, serve the coffee with cinnamon sticks.

FOR A BETTER CUP OF JOE...

Use freshly ground coffee within seven days after opening or store it in the freezer. (Remember, the finer your grind, the stronger the flavor becomes.) Keep in mind that coffee absorbs flavors from anything nearby, so store it in an airtight container in a cool, dry place.

Favorite Mint Hot Chocolate

This is one of my husband's favorite winter drinks. I love the minty, chocolaty recipe because it's like Christmas in a cup. Be sure to make extra chocolate-covered mint leaves for the garnish. For some people, that's the best part!

—ALYSSA PONTICELLO BROOKLYN, NY

START TO FINISH: 25 MIN.
MAKES: 4 SERVINGS

8 fresh mint leaves
1 ounce dark baking chocolate, melted

WHIPPED CREAM

½ cup heavy whipping cream
3 tablespoons sugar
⅛ teaspoon peppermint extract

HOT CHOCOLATE

4 cups 2% milk
½ cup heavy whipping cream
4 teaspoons minced fresh mint (about 16 leaves)
1 cup (6 ounces) semisweet chocolate chips

1. Brush both sides of mint leaves with melted chocolate. Place on a waxed paper-lined baking sheet; refrigerate until set.
2. In a small bowl, beat cream until it begins to thicken. Add the sugar and extract; beat until soft peaks form. Refrigerate until time to serve.
3. In a large saucepan, heat milk and cream over medium heat just to simmering (do not boil). Remove from heat; add mint. Whisk in the chocolate chips until melted; return to heat and heat through.
4. If desired, pour hot chocolate through a strainer to remove the mint leaves. Top servings with whipped cream and chocolate leaves.

December reigns supreme as the month of special desserts, and rightfully so. But as the usual suspects—the gingerbread men, the frosted sugar cookies, the endless flavors of fudge—make their rounds at holiday parties across the country, you might find yourself craving something a bit more exotic.

'Tis the season to introduce your family and holiday guests to an international mix of desserts so delicious you'll wonder why you've never tried them before. From German Lebkuchen (p. 50) to Austrian Sachertorte Bites (p. 54), here you'll find a collection of confections from more than 10 different countries. So go on, join these cooks with global flair in the kitchen and start spreading cheer from around the world.

Blood Orange & Goat Cheese Galette (p. 57)
Flan de Vanilla (p. 54)

DESSERTS AROUND THE WORLD

Lebkuchen

It's tradition for my family to get together on Thanksgiving weekend and bake these spice-filled German treats. The recipe came from my great-grandmother's cookbook and, judging from the amount of requests I get each year, I'd say it's a keeper.
—ESTHER KEMPKER JEFFERSON CITY, MO

PREP: 25 MIN. • **BAKE:** 25 MIN. + COOLING • **MAKES:** 3 DOZEN

- **½ cup butter, softened**
- **½ cup sugar**
- **⅓ cup packed brown sugar**
- **2 eggs**
- **1 cup molasses**
- **¼ cup buttermilk**
- **½ teaspoon anise extract**
- **4½ cups all-purpose flour**
- **1½ teaspoons baking powder**
- **1 teaspoon baking soda**
- **1 teaspoon ground cinnamon**
- **½ teaspoon salt**
- **½ teaspoon each ground allspice, cardamom and cloves**
- **½ cup ground walnuts**
- **½ cup raisins**
- **½ cup pitted dates**
- **½ cup candied lemon peel**
- **⅓ cup flaked coconut**
- **¼ cup candied orange peel**
- **3 tablespoons candied pineapple**

GLAZE

- **½ cup sugar**
- **¼ cup water**
- **2 tablespoons confectioners' sugar**

1. Preheat oven to 350°. Line a 15x10x1-in. baking pan with parchment paper.

2. In a large bowl, cream butter and sugars until light and fluffy. Add eggs, one at a time, beating well after each addition. Beat in molasses, buttermilk and extract. In another bowl, whisk flour, baking powder, baking soda, cinnamon, salt, allspice, cardamom and cloves; gradually add to creamed mixture and beat well. Stir in walnuts.

3. Place raisins, dates, lemon peel, coconut, orange peel and pineapple in a food processor; pulse until chopped. Stir into batter; press into prepared pan. Bake 25-28 minutes or until lightly browned.

4. For glaze, in a small saucepan, bring sugar and water to a boil; boil 1 minute. Remove from heat; whisk in confectioners' sugar. Spread over warm bars. Cool completely in pan on a wire rack.

Coconut-Ricotta Balls

A common sweet in India, these coconut laddus are simple no-bake cookies that require only a handful of ingredients. My guests always appreciate when I serve these tasty treats.
—NIDHI PATHAK NOIDA, IN

START TO FINISH: 30 MIN. • **MAKES:** 10 BALLS

- **1 cup ricotta cheese**
- **2 cups finely shredded unsweetened coconut**
- **½ cup sugar**
- **2 tablespoons chopped cashews**
- **4 teaspoons chopped almonds**
- **¼ teaspoon ground cardamom**
- **10 unblanched almonds**

1. In a large nonstick skillet, heat ricotta cheese over medium-low heat; cook 20-25 minutes or until reduced by almost half, stirring occasionally. Transfer to a small bowl; cool 5 minutes.

2. Stir in coconut, sugar, cashews, chopped almonds and cardamom. Shape mixture into 1½-in. balls; press one whole almond into each ball. Store between layers of waxed paper in an airtight container in the refrigerator.

Hazelnut Toffee Zuccotto

As a grandmother and great-grandmother, I've always enjoyed cooking and creating recipes. In our home, we love to make Italian food because it's our favorite type of cuisine. Zuccotto, which means "little pumpkin" in Italian, is a traditional Italian dessert.

—PATRICIA HARMON BADEN, PA

PREP: 30 MIN. + CHILLING
MAKES: 10 SERVINGS

1 loaf (10¾ ounces) frozen pound cake, thawed
⅓ cup Kahlua (coffee liqueur)
1 package (8 ounces) cream cheese, softened
⅔ cup confectioners' sugar
1½ teaspoons instant espresso powder
1 teaspoon vanilla extract
⅔ cup heavy whipping cream
3 English toffee candy bars (1.4 ounces each), chopped
½ cup chopped hazelnuts, toasted
Baking cocoa and additional confectioners' sugar

1. Line a 1½-qt. bowl with plastic wrap; set aside. Cut pound cake into ¼-in. slices; set aside six slices for the top. Line bottom and sides of prepared bowl with remaining cake, trimming slices to fit snugly. Brush cake in bowl with some Kahlua.

2. In a small bowl, beat cream cheese, confectioners' sugar, espresso powder and vanilla until blended. In another bowl, beat cream until stiff peaks form; fold into cream cheese mixture. Fold in chopped candy bars and hazelnuts. Spoon over cake.

3. Brush one side of reserved cake slices with remaining Kahlua; place brushed sides down over the filling, trimming slices to fit. Refrigerate, covered, 5 hours or overnight.

4. To serve, unmold onto a serving plate. Remove bowl and plastic wrap; dust cake with cocoa and additional confectioners' sugar. Cut into wedges.

NOTE *To toast nuts, spread in a 15x10x1-in. baking pan. Bake at 350° for 5-10 minutes or until lightly browned, stirring occasionally. Or, spread in a dry nonstick skillet and heat over low heat until lightly browned, stirring occasionally.*

Lamington Roulade

I am a teacher, born in Australia, who came to the United States seven years ago via a teacher exchange program. I'm now married to an American and have two beautiful children. This dessert is made often for special occasions in my mother country, and when I make it for my teacher co-workers here in the U.S., it goes quickly!
—**SUSAN FAGAN** LEXINGTON, SC

PREP: 45 MIN.
BAKE: 10 MIN. + CHILLING
MAKES: 12 SERVINGS

3 eggs
½ cup superfine sugar
¾ cup all-purpose flour
1 teaspoon baking powder
¼ teaspoon salt
2 tablespoons plus ½ cup finely shredded unsweetened coconut, divided
¾ cup plus 2 tablespoons heavy whipping cream, divided
½ cup red raspberry preserves
4 ounces bittersweet chocolate, coarsely chopped
2 tablespoons butter, cubed

1. Preheat oven to 400°. Line the bottom of a greased 15x10x1-in. baking pan with waxed paper and grease paper.
2. In a large bowl, beat eggs on high speed 5 minutes. Gradually add sugar, beating until thick and lemon-colored. In another bowl, whisk flour, baking powder and salt; fold into egg mixture. Transfer to the prepared pan, spreading evenly.
3. Bake 7-9 minutes or until top springs back when lightly touched. Cool 5 minutes. Invert onto a kitchen towel sprinkled with 2 tablespoons coconut. Gently peel off paper. Roll up cake in the towel jelly-roll style, starting with a short side. Cool completely on a wire rack.
4. In a small bowl, beat ¾ cup cream until stiff peaks form. Unroll cake; spread preserves over cake to within ½ in. of edges. Spread whipped cream over preserves. Roll up again, without towel. Place on a platter, seam side down. Refrigerate, covered, at least 1 hour.
5. In a microwave, melt chocolate and butter with remaining cream; stir until smooth. Spread over top and sides of cake. Sprinkle with remaining coconut; let stand until set.
NOTE *Look for unsweetened coconut in the baking or health food section.*

Chocolate Alfajores

Alfajores are a popular South American dessert made of slightly sweetened shortbread cookies filled with a rich and creamy milk caramel called dulce de leche. It's best to chill the dough for at least 2 hours so that the cookies hold when baking.
—**KIMBERLY SCOTT** KOSCIUSKO, MS

PREP: 40 MIN. + CHILLING • **BAKE:** 5 MIN./BATCH + COOLING • **MAKES:** ABOUT 1½ DOZEN

- **½ cup butter, softened**
- **⅓ cup sugar**
- **3 egg yolks**
- **2 teaspoons rum extract or vanilla extract**
- **1 cup all-purpose flour**
- **½ cup cornstarch**
- **¼ cup baking cocoa**
- **½ teaspoon baking soda**
- **⅛ teaspoon salt**
- **1 can (13.4 ounces) dulce de leche**
- **½ cup flaked coconut, finely chopped**

1. In a large bowl, cream butter and sugar until light and fluffy. Beat in egg yolks and extract. In another bowl, whisk flour, cornstarch, cocoa, baking soda and salt; gradually beat into creamed mixture. Shape dough into a disk; wrap in plastic wrap. Refrigerate 2 hours or until firm enough to roll.

2. Preheat oven to 350°. On a lightly floured surface, roll dough to ⅛-in. thickness. Cut with a floured 2-in. round cookie cutter. Place cookies 1 in. apart on greased baking sheets.

3. Bake 5-7 minutes or until just set. Remove from pans to wire racks to cool completely.

4. Spread dulce de leche on bottoms of half of the cookies; cover with remaining cookies. Press edges into coconut. Refrigerate in airtight containers.

NOTE *This recipe was tested with Nestle La Lechera dulce de leche; look for it in the international foods section. If using Eagle Brand dulce de leche (caramel flavored sauce), thicken according to package directions before using.*

Sticky Rice with Mango-Coconut Sauce

As a nice contrast to traditional Christmastime desserts, sweet sticky rice is a refreshing Thai treat made even better with a mango-coconut sauce.
—**MONNIE NORASING** MANSFIELD, TX

PREP: 15 MIN. + SOAKING • **MAKES:** 8 SERVINGS (3 CUPS SAUCE)

- **2 cups uncooked sweet rice**
- **2 medium mangoes**
- **1 can (13.66 ounces) coconut milk**
- **½ cup packed light brown sugar**
- **¼ teaspoon salt**

1. Rinse rice and place in a 3-qt. microwave-safe dish. Cover with water; let stand 1 hour.

2. Drain rice and return to dish; add 2 cups water. Microwave, covered, on high for 8-12 minutes or until the rice is tender, stirring every 3 minutes. Let stand 10 minutes.

3. Meanwhile, peel and thinly slice ½ of a mango; reserve for serving. Peel and coarsely chop remaining mangoes.

4. In a large saucepan, combine coconut milk, brown sugar and salt; cook and stir until heated through and the brown sugar is dissolved. Remove from heat; stir in the chopped mangoes. Cool slightly.

5. Process mango mixture in batches in a blender until smooth. To serve, place warm or room-temperature rice in serving dishes. Spoon sauce over rice; top with sliced mango.

IF USING FROZEN MANGO CHUNKS

Thaw to room temperature and use 2 cups of chopped mango. Remember that 1 fresh mango will yield about 1 cup of chopped fruit.

Flan de Vanilla

PICTURED ON PAGE 49

Flan is a traditional Mexican dessert with many variations. My version is sweet with a pleasant vanilla flavor and luscious caramel sauce.
—SHELISA TERRY HENDERSON, NV

PREP: 35 MIN. • **BAKE:** 35 MIN. + CHILLING • **MAKES:** 6 SERVINGS

- **1¾ cups sugar, divided**
- **1⅓ cups whole milk**
- **1⅓ cups half-and-half cream**
- **3 eggs**
- **4 egg yolks**
- **Dash salt**
- **2 teaspoons vanilla extract**
- **½ cup pomegranate seeds**

1. Preheat oven to 325°. In a small heavy saucepan, spread ¾ cup sugar; cook, without stirring, over medium-low heat until it begins to melt. Gently drag melted sugar to center of pan so sugar melts evenly. Cook, without stirring, until melted sugar turns a medium amber color, about 5 minutes. Quickly pour into six ungreased 6-oz. custard cups.

2. In a small saucepan, heat milk and cream until bubbles form around sides of pan; remove from heat. In a large bowl, whisk eggs, egg yolks, salt and remaining sugar until blended but not foamy. Slowly whisk in hot milk mixture. Stir in vanilla.

3. Place custard cups in a baking pan large enough to hold them without touching. Pour egg mixture into cups. Place pan on oven rack; add very hot water to pan to within ½ in. of top of cups. Bake 35-40 minutes or until center is just set (mixture will jiggle). Remove cups from water bath immediately to a wire rack; cool 10 minutes. Refrigerate until cold.

4. To unmold, run a knife around edges and invert onto individual rimmed dishes. Sprinkle with pomegranate seeds.

Sachertorte Bites

Elegant and simple, these rich confection-like bars are a bite-sized take on the famous Viennese Sachertorte. It's traditionally made with apricot jam, but raspberry would be a fun twist.
—DEIRDRE DEE COX KANSAS CITY, KS

PREP: 25 MIN. • **BAKE:** 15 MIN.+ COOLING • **MAKES:** 40 BARS

- **¾ cup butter, softened**
- **3 ounces unsweetened chocolate**
- **3 eggs**
- **1½ cups sugar**
- **1½ teaspoons vanilla extract**
- **1¼ cups all-purpose flour**
- **1 jar (12 ounces) apricot preserves or seedless raspberry jam**
- **6 ounces semisweet chocolate chips**
- **1 teaspoon shortening**

1. Preheat oven to 325°. In a large saucepan, melt butter and chocolate over low heat; stir until smooth. Remove from heat; cool until mixture is warm.

2. In a large bowl, whisk eggs, sugar and vanilla. Whisk into chocolate mixture. Gradually add flour, mixing well.

3. Spread into a greased 15x10x1-in. baking pan. Bake 15-17 minutes or until the center is set. Cool completely in pan on a wire rack.

4. Microwave preserves on high for 30 seconds, stirring halfway; spread over bars. Let stand until set. Cut into four rectangles; remove rectangles from pan. Layer two rectangles, jam side up. Cut into 20 bars. Repeat with remaining rectangles. Place the bars on waxed paper-lined baking sheets.

5. In a microwave, melt chocolate chips and shortening; stir until smooth. Drizzle over bars; refrigerate until set. Store between layers of waxed paper in an airtight container.

Baklava Pastry Rolls

My niece gave me this recipe for a chocolate twist on traditional baklava—it's a sweet way to end a Greek-inspired meal.

—AGNES WARD STRATFORD, ON

PREP: 1 HOUR + COOLING
BAKE: 15 MIN./BATCH
MAKES: 40 ROLLS

- **3 cups sugar**
- **2 cups water**
- **2 teaspoons lemon juice**
- **2 cinnamon sticks (3 inches)**
- **6 cups finely chopped walnuts**
- **1 teaspoon almond extract**
- **2 packages (16 ounces each, 14x9-inch sheets) frozen phyllo dough, thawed**
- **1½ cups butter, melted**

TOPPING

- **⅓ cup butter, cubed**
- **2½ ounces unsweetened chocolate, chopped**
- **1 cup confectioners' sugar**
- **⅓ cup 2% milk**
- **½ cup finely chopped walnuts**

1. In a large saucepan, bring sugar, water, lemon juice and cinnamon sticks to a boil. Reduce heat; simmer, uncovered, for 20 minutes. Let cool. Discard cinnamon sticks.

2. Preheat oven to 350°. In a large bowl, combine walnuts and extract. Stir in 2 cups syrup. Place one sheet of phyllo dough on a work surface; brush with butter. Layer with an additional phyllo sheet, brush with butter. (Keep remaining phyllo covered with plastic wrap and a damp towel to prevent it from drying out.)

3. Place about 2 tablespoons walnut mixture along one short side; fold sides of phyllo over filling. Roll up tightly, pressing edges to seal. Repeat with remaining phyllo dough, butter and walnut mixture. Place 2 in. apart on ungreased 15x10x1-in. baking pans; brush tops with butter. Bake 15-20 minutes or until golden brown.

4. For topping, in a small heavy saucepan, melt butter and chocolate over medium heat. Add confectioners' sugar and milk; cook and stir for 4-5 minutes or until thickened. Brush remaining syrup over warm pastries. Drizzle with chocolate sauce; sprinkle with walnuts.

Warm Sticky Toffee Pudding

Sticky toffee pudding is a very rich English spiced cake, replete with mincemeat and toasted walnuts and drizzled with buttery warm toffee sauce. Serve it warm or at room temperature. The toffee sauce should be heated just before serving.

—DENISE NYLAND PANAMA CITY, FL

PREP: 25 MIN. • **BAKE:** 45 MIN.
MAKES: 9 SERVINGS

- **¼ cup butter, softened**
- **¾ cup packed brown sugar**
- **1 egg**
- **1 teaspoon vanilla extract**
- **1 cup plus 1 tablespoon all-purpose flour**
- **1 teaspoon baking powder**
- **1 teaspoon baking soda**
- **½ teaspoon salt**
- **2⅓ cups prepared mincemeat**
- **¾ cup chopped walnuts, toasted**

TOFFEE SAUCE

- **½ cup butter, cubed**
- **1 cup packed brown sugar**
- **½ cup heavy whipping cream**

1. Preheat oven to 325°. Grease a 9-in.-square baking pan. In a large bowl, cream butter and brown sugar until blended. Beat in egg and vanilla. In another bowl, whisk flour, baking powder, baking soda and salt; gradually beat into creamed mixture. Stir in mincemeat and walnuts.

2. Transfer batter to prepared pan. Bake 45-50 minutes or until a toothpick inserted in center comes out clean. Cool slightly in pan on a wire rack.

3. Meanwhile, in a small saucepan, melt butter over medium heat; stir in brown sugar and cream. Bring to a boil, stirring to dissolve sugar. Reduce heat; simmer about 5 minutes or until slightly thickened, stirring constantly. Remove from heat. Serve with warm cake.

NOTE *To toast nuts, spread in a 15x10x1-in. baking pan. Bake at 350° for 5-10 minutes or until lightly browned, stirring often. Or, spread in a dry nonstick skillet and heat over low heat until lightly browned, stirring occasionally.*

Blood Orange & Goat Cheese Galette

PICTURED ON PAGE 48

I made this French galette for my mother-in-law's birthday, and it was a sensational hit! There is something about the gorgeous hue of the blood oranges that transforms this rustic pie into an elegant dessert.

—TIA LAWS ENTERPRISE, OR

PREP: 1 HOUR + FREEZING • **BAKE:** 1 HOUR + COOLING • **MAKES:** 8 SERVINGS (⅔ CUP SAUCE)

- **1 cup all-purpose flour**
- **2 tablespoons sugar**
- **½ teaspoon salt**
- **⅓ cup cold butter, cubed**
- **¼ cup quick-cooking oats**
- **4 to 6 tablespoons ice water**

FILLING

- **10 medium blood oranges**
- **¾ cup crumbled goat cheese**
- **3 ounces cream cheese, softened**
- **⅓ cup sour cream**
- **¼ cup honey**
- **¼ teaspoon salt**
- **3 tablespoons coarse sugar, divided**
- **1 tablespoon butter**
- **1 egg yolk**
- **1 tablespoon water**

SAUCE

- **¼ cup butter, cubed**
- **½ cup packed brown sugar**
- **2 tablespoons half-and-half cream**
- **2 tablespoons honey**
- **½ teaspoon ground cinnamon**

1. In a large bowl, mix flour, sugar and salt; cut in butter until crumbly. Stir in oats. Gradually add ice water, tossing with a fork until dough holds together when pressed. Shape into a disk; wrap in plastic wrap. Refrigerate for 1 hour or overnight.

2. On a lightly floured surface, roll dough to a 13-in. circle. Transfer to a parchment paper-lined 14-in. pizza pan. Refrigerate, covered, while preparing the filling.

3. For filling, cut a thin slice from the top and bottom of oranges; stand oranges upright on a cutting board. With a knife, cut peel and outer membrane from oranges. Cut along the membrane of each segment to remove fruit from eight oranges. Thinly slice remaining oranges; remove seeds.

4. In a small bowl, beat goat cheese, cream cheese, sour cream, honey and salt until smooth. Spread over pastry to within 2 in. of edge. Arrange orange segments over cheese mixture. Sprinkle with 2 tablespoons coarse sugar; dot with butter.

5. Fold pastry edge over filling, pleating as you go and leaving an opening in the center. Whisk egg yolk and water; brush over folded pastry. Arrange orange slices over pastry to within 1 in. of edge. Sprinkle with remaining coarse sugar. Freeze, covered, overnight.

6. Preheat oven to 375°. Bake for 60-70 minutes or until the crust is golden and the filling is bubbly. Transfer tart to a wire rack to cool.

7. For sauce, in a small saucepan, melt butter over medium heat. Add brown sugar, cream, honey and cinnamon; bring to a boil. Boil 1 minute, stirring constantly to dissolve the sugar. Serve with the galette.

FRENCH FACT OR FICTION

When you think of French desserts, it's not uncommon to start craving chocolate souffle or the sugary glazed topping of a perfectly prepared creme brulee. But did you know the most common dessert in France is not a super-sweet confection or buttery pastry? It's a simple selection of fresh seasonal fruits paired with savory semi-soft cheeses such as Muenster and goat cheese.

Since being published in December 1843, Charles Dickens' *A Christmas Carol* has remained a popular tale for bookworms, theatergoers and movie lovers. The classic story of Scrooge's transformation from a bitter old man to a character showing generosity and goodwill is credited with reviving the Christmas season as a time for merriment and tradition.

That's exactly what makes this Victorian-era novella such a heartwarming theme for an unforgettable holiday dinner. In this modern approach, invite the family to feast on meat pie and plum pudding as you recount your favorite Dickens' quotes—or maybe a few of your own family anecdotes from Christmases past.

Braised Brussels Sprouts (p. 65)
Garlic-Mustard Rib Roast (p. 66)
Hot Spiced Wine (p. 63)
Squash-Stuffed Baked Apples (p. 64)

CHARLES DICKENS
CHRISTMAS DINNER

Cheddar Cheese & Beer Soup

The taste of beer is subtle, but it's just enough to complement the cheese in this rich and creamy soup. For a slightly sweeter version, you can use apple juice instead of beer.
—**HOLLY LEWIS** SWINK, CO

PREP: 15 MIN. • **COOK:** 25 MIN.
MAKES: 6 SERVINGS

- **¼ cup butter, cubed**
- **¾ pound potatoes, peeled and chopped (about 2 cups)**
- **4 celery ribs, chopped (about 2 cups)**
- **2 medium onions, chopped (about 1½ cups)**
- **2 medium carrots, sliced (about 1 cup)**
- **½ cup all-purpose flour**
- **1½ teaspoons salt**
- **1 teaspoon ground mustard**
- **⅛ teaspoon cayenne pepper**
- **3 cups chicken stock**
- **3 cups (12 ounces) shredded sharp cheddar cheese**
- **2 cups 2% milk**
- **½ cup beer or apple juice**

1. In a Dutch oven, heat butter over medium-high heat. Add potatoes, celery, onions and carrots; cook and stir 5-7 minutes or until onions are tender.
2. Stir in flour, salt, mustard and cayenne until blended; gradually stir in stock. Bring to a boil, stirring occasionally. Reduce heat; simmer, uncovered, 10-12 minutes or until potatoes are tender. Add remaining ingredients; cook and stir until cheese is melted.

Raisin & Walnut Dark Rye Bread

PICTURED AT LEFT

Cocoa and molasses give this rye loaf a deep dark-brown color and rich flavor. The recipe can be made with or without the raisins or walnuts, and can also be turned into buns or rolls.

—BEE ENGELHART BLOOMFIELD TOWNSHIP, MI

PREP: 15 MIN. + RISING • **BAKE:** 30 MIN. + COOLING • **MAKES:** 1 LOAF (1½ POUNDS, 12 SLICES)

- **¾ cup water (70° to 80°)**
- **¼ cup molasses**
- **1 tablespoon butter**
- **2 tablespoons baking cocoa**
- **1 tablespoon caraway seeds**
- **1 teaspoon salt**
- **1¼ cups bread flour**
- **1 cup rye flour**
- **1 tablespoon quick-rise yeast**
- **1 teaspoon cornmeal**
- **½ cup golden raisins**
- **½ cup chopped walnuts, toasted**

1. In bread machine pan, place the first nine ingredients in order suggested by manufacturer. Select dough setting. Check dough after 5 minutes of mixing; add 1-2 tablespoons water or flour if needed.

2. Grease a baking sheet; sprinkle with cornmeal. When cycle is completed, turn dough onto a lightly floured surface. Knead in raisins and walnuts. Shape into a round loaf; transfer to prepared pan. Cover with a kitchen towel; let rise in a warm place until doubled, about 45 minutes. Preheat oven to 375°.

3. Bake 30-35 minutes or until dark golden brown. Remove from pan to a wire rack to cool.

NOTE *To toast nuts, spread in a 15x10x1-in. baking pan. Bake at 350° for 5-10 minutes or until lightly browned, stirring occasionally. Or, spread in a dry nonstick skillet and heat over low heat until lightly browned, stirring occasionally.*

Spiced Baked Beets

Especially when served family-style, this shredded beet casserole is a nice way to dress up the table during Christmastime. A little dash of cloves is all you need to spice it right for the holidays.

—MARGERY RICHMOND LACOMBE, AB

PREP: 20 MIN. • **BAKE:** 1 HOUR • **MAKES:** 10 SERVINGS

- **4 cups shredded peeled beets (about 4 to 5 medium)**
- **1 medium onion, shredded**
- **1 medium potato, shredded**
- **3 tablespoons brown sugar**
- **3 tablespoons canola oil**
- **2 tablespoons water**
- **1 tablespoon cider vinegar**
- **½ teaspoon salt, optional**
- **¼ teaspoon celery seed**
- **¼ teaspoon pepper**
- **⅛ to ¼ teaspoon ground cloves**

1. Preheat oven to 350°. In a large bowl, combine beets, onion and potato. In a small bowl, mix remaining ingredients; pour over vegetables and toss to coat. Transfer to a greased 1½-qt. baking dish.

2. Bake, covered, 45 minutes, stirring occasionally. Uncover; bake 15-25 minutes longer or until vegetables are tender.

ADD A LITTLE GREEN TO YOUR RED

When it comes to beets, you can eat the greens, too. Simply snip off the stems, wash the leaves thoroughly, pat dry and saute them in oil with a little bit of garlic, then season them to your liking.

Christmas Eve Meat Pie

When this pie is baking, my daughter says that the house smells like Christmas. The recipe evolved over the years and is served as part of our family's Christmas Eve celebration. It's a soul-satisfying dinner on a cold winter day.

—MICHELE BOUCHARD KANSAS CITY, MO

PREP: 40 MIN. • **BAKE:** 55 MIN. • **MAKES:** 8 SERVINGS

- **2 tablespoons butter**
- **2 large onions, chopped (about 2 cups)**
- **2 garlic cloves, minced**
- **1 pound lean ground beef (90% lean)**
- **½ pound ground pork**
- **1 can (8 ounces) tomato sauce**
- **1½ teaspoons salt**
- **½ teaspoon dried thyme**
- **¼ teaspoon each ground cloves, ground mace and ground nutmeg**
- **¼ teaspoon pepper**
- **1 package (10 ounces) frozen chopped spinach, thawed and squeezed dry**
- **1 cup frozen shredded hash brown potatoes**
- **1 package (14.1 ounces) refrigerated pie pastry**

1. Preheat oven to 400°. In a Dutch oven, heat butter over medium heat. Add onions; cook and stir 4-6 minutes or until tender. Add garlic; cook 1 minute longer. Add beef and pork; cook 8-10 minutes or until no longer pink, breaking up meat into crumbles. Drain.

2. Stir tomato sauce and seasonings into meat mixture. Stir in spinach and potatoes. Remove from heat.

3. Unroll one pastry sheet into a 9-in. pie plate; trim even with rim. Add filling. Unroll remaining pastry; place over filling. Trim, seal and flute edge. Cut slits in top. Bake 10 minutes.

4. Reduce oven setting to 350°. Bake 45-55 minutes longer or until crust is golden brown. Cover edge loosely with foil during the last 15 minutes if needed to prevent overbrowning.

FINISHING TOUCHES

Do you want your pie to truly shine? Use a pastry brush to lightly and evenly apply one of the following washes to your top crust.

For shine and light browning: Brush with an egg white that was beaten with 1 teaspoon of water.

For gloss: Brush with an egg yolk that was beaten with 1 teaspoon of water.

For a crisp brown crust: Brush with water.

For a slight shine: Brush with half-and-half cream.

Hot Spiced Wine

PICTURED ON PAGE 59

My friends, family and I enjoy this spiced wine during cold-weather gatherings. This warm drink will be especially pleasing to people who enjoy dry red wines.

—NOEL LICKENFELT BOLIVAR, PA

PREP: 15 MIN. • **COOK:** 4 HOURS
MAKES: 8 SERVINGS

- **2 cinnamon sticks (3 inches)**
- **3 whole cloves**
- **2 bottles (750 milliliters each) dry red wine**
- **3 medium tart apples, peeled and sliced**
- **½ cup sugar**
- **1 teaspoon lemon juice**

1. Place cinnamon sticks and cloves on a double thickness of cheesecloth. Gather corners of cloth to enclose seasonings; tie securely with string.

2. In a 3-qt. slow cooker, combine remaining ingredients. Add spice bag. Cook, covered, on low 4-5 hours or until heated through. Discard the spice bag. Serve warm.

Squash-Stuffed Baked Apples

I've tried this dish with different squash and baking apples, and I found that most any will do. It also works well to prepare it several days in advance and refrigerate, then do the final 30 minutes of baking just before serving. My husband and four children all really enjoy my cooking creations.
—CAROLYN BUSCHKAMP EMMETSBURG, IA

PREP: 25 MIN. • **BAKE:** 1½ HOURS • **MAKES:** 8 SERVINGS

- **8 medium tart apples**
- **½ cup plus 1 tablespoon packed brown sugar, divided**
- **½ cup orange juice**
- **½ cup water**
- **2 tablespoons butter**
- **2½ cups mashed cooked butternut squash**
- **¼ teaspoon salt**
- **½ teaspoon ground nutmeg, divided**

1. Preheat oven to 325°. Core apples, leaving bottoms intact; peel top third of each. Remove centers of apples, leaving ½-in. shells; chop removed apple and set aside.
2. Place cored apples in an ungreased 13x9-in. baking dish. In a small bowl, mix ½ cup brown sugar, orange juice and water; pour over apples. Bake, uncovered, 1 hour or until apples are tender, basting occasionally with juice mixture.
3. In a large saucepan, heat butter over medium-high heat. Add chopped apple; cook and stir until tender. Stir in squash; bring to a boil. Reduce heat; simmer, covered, 5 minutes, stirring frequently. Stir in the salt, ¼ teaspoon nutmeg and remaining brown sugar. Spoon into apples; sprinkle with the remaining nutmeg.
4. Bake 30-35 minutes longer or until heated through, basting occasionally. Drizzle with pan juices before serving.

Braised Brussels Sprouts

PICTURED ON PAGE 58

Bacon, caraway and onion give this side dish a homey flavor that goes great with beef roast. Here's a little trick for preparing it: Cutting the core of the Brussels sprouts helps the hot water reach the centers—so they cook more quickly and evenly.

—**YVONNE ANDERSON** NEW PHILADELPHIA, OH

START TO FINISH: 30 MIN. • **MAKES:** 8 SERVINGS

- **2 pounds Brussels sprouts**
- **2 bacon strips, chopped**
- **1 medium onion, chopped**
- **1 cup chicken broth**
- **1 teaspoon caraway seeds**
- **¼ teaspoon salt**
- **⅛ teaspoon pepper**

1. Trim Brussels sprout stems; using a paring knife, cut an "X" in the bottom of each. In a large saucepan, bring ½ in. of water to a boil. Add sprouts; cook, covered, 8-10 minutes or until crisp-tender. Drain.

2. Meanwhile, in a large skillet, cook bacon over medium heat until crisp. Remove with a slotted spoon; drain on paper towels.

3. Cook and stir onion in bacon drippings until tender. Stir in remaining ingredients. Bring to a boil. Reduce heat; simmer, uncovered, until liquid is almost evaporated. Add Brussels sprouts; stir in bacon.

Christmas Wassail

After everyone is served cups of steaming, spiced cider, we all give the wassail toast, "Be whole. Good health to you."

—**PATRICIA ATKINS** PALMER LAKE, CO

PREP: 40 MIN. • **COOK:** 25 MIN. • **MAKES:** 42 SERVINGS (¾ CUP EACH)

- **3 medium McIntosh or Rome apples, halved and cored**
- **½ cup water**
- **2 gallons apple cider or juice, divided**
- **2 medium navel oranges, halved and sliced**
- **2 medium lemons, halved and sliced**
- **1½ cups sugar**
- **1 cinnamon stick (3 inches), halved**
- **½ teaspoon ground nutmeg**
- **½ teaspoon ground cloves**

1. Preheat oven to 375°. Place apples in an 8-in.-square baking dish, cut side down. Pour water around apples. Bake, uncovered, 20-25 minutes or until tender. Cool slightly.

2. When cool enough to handle, scoop out pulp from apples and place in a blender; discard apple peel. Add ½ cup cider to blender; cover and process until smooth.

3. In a stockpot, combine the remaining ingredients, apple puree and remaining cider. Bring to a boil. Reduce heat; simmer, uncovered, 15 minutes. If desired, discard citrus slices and cinnamon stick before serving.

Garlic-Mustard Rib Roast

PICTURED ON PAGE 59

This is one of my favorite ways to prepare a roast because it turns out so tender and flavorful. My husband and our six children just love it!

—DONNA CONLIN GILMOUR, ON

PREP: 5 MIN. • **BAKE:** 2¼ HOURS + STANDING • **MAKES:** 10 SERVINGS

- **1 bone-in beef rib roast (6 to 8 pounds)**
- **1 tablespoon garlic powder**
- **1 tablespoon ground mustard**
- **1 to 2 teaspoons salt**
- **1 to 2 teaspoons pepper**
- **¼ cup water**
- **¼ cup beef broth**
- **1 tablespoon red wine vinegar**

1. Preheat oven to 350°. Place roast in a shallow roasting pan, fat side up. Mix seasonings; rub over roast. Add water, broth and vinegar to pan.

2. Roast 2¼ to 2¾ hours or until meat reaches desired doneness (for medium-rare, a thermometer should read 145°; medium, 160°; well-done, 170°). Baste occasionally with pan juices. Remove roast from oven; tent with foil. Let stand 15 minutes before carving.

Lemon Cream Scones

As a quick way to warm everyone up, I make these lemony scones to go with a pot of hot tea. Sometimes I like to add dried cherries to the batter to jazz it up a little.

—ANGELA MATZ WEST ALLIS, WI

PREP: 15 MIN. • **BAKE:** 20 MIN. • **MAKES:** 8 SCONES

- **3 cups all-purpose flour**
- **⅓ cup plus 1 tablespoon sugar, divided**
- **3 teaspoons baking powder**
- **¼ teaspoon salt**
- **½ cup cold butter**
- **¾ cup plus 1 tablespoon heavy whipping cream, divided**
- **2 eggs**
- **2 teaspoons lemon extract**
- **¼ teaspoon ground cinnamon**

1. Preheat oven to 400°. In a large bowl, whisk flour, ⅓ cup sugar, baking powder and salt. Cut in butter until mixture resembles coarse crumbs. In another bowl, whisk ¾ cup cream, eggs and lemon extract until blended; stir into crumb mixture just until moistened.

2. Turn onto a lightly floured surface; knead gently 10 times. Pat dough into an 8-in. circle. Cut into eight wedges.

3. Place wedges on a greased baking sheet. Mix cinnamon and remaining sugar. Brush tops with remaining cream; sprinkle with cinnamon-sugar. Bake 20-25 minutes or until golden brown. Serve warm.

SCONE CRUST: SOFT OR CRISP?

Scones are generally patted into a circle and cut into wedges. If the wedges are separated, the scones will have a crisper crust. If the wedges are cut and not separated, the scones will have a softer crust. Either way, they should be stored in an airtight container and eaten within 1 to 2 days or frozen for up to 3 months.

Tiny Tim's Plum Pudding

We first read about this English tradition in *A Christmas Carol*. In the story, everyone clapped for plum pudding. Since then, we made this pudding every year.

—RUTHANNE KAREL
HUDSONVILLE, MI

PREP: 30 MIN. • **COOK:** 2 HOURS
MAKES: 12 SERVINGS (1½ CUPS SAUCE)

- **½ cup butter, softened**
- **¾ cup packed brown sugar**
- **3 eggs**
- **¾ cup dry bread crumbs**
- **½ cup all-purpose flour**
- **1 tablespoon grated orange peel**
- **1 teaspoon ground cinnamon**
- **½ teaspoon baking soda**
- **½ teaspoon ground nutmeg**
- **¼ teaspoon salt**
- **¼ teaspoon ground cloves**
- **2 cans (15 ounces each) plums, drained, pitted and chopped**
- **1¾ cups chopped dates**
- **1 cup golden raisins**
- **1 cup shredded carrots**
- **½ cup dried currants**

HARD SAUCE

- **½ cup butter, softened**
- **3 cups confectioners' sugar**
- **¼ cup dark rum or orange juice**

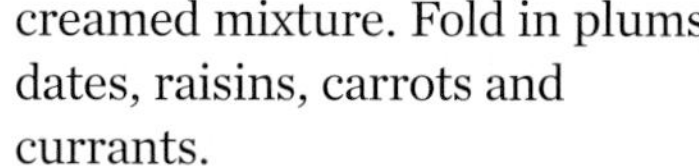

1. Generously grease an 8-cup pudding mold, metal gelatin mold or ovenproof bowl.

2. In a large bowl, cream butter and brown sugar until light and fluffy. Add eggs, one at a time, beating well after each addition. In another bowl, mix bread crumbs, flour, orange peel, cinnamon, baking soda, nutmeg, salt and cloves; gradually add to creamed mixture. Fold in plums, dates, raisins, carrots and currants.

3. Transfer to prepared pudding mold. Cover tightly with heavy-duty foil; tie foil with kitchen string to secure.

4. Place on a rack in a stockpot; add 3 in. of hot water to pot. Bring water to a gentle boil; steam cake, covered, for 2 to 2½ hours or until a toothpick inserted in center comes out clean; add additional water to pot as needed. Remove pudding from pot; let stand 5 minutes before unmolding.

5. Meanwhile, in a bowl, beat hard sauce ingredients until smooth and creamy. Unmold pudding onto a serving plate; serve warm with sauce.

Those aren't just any cookies...those are about to make the most memorable Christmas gift of the year. They're also the kind of cookies that can save you countless trips to a crowded shopping center and spare you the stress of deciding what to get for your neighbors, co-workers and friends. With varieties like Key-Lime Butter Cookies (p. 70) and Merry Cherry Cookie Tarts (p.77), 'tis the season to give extraordinary and unforgettable Christmas treats. The only problem you'll have is trying to top this gift next year.

Red Velvet Peppermint Thumbprints (p. 75)

THE GIFT OF **COOKIES**

Key-Lime Butter Cookies

I love limes so much that if a recipe calls for lemons, I almost always use limes instead. With their pretty green color, these are perfect for Christmas—you can also make them as sandwich cookies and use lime curd for the filling.

—DEIRDRE DEE COX KANSAS CITY, KS

PREP: 25 MIN.
BAKE: 10 MIN./BATCH + COOLING
MAKES: 3 DOZEN

1 cup butter, softened
½ cup confectioners' sugar
1 tablespoon grated lime peel
½ teaspoon vanilla extract
1¾ cups all-purpose flour
¼ cup cornstarch
Sugar

GLAZE

½ cup confectioners' sugar
4 teaspoons Key lime or regular lime juice
1 teaspoon grated lime peel
Green decorating gel, optional

1. Preheat oven to 350°. In a large bowl, cream butter and confectioners' sugar until light and fluffy. Beat in lime peel and vanilla. In another bowl, whisk flour and cornstarch; gradually beat into creamed mixture.

2. Shape dough into 1-in. balls; place 1 in. apart on ungreased baking sheets. Flatten to ¼-in. thickness with bottom of a glass dipped in sugar. Bake 8-10 minutes or until bottoms are light brown. Remove from pans to wire racks to cool completely.

3. In a small bowl, mix confectioners' sugar, lime juice and peel. Brush over cookies. Let stand until set. If desired, decorate with gel just before serving.

Star-Bright Cookies

PICTURED AT LEFT

Sugar cookies are a must-have on any holiday cookie tray. These sweet star cookies are super-cute and buttery, and they require no frosting.

—ANETA KISH LA CROSSE, WI

PREP: 40 MIN. + CHILLING • **BAKE:** 10 MIN./BATCH • **MAKES:** ABOUT 2 DOZEN

- **½ cup butter, softened**
- **½ cup sugar**
- **1 egg yolk**
- **3 tablespoons milk**
- **1½ teaspoons vanilla extract**
- **1½ cups all-purpose flour**
- **½ teaspoon baking powder**
- **¼ teaspoon salt**
- **½ teaspoon peppermint extract**
- **4 drops red food coloring**
- **Edible glitter**

1. In a large bowl, cream butter and sugar until light and fluffy. Gradually beat in egg yolk, milk and vanilla. In another bowl, whisk flour, baking powder and salt; gradually beat into the creamed mixture.

2. Remove ½ cup dough; stir in peppermint extract and food coloring. Wrap both portions of dough in plastic wrap and refrigerate until easy to handle.

3. Preheat oven to 375°. On a lightly floured surface, roll plain dough to ⅛-in. thickness; cut with a floured 2-in. round cookie cutter. Place 1 in. apart on greased baking sheets. Roll the peppermint dough to ⅛-in. thickness; cut with a floured 1½-in. star-shaped cookie cutter. Place one star in the center of each round cutout; sprinkle with glitter.

4. Bake 9-11 minutes or until edges are lightly browned. Cool on pans for 1 minute. Remove to wire racks to cool.

NOTE *Edible glitter is available from Wilton Industries. Call 800-794-5866 or visit wilton.com.*

Cinnamon-Sour Cream Pinwheels

My grandmother would make these for holidays and special occasions. Since they are my favorite cookie, she brought me some at the hospital the day my son was born in lieu of flowers. It was very much appreciated and a tasty surprise.

—LAURA BERLINGUETTE GATINEAU, QC

PREP: 35 MIN. + CHILLING • **BAKE:** 10 MIN./BATCH • **MAKES:** 6½ DOZEN

- **1 cup butter, softened**
- **½ cup sugar**
- **2 egg yolks**
- **¾ cup sour cream**
- **3½ cups all-purpose flour**
- **1 teaspoon baking powder**
- **½ teaspoon salt**

FILLING

- **1 cup finely chopped walnuts**
- **⅓ cup sugar**
- **1 teaspoon ground cinnamon**
- **1 egg white, lightly beaten**

1. In a large bowl, cream butter and sugar until light and fluffy. Beat in egg yolks and sour cream. In another bowl, whisk flour, baking powder and salt; gradually add to creamed mixture. Divide dough in half. Shape each half into a disk; wrap in plastic wrap. Refrigerate at least 2 hours or until easy to handle.

2. In a small bowl, mix walnuts, sugar and cinnamon. On a lightly floured surface, roll each portion of dough into a 12x9-in. rectangle. Brush with egg white; sprinkle each with half of the walnut mixture. Roll up jelly-roll style, starting with a long side. Wrap in plastic wrap and refrigerate 1 hour or overnight.

3. Preheat oven to 350°. Unwrap and cut dough crosswise into ¼-in. slices. Place 1 in. apart on greased baking sheets. Bake 10-12 minutes or until bottoms are golden brown. Remove to wire racks to cool.

Espresso Shortbread Squares

I developed this recipe several years ago to leave out for Santa on Christmas Eve. The delightful espresso offers a jolly jolt for his last-minute toy assembly!
—LISA RENSHAW KANSAS CITY, MO

PREP: 15 MIN. + CHILLING • **BAKE:** 20 MIN./BATCH + COOLING • **MAKES:** 25 COOKIES

- **1 tablespoon instant espresso powder**
- **1 tablespoon hot water**
- **1 cup butter, softened**
- **⅔ cup confectioners' sugar**
- **½ teaspoon vanilla extract**
- **2 cups all-purpose flour**
- **1 cup white baking chips**
- **½ cup dried cherries, coarsely chopped**
- **Additional confectioners' sugar**

1. In a small bowl, dissolve espresso powder in hot water. In a large bowl, cream butter and confectioners' sugar until light and fluffy. Beat in vanilla and dissolved espresso mixture. Gradually beat in flour. Stir in baking chips and cherries.

2. On a sheet of plastic wrap, pat dough into a 10-in. square; wrap tightly and refrigerate at least 2 hours or until firm.

3. Preheat oven to 325°. Unwrap dough; cut into 2-in. squares. Place 1 in. apart on a parchment paper-lined baking sheet. Prick holes in each cookie with a fork. Bake 20-25 minutes or until set.

4. Remove from pans to wire racks to cool completely. Dust lightly with additional confectioners' sugar. Store in airtight containers.

Crunchy Apricot-Coconut Balls

My mom gave me this no-bake cookie recipe years ago when she had them on her Christmas buffet. I can't believe how simple they are to make.
—JANE MCMILLAN DANIA BEACH, FL

START TO FINISH: 30 MIN. • **MAKES:** 2 DOZEN

- **1¼ cups flaked coconut**
- **1 cup dried apricots, finely chopped**
- **⅔ cup chopped pecans**
- **½ cup fat-free sweetened condensed milk**
- **½ cup confectioners' sugar**

1. In a small bowl, combine coconut, apricots and pecans. Add condensed milk; mix well (mixture will be sticky).

2. Shape into 1¼-in. balls and roll in confectioners' sugar. Store in an airtight container in the refrigerator.

REVIVING COCONUT

To soften shredded coconut that's turned hard, soak it in milk for 30 minutes. Then drain the coconut and pat dry on paper towels before using. The leftover coconut-flavored milk can be used within 5 days in baked goods or blended with fresh fruit for a tasty beverage.

Cranberry-Pistachio Christmas Cookies

The cranberries and pistachios are what make this cookie look and taste like Christmas. I particularly enjoy the contrasting tartness of the cranberries with the sweetness of the cookie and filling.

—DION FRISCHER

ANN ARBOR, MI

PREP: 40 MIN.+ CHILLING
BAKE: 10 MIN./BATCH + COOLING
MAKES: 3 DOZEN

½ cup butter, softened
¼ cup sugar
¼ cup packed brown sugar
1 egg yolk
1 teaspoon grated orange peel
1 cup all-purpose flour
1 cup dried cranberries
¾ cup plus 2 tablespoons finely chopped pistachios, divided
⅔ cup white baking chips
¼ cup heavy whipping cream
36 dried cranberries

1. Preheat oven to 350°. In a small bowl, cream butter and sugars until light and fluffy. Beat in egg yolk and orange peel. Gradually beat in flour. Stir in cranberries and ¾ cup of the pistachios.

2. Shape dough into 1-in. balls. Place 2 in. apart on ungreased baking sheets. Press a deep indentation in the center of each with the end of a wooden spoon handle.

3. Bake 9-11 minutes or until edges are light brown. Remove from pans to wire racks to cool completely.

4. Meanwhile, place baking chips in a small bowl. In a small saucepan, bring cream just to a boil. Pour over baking chips; stir with a whisk until smooth. Cool to room temperature, stirring occasionally. Refrigerate, covered, until thickened.

5. Spoon ganache onto cookies; sprinkle with remaining pistachios. Top each with cranberry pieces. Refrigerate leftovers.

Almond-Ricotta Twists

A very dear friend gave me this recipe, so I make these to remind me of our time together. I like to drizzle melted white chocolate or chocolate chips over the baked cookies.
—PAULA J. PRECHTL BROCKPORT, PA

PREP: 45 MIN. + CHILLING
BAKE: 15 MIN./BATCH + COOLING
MAKES: ABOUT 6½ DOZEN

- **1 cup sugar**
- **1 cup butter, melted and cooled**
- **2 eggs**
- **1 cup ricotta cheese**
- **2 teaspoons almond extract**
- **4 cups all-purpose flour**
- **2 teaspoons baking powder**
- **1 teaspoon baking soda**
- **1 teaspoon salt**
- **1 cup white baking chips, melted**

1. In a large bowl, beat sugar and butter until blended. Beat in eggs, then ricotta cheese and extract. In another bowl, whisk flour, baking powder, baking soda and salt; gradually beat into the creamed mixture. Refrigerate, covered, 2 hours or until firm enough to shape.
2. Preheat oven to 350°. Using 1 tablespoon of dough for each cookie, divide in half and shape each into a 3-in. rope. (If dough is soft, work in batches and keep remaining dough chilled until ready to shape.) Twist two ropes around each other, pinching and tucking under ends. Place 2-in. apart on ungreased baking sheets.
3. Bake 12-15 minutes or until golden brown. Cool 1 minute before removing to wire racks to cool completely.
4. Drizzle melted chocolate over cookies; let stand until set. Store in airtight containers.

Red Velvet Peppermint Thumbprints

PICTURED ON PAGE 69

I love red velvet cookies and cakes but always wish they had a little more taste. So, for this thumbprint cookie, I added my favorite holiday flavor, peppermint!

—**PRISCILLA YEE** CONCORD, CA

PREP: 30 MIN. • **BAKE:** 10 MIN./BATCH + COOLING • **MAKES:** 4 DOZEN

- **1 cup butter, softened**
- **1 cup sugar**
- **1 egg**
- **4 teaspoons red food coloring**
- **1 teaspoon peppermint extract**
- **2½ cups all-purpose flour**
- **3 tablespoons baking cocoa**
- **1 teaspoon baking powder**
- **¼ teaspoon salt**
- **2 cups white baking chips**
- **2 teaspoons canola oil**
- **¼ cup crushed peppermint candies**

1. Preheat oven to 350°. In a large bowl, cream butter and sugar until light and fluffy. Beat in egg, food coloring and extract. In another bowl, whisk flour, baking cocoa, baking powder and salt; gradually beat into the creamed mixture.

2. Shape dough into 1-in. balls. Place 1 in. apart on ungreased baking sheets. Press a deep indentation in center of each with the end of a wooden spoon handle. Bake 9-11 minutes or until set. Remove from pans to wire racks to cool completely.

3. In a microwave, melt baking chips with oil; stir until smooth. Fill each cookie with a scant teaspoon of filling. Drizzle remaining mixture over tops; sprinkle with crushed candies. Cool completely. Store in airtight containers.

Pistachio-Mint Meringue Cookies

This was one of my mom's favorite holiday cookie recipes. Light as air and with the flavors and colors of Christmas, each batch I bake is a sweet reminder of how precious those times with her were.

—**LISA RENSHAW** KANSAS CITY, MO

PREP: 15 MIN. • **BAKE:** 1 HOUR + COOLING • **MAKES:** 10 DOZEN

- **4 egg whites**
- **1 teaspoon vanilla extract**
- **¼ teaspoon cream of tartar**
- **¼ teaspoon salt**
- **¾ cup sugar**
- **1 package (10 to 12 ounces) white baking chips**
- **1 cup chopped pistachios**
- **1 cup finely crushed peppermint candies**
- **Additional chopped pistachios, optional**

1. Place egg whites in a large bowl; let stand at room temperature 30 minutes.

2. Preheat oven to 225°. Add vanilla, cream of tartar and salt to egg whites; beat on medium speed until foamy. Gradually add sugar, 1 tablespoon at a time, beating on high after each addition until sugar is dissolved. Continue beating until stiff glossy peaks form. Fold in baking chips, pistachios and crushed candies.

3. Drop by rounded teaspoonfuls 1 in. apart onto parchment paper-lined baking sheets. If desired, sprinkle with additional pistachios. Bake 1 to 1¼ hours or until firm to the touch. Remove to wire racks to cool completely. Store in airtight containers.

Toffee Snowman Cookies

My family loves toffee, so I'm always trying to find new ways to bake with it. These cookies are so easy to make and are wonderful for a Christmas cookie exchange. Chilling the dough before baking and paying attention to the baking time are essential so they don't turn too brown.
—CHRISTINE MERTEN MENOMONEE FALLS, WI

PREP: 30 MIN. + CHILLING • **BAKE:** 15 MIN. + COOLING • **MAKES:** ABOUT 5 DOZEN

1 cup butter, softened
1⅔ cups confectioners' sugar, divided
¼ teaspoon salt
½ teaspoon vanilla extract
2¼ cups all-purpose flour
1 cup (6 ounces) miniature semisweet chocolate chips
1 cup brickle toffee bits
⅔ cup finely chopped pecans, toasted
Green, orange and red confetti sprinkles

1. Preheat oven to 350°. In a large bowl, cream butter, ⅓ cup confectioners' sugar and salt until light and fluffy. Beat in vanilla. Gradually beat in flour. Stir in chocolate chips, toffee bits and pecans. Refrigerate, covered, 1 hour or until easy to handle.

2. Shape dough into 1-in. balls; place 1 in. apart on ungreased baking sheets. Bake 12-15 minutes or until set. Cool on pans for 2 minutes. Remove to wire racks. Roll warm cookies in remaining confectioners' sugar. Cool completely on wire racks.

3. Reroll cookies in the remaining confectioners' sugar. Decorate using green sprinkles for snowman eyes, orange sprinkles for nose, and red sprinkles for mouth.

NOTE *To toast nuts, spread in a 15x10x1-in. baking pan. Bake at 350° for 5-10 minutes or until lightly browned, stirring occasionally. Or, spread in a dry nonstick skillet and heat over low heat until lightly browned, stirring occasionally.*

Candy Cane Drop Cookies

One of our family's favorites, this recipe came about by combining my love of peppermint candy canes and sugar cookies. We drizzle melted white chocolate over the cookies and sprinkle them with coarsely-crushed candy canes for a Christmastime look.
—MEG BAGLEY LOGAN, UT

PREP: 20 MIN. • **BAKE:** 10 MIN./BATCH + COOLING • **MAKES:** 3 DOZEN

½ cup plus 2 tablespoons unsalted butter, softened
1 cup sugar
1 egg
1 egg yolk
1 teaspoon vanilla extract
2 cups all-purpose flour
½ teaspoon salt
½ teaspoon baking powder
⅔ cup crushed candy canes (about 8), divided
6 ounces white baking chocolate, melted

1. Preheat oven to 350°. In a large bowl, cream butter and sugar until light and fluffy. Beat in egg, egg yolk and vanilla. In another bowl, whisk flour, salt and baking powder; gradually beat into creamed mixture. Stir in ⅓ cup crushed candy canes.

2. Drop dough by tablespoonfuls 2 in. apart onto greased baking sheets. Bake 9-11 minutes or until firm. Cool on pans for 2 minutes. Remove to wire racks to cool completely.

3. Drizzle melted chocolate over cookies; sprinkle with the remaining crushed candy canes. Refrigerate until set. Store in airtight containers.

Merry Cherry Cookie Tarts

I love to cook and bake, and I think these are the best-ever Christmas cookies! Tender almond-flavored dough with a sweet cherry filling and thin glaze just feels like the holidays.
—JANICE CHRISTOFFERSON EAGLE RIVER, WI

PREP: 45 MIN. + CHILLING • **BAKE:** 15 MIN./BATCH + COOLING • **MAKES:** 3 DOZEN

- **¾ cup unsalted butter, softened**
- **¾ cup sugar**
- **1 egg**
- **2 tablespoons 2% milk**
- **1 teaspoon almond extract**
- **2½ cups all-purpose flour**
- **¼ teaspoon baking soda**
- **¼ teaspoon salt**
- **¾ cup cherry preserves**
- **1 egg white, lightly beaten**

GLAZE

- **1 cup confectioners' sugar**
- **2 tablespoons 2% milk**
- **½ teaspoon vanilla extract**

1. In a large bowl, cream butter and sugar until light and fluffy. Beat in egg, milk and extract. In another bowl, whisk flour, baking soda and salt; gradually beat into creamed mixture. Divide dough in half. Shape each into a disk; wrap in plastic wrap. Refrigerate 1 hour or until easy to handle.
2. Preheat oven to 350°. On a lightly floured surface, roll one portion of dough to ⅛-in. thickness. Cut with a floured 2-in. round cookie cutter.
3. Place half of the cutouts 2 in. apart on greased baking sheets. Top each with a heaping teaspoonful of preserves; top with remaining cutouts. Crimp edges together with a fork to seal. With a sharp knife, cut an "X" in the top of each cookie. Brush tops with egg white.
4. Bake 12-15 minutes or until edges are light brown. Remove to wire racks to cool completely.
5. In a small bowl, mix the glaze ingredients; spread over cooled cookies. Let stand until set.

Chocolate Orange Checkerboard Cookies

I use these for gifts during the holidays because I like the elegant flavor combination of chocolate and orange. The shortbread texture melts in your mouth, and the walnuts add a nice crunch.

—SANDY PAIGE APO, AE

PREP: 30 MIN. + CHILLING • **BAKE:** 10 MIN./BATCH • **MAKES:** ABOUT 3½ DOZEN

1¼ cups butter, softened
1½ cups confectioners' sugar
¼ teaspoon salt
1 egg
1 teaspoon vanilla extract
3 cups cake flour
1½ cups finely chopped pecans
¼ cup baking cocoa
1 teaspoon grated orange peel
½ teaspoon orange extract

1. In a large bowl, cream butter, confectioners' sugar and salt until blended. Beat in egg and vanilla. Gradually beat in flour. Stir in pecans.

2. Divide dough in half. Mix baking cocoa into one half; mix orange peel and extract into the remaining half.

3. Shape each portion into a 5½x2x2-in. block. Wrap each block in plastic wrap; refrigerate 30 minutes. Unwrap dough; cut each block lengthwise into quarters, making four 5½x1x1-in. sticks. Switch two of the chocolate sticks with two of the orange sticks, forming two checkerboard blocks. Gently press sticks together to adhere. Rewrap in plastic wrap; refrigerate 2 hours or until firm.

4. Preheat oven to 350°. Unwrap and cut dough crosswise into ¼-in. slices. Place 1 in. apart on ungreased baking sheets. Bake 9-11 minutes or until set. Remove from pans to wire racks to cool.

Chocolate-Dipped Triple-Ginger Cookies

My mother always enjoyed chocolate-covered ginger, so she decided to turn her favorite treat into a cookie. In retrospect, the cookie is an expression of her own character, which is unforgettable and always delightful.

—BETHANY HAMMOND VANCOUVER, WA

PREP: 35 MIN. + CHILLING • **BAKE:** 10 MIN./BATCH + COOLING • **MAKES:** ABOUT 3 DOZEN

- **1 cup shortening**
- **½ cup sugar**
- **½ cup packed brown sugar**
- **1 egg**
- **1 cup molasses**
- **2 tablespoons finely chopped crystallized ginger**
- **2 teaspoons grated fresh gingerroot**
- **4⅔ cups all-purpose flour**
- **1½ teaspoons baking powder**
- **¾ teaspoon baking soda**
- **2 teaspoons ground ginger**
- **½ teaspoon salt**
- **½ teaspoon ground cinnamon**
- **½ teaspoon ground nutmeg**
- **2 packages (10 ounces each) 60% cacao bittersweet chocolate baking chips, melted**
- **4 ounces white baking chocolate, melted**

1. In a large bowl, cream shortening and sugars until light and fluffy. Beat in egg, then molasses, crystallized ginger and gingerroot. In another bowl, whisk flour, baking powder, baking soda and seasonings; gradually beat into the creamed mixture.

2. Divide dough in half. Shape each half into a disk; wrap in plastic wrap. Refrigerate 1 hour or until firm enough to roll.

3. Preheat oven to 375°. On a lightly floured surface, roll each portion of dough to ⅛-in. thickness. Cut with a floured 2½-in. round, 3-in. gingerbread man cookie cutter or cookie cutter of your choice. Place 2 in. apart on ungreased baking sheets. Bake 8-10 minutes or until set. Remove from pans to wire racks to cool completely.

4. Dip each cookie halfway into melted dark chocolate, allowing excess to drip off. Place on waxed paper; let stand until set. Drizzle with melted white chocolate; let stand until set.

PIPE ON ROYAL ICING

1. Cut a small hole in the corner of a plastic bag. Insert a round tip. Fill bag with icing. Hold bag at 45° angle and pipe around edge. Stop squeezing before you lift the tip from the cookie.

2. Thin the remaining icing. Fill another bag with thinned icing. Starting in the middle, fill in the cookie with icing, letting the icing flow up to the outline. Let dry overnight.

3. With a new small paintbrush, paint your own designs on the cookies with liquid food coloring.

You resolved to cook more at home, eat healthier with your family and entertain friends more often. With all that you've pledged for the upcoming months, and with the hustle and bustle of the holiday season behind you, you're ready to kick off the New Year with the new you. Get started with five dinner-party menus that are as impressive and delicious as they are healthy and light—and that includes dessert! Here's to a fresh new start.

FIVE HEALTHY MENUS

Pear & Peanut Spinach Salad (p. 88)
Grapefruit-Gremolata Salmon (p. 89)

NEW YEAR **NEW YOU**

Sesame Asparagus Risotto

Asparagus is one of my favorite ingredients to work into recipes. It gives this nutty risotto a beautiful pop of color.
—SHERRY JOHNSTON GREEN COVE SPRINGS, FL

PREP: 10 MIN. • **COOK:** 35 MIN. • **MAKES:** 8 SERVINGS

- **5 cups vegetable broth**
- **2 tablespoons butter**
- **1½ cups uncooked arborio rice**
- **1 pound cut fresh asparagus (1-inch pieces)**
- **½ teaspoon grated orange peel**
- **1 tablespoon sesame oil**
- **⅓ cup sliced almonds, toasted**
- **4 teaspoons sesame seeds, toasted**

1. In a large saucepan, bring broth to a simmer; keep hot. In another large saucepan, heat butter over medium heat. Add rice; cook and stir 1-2 minutes or until rice is coated.

2. Stir in 1 cup hot broth. Reduce heat to maintain a simmer; cook and stir until broth is absorbed. Add an additional 2 cups broth, ½ cup at a time, cooking and stirring until broth has been absorbed after each addition. Stir in asparagus.

3. Continue stirring in remaining broth, ½ cup at a time, until rice is tender but firm to the bite and risotto is creamy. Remove from heat; stir in orange peel.

4. Serve immediately. Drizzle top with sesame oil; sprinkle with almonds and sesame seeds.

NOTE *To toast almonds and sesame seeds, place each separately in a dry nonstick skillet and heat over low heat until lightly browned, stirring frequently.*

LAVA-LICIOUS AND LIGHT

The chocolaty insides of this cake ooze out like lava when you break into it. It's so rich and decadent, you'd never guess that each serving has only 207 calories and just 4 grams of fat.

Slow Cooker Lava Cake

Because I love chocolate, this lava cake has long been a family favorite. We like to eat it while the cake is still slightly warm.
—ELIZABETH FARRELL HAMILTON, MT

PREP: 15 MIN. • **COOK:** 2 HOURS + STANDING • **MAKES:** 8 SERVINGS

- **1 cup all-purpose flour**
- **1 cup packed brown sugar, divided**
- **5 tablespoons baking cocoa, divided**
- **2 teaspoons baking powder**
- **¼ teaspoon salt**
- **½ cup fat-free milk**
- **2 tablespoons canola oil**
- **½ teaspoon vanilla extract**
- **⅛ teaspoon ground cinnamon**
- **1¼ cups hot water**

1. In a large bowl, whisk the flour, ½ cup brown sugar, 3 tablespoons cocoa, baking powder and salt. In another bowl, whisk milk, oil and vanilla until blended. Add to flour mixture; stir just until moistened.

2. Spread into a 3-qt. slow cooker coated with cooking spray. In a small bowl, mix cinnamon and the remaining brown sugar and cocoa; stir in hot water. Pour over batter (do not stir).

3. Cook, covered, on high 2 to 2½ hours or until a toothpick inserted in cake portion comes out clean. Turn off slow cooker; let cake stand 15 minutes; serve.

Makeover Spinach-Stuffed Chicken Pockets

For an easy, upscale chicken dish, you'll love these spinach-stuffed chicken breasts. You can also double the recipe without much effort.
—TASTE OF HOME TEST KITCHEN

START TO FINISH: 30 MIN.
MAKES: 4 SERVINGS

3 teaspoons olive oil, divided
4 cups fresh baby spinach
1 garlic clove, minced
½ cup reduced-fat garlic-herb spreadable cheese
1 teaspoon Italian seasoning, divided
⅓ cup plus ½ cup panko (Japanese) bread crumbs, divided
4 boneless skinless chicken breast halves (6 ounces each)
¼ teaspoon salt
¼ teaspoon pepper
1 egg white
1 tablespoon water

1. Preheat oven to 400°. In a large skillet, heat 1 teaspoon oil over medium-high heat. Add spinach; cook and stir 1-2 minutes or until wilted. Add garlic; cook 1 minute longer. Remove from heat. Stir in spreadable cheese, 1/4 teaspoon Italian seasoning and 1/3 cup bread crumbs.
2. Cut a pocket horizontally in the thickest part of each chicken breast. Fill with spinach mixture; secure with toothpicks.
3. In a shallow bowl, toss the remaining bread crumbs with salt, pepper and remaining Italian seasoning. In a separate shallow bowl, whisk egg white and water. Dip both sides of chicken in egg white mixture, then in crumb mixture, patting to help the coating adhere.
4. In a large ovenproof skillet, heat remaining oil over medium heat. Brown chicken on each side. Place in oven; bake for 15-18 minutes or until a thermometer inserted in chicken reads 165°. Discard toothpicks before serving.

Slow Cooker Beef Bourguignon

I've wanted to make Beef Burgundy ever since I got one of Julia Child's cookbooks, but I wanted to find a way to fix it in a slow cooker. My version of this popular beef stew is still rich, hearty and delicious, but without the need to watch it on the stovetop or in the oven.

—**CRYSTAL BRUNS** ILIFF, CO

PREP: 30 MIN. + MARINATING • **COOK:** 8 HOURS • **MAKES:** 12 SERVINGS

- **3 pounds beef stew meat**
- **1½ cups dry red wine**
- **3 tablespoons olive oil**
- **2 tablespoons dried minced onion**
- **2 tablespoons dried parsley flakes**
- **1 bay leaf**
- **1 teaspoon dried thyme**
- **¼ teaspoon pepper**
- **8 bacon strips, finely chopped**
- **1 pound whole fresh mushrooms, quartered**
- **24 pearl onions, peeled**
- **2 garlic cloves, minced**
- **⅓ cup all-purpose flour**
- **1 teaspoon salt**
- **Hot cooked whole wheat egg noodles, optional**

1. Place beef in a large resealable plastic bag; add wine, oil and seasonings. Seal bag and turn to coat. Refrigerate overnight.
2. In a large skillet, cook bacon over medium heat until crisp, stirring occasionally. Remove with a slotted spoon; drain on paper towels. Discard drippings, reserving 1 tablespoon in pan.
3. Add mushrooms and onions to drippings; cook and stir over medium-high heat until tender. Add garlic; cook 1 minute longer.
4. Drain beef, reserving 1 cup of marinade and bay leaf; transfer beef to a 4- or 5-qt. slow cooker. Sprinkle beef with flour and salt; toss to coat. Top with bacon and mushroom mixture. Add reserved marinade and bay leaf.
5. Cook, covered, on low 8-10 hours or until beef is tender. Remove bay leaf. If desired, serve beef mixture with noodles.

Roasted Garlic Tomato Soup

Roasting the garlic for this soup adds a sweet, robust flavor that you won't find in its canned counterpart. Using fresh thyme enhances the taste even further.
—LIZZIE MUNRO BROOKLYN, NY

PREP: 55 MIN. • **COOK:** 30 MIN. • **MAKES:** 4 SERVINGS

- **3 whole garlic bulbs**
- **3 tablespoons olive oil, divided**
- **2½ pounds large tomatoes, quartered and seeded**
- **¼ teaspoon salt, divided**
- **¼ teaspoon pepper, divided**
- **1 medium onion, chopped**
- **5 garlic cloves, minced**
- **1 tablespoon minced fresh or 1 teaspoon dried thyme**
- **2 cups chicken stock**
- **½ cup half-and-half cream**

1. Preheat oven to 350°. Remove papery outer skin from garlic bulbs, but do not peel or separate the cloves. Cut off top of garlic bulbs, exposing individual cloves. Drizzle the cut cloves with 2 tablespoons oil. Wrap in foil; place on a foil-lined 15x10x1-in. baking pan.
2. Place tomatoes on same pan; sprinkle with ⅛ teaspoon salt and ⅛ teaspoon pepper. Bake 40-45 minutes or until garlic cloves and tomatoes are soft. Unwrap the garlic and cool for 10 minutes.
3. In a large saucepan, heat remaining oil over medium heat. Add onion; cook and stir until tender. Add minced garlic, thyme and tomatoes. Squeeze garlic from skins and add to tomato mixture. Add stock; bring to a boil. Reduce heat; simmer, uncovered, 20-25 minutes or until the flavors are blended, stirring occasionally.
4. Remove soup from heat; cool slightly. Process in batches in a blender until smooth; return to saucepan. Add cream and the remaining salt and pepper; heat through, stirring occasionally.

Citrus Compote with Grapefruit Granita

Make granita no more than a day ahead of time for best texture. If it freezes solid, it can be revived by pulsing in a food processor. This recipe was inspired by a trip I took with my husband to Italy.
—JENNIFER BECKMAN FALLS CHURCH, VA

PREP: 25 MIN. + FREEZING • **MAKES:** 6 SERVINGS

- **½ cup sugar**
- **½ cup water**
- **1½ cups ruby red grapefruit juice**
- **2 small navel oranges, peeled and sectioned**
- **2 small grapefruit, peeled and sectioned**
- **2 clementines, peeled and sectioned**
- **⅓ cup pomegranate seeds**

1. In a small saucepan, bring sugar and water to a boil. Cook and stir until sugar is dissolved. Remove from heat; cool slightly.
2. Stir in grapefruit juice. Transfer to an 8-in.-square dish. Freeze 1 hour. Stir with a fork. Freeze 2-3 hours longer or until completely frozen, stirring every 30 minutes.
3. Cut a thin slice from the top and bottom of each orange. Stand oranges upright on a cutting board. With a knife, cut off peel and outer membrane from oranges. Working over a bowl to catch juices, cut along the membrane of each segment to remove fruit. Place fruit in bowl. Repeat with grapefruit, removing any seeds.
4. Peel and separate clementines into segments; add to bowl. Gently stir in pomegranate seeds.
5. To serve, stir granita with a fork. Alternately layer the granita and the fruit mixture into six dessert dishes.

Light & Lemony Sorbet

Whether you offer it as a dessert or as a palate cleanser between courses, this sweet-tart sorbet will hit the spot. I recommend letting it freeze for a day before eating.
—GWEN PRATESI SMYRNA, GA

PREP: 15 MIN. + CHILLING • **PROCESS:** 30 MIN. + FREEZING • **MAKES:** 3 CUPS

- **1¾ cups sugar**
- **2 cups water**
- **¾ cup lemon juice**
- **2 tablespoons pasteurized egg white**
- **2 teaspoons grated lemon peel**
- **1 tablespoon vodka, optional**

1. In a small heavy saucepan, bring sugar and water to a boil. Cook and stir until sugar is dissolved. Transfer to a large bowl; cool completely.

2. Stir in the lemon juice. Refrigerate, covered, several hours or overnight.

3. In a small bowl, beat egg white until foamy; add to cold syrup. Stir in lemon peel and, if desired, vodka. Pour into cylinder of ice cream freezer; freeze according to manufacturer's directions.

4. Transfer sorbet to a freezer container, allowing headspace for expansion. Freeze 2-4 hours or until firm.

Warm Garbanzo & Tomato Salad

I created this salad on a whim while on a trip with friends. We put together a bunch of ingredients we had on hand, and the result was a winner!
—BRITTANY DESALVO NEW RICHMOND, OH

START TO FINISH: 25 MIN. • **MAKES:** 12 SERVINGS (1 CUP EACH)

- **½ cup red wine vinegar**
- **3 tablespoons olive oil, divided**
- **2 tablespoons honey**
- **½ teaspoon Italian seasoning**
- **½ teaspoon ground cinnamon**
- **1 can (16 ounces) garbanzo beans or chickpeas, rinsed and drained**
- **24 cherry tomatoes**
- **⅛ teaspoon onion salt**
- **⅛ teaspoon garlic salt**
- **1 medium bunch romaine, torn (about 8 cups)**
- **1 cup salad croutons**

1. In a small bowl, whisk vinegar, 2 tablespoons oil, honey, Italian seasoning and cinnamon.

2. In a large skillet, heat the remaining oil over medium-high heat. Add the beans, tomatoes, onion salt and garlic salt; cook and stir 5-7 minutes or until heated through.

3. In a large bowl, combine romaine and croutons. Add bean mixture; drizzle with dressing and toss to coat. Serve immediately.

Cheese Manicotti

This is the first meal I ever cooked for my husband, and years later, he still enjoys my manicotti!
—**JOAN HALLFORD**
NORTH RICHLAND HILLS, TX

PREP: 25 MIN. • **BAKE:** 1 HOUR
MAKES: 7 SERVINGS

- **1 carton (15 ounces) reduced-fat ricotta cheese**
- **½ cup shredded part-skim mozzarella cheese**
- **1 small onion, finely chopped**
- **1 egg, lightly beaten**
- **2 tablespoons minced fresh parsley**
- **½ teaspoon pepper**
- **¼ teaspoon salt**
- **1 cup grated Parmesan cheese, divided**
- **4 cups marinara sauce**
- **½ cup water**
- **1 package (8 ounces) manicotti shells**

1. Preheat oven to 350°. In a small bowl, mix the first seven ingredients; stir in ½ cup Parmesan cheese. In another bowl, mix marinara sauce and water; spread ¾ cup sauce onto bottom of a 13x9-in. baking dish coated with cooking spray. Fill uncooked manicotti shells with ricotta mixture; arrange over sauce. Top with remaining sauce.
2. Bake, covered, 50 minutes or until pasta is tender. Sprinkle with remaining Parmesan cheese. Bake, uncovered, 10-15 minutes longer or until cheese is melted.

Pear & Peanut Spinach Salad

PICTURED ON PAGE 80

A creamy pear-flavored dressing coats this delightful mixed salad made of spinach, pears, peanuts and raisins. My guests are always impressed by it.

—**KRISTIN BRADY** SOUTH BEND, IN

START TO FINISH: 20 MIN. • **MAKES:** 6 SERVINGS

- **1 package (6 ounces) fresh baby spinach**
- **3 medium pears, chopped**
- **¼ cup dry roasted peanuts**
- **¼ cup golden raisins**
- **1 green onion, sliced**
- **1 star fruit, optional**
- **¼ cup fat-free mayonnaise**
- **3 tablespoons pear juice**
- **2 tablespoons vanilla yogurt**
- **1 teaspoon cider vinegar**
- **Dash salt**

1. In a large bowl, combine the first five ingredients. If desired, slice star fruit and add to bowl.

2. In a small bowl, whisk remaining ingredients. Add to salad and toss to coat. Serve immediately.

Cranberry-Orange Snack Cake

This recipe contains so many great holiday flavors, including pecans, orange, and cranberry, without the post-holiday guilt! I also love the cream cheese icing that really makes this cake stand out.

—**LISA VARNER** EL PASO, TX

PREP: 30 MIN. • **BAKE:** 20 MIN. + COOLING • **MAKES:** 24 SERVINGS

APPLES AND BANANAS

Applesauce is often used to replace some of the fat in baked goods such as cakes and quick breads. But remember that other fruit purees work, too. Try pureed banana, mango or pumpkin if you don't have applesauce handy.

- **1 cup packed light brown sugar**
- **½ cup butter, melted**
- **½ cup egg substitute**
- **½ cup unsweetened applesauce**
- **2 teaspoons grated orange peel, divided**
- **1 teaspoon vanilla extract**
- **2 cups all-purpose flour**
- **1½ teaspoons baking powder**
- **⅛ teaspoon salt**
- **½ cup dried cranberries**
- **½ cup white baking chips**
- **8 ounces reduced-fat cream cheese**
- **1 cup confectioners' sugar**
- **½ cup chopped pecans**

1. Preheat oven to 350°. Coat a 13x9-in. baking pan with cooking spray.

2. In a large bowl, beat the brown sugar, melted butter, egg substitute, applesauce, 1 teaspoon orange peel and vanilla until well blended. In another bowl, whisk flour, baking powder and salt; gradually beat into brown sugar mixture. Stir in cranberries and baking chips.

3. Transfer batter to prepared pan. Bake 20-25 minutes or until a toothpick inserted in center comes out clean. Cool completely on a wire rack.

4. In a small bowl, beat cream cheese and confectioners' sugar until blended. Beat in the remaining orange peel. Spread over cake. Sprinkle with pecans. Refrigerate leftovers.

Grapefruit-Gremolata Salmon

If you're looking for a simple fish dish, make this Italian-inspired recipe that combines salmon, broiled grapefruit and a fragrant gremolata. Halibut may be substituted for the salmon.
—GILDA LESTER MILLSBORO, DE

START TO FINISH: 30 MIN.
MAKES: 4 SERVINGS

- **2 medium grapefruit**
- **¼ cup minced fresh parsley**
- **1 garlic clove, minced**
- **1 tablespoon plus 1 teaspoon brown sugar, divided**
- **4 salmon fillets (6 ounces each)**
- **1 tablespoon cumin seeds, crushed**
- **½ teaspoon salt**
- **½ teaspoon coarsely ground pepper**

1. Preheat broiler. Finely grate enough peel from grapefruit to measure 2 tablespoons. In a small bowl, mix parsley, garlic and grapefruit peel.
2. Cut a thin slice from the top and bottom of each grapefruit; stand grapefruit upright on a cutting board. With a knife, cut off peel and outer membrane from grapefruit. Cut along the membrane of each segment to remove fruit. Arrange sections in a single layer on one half of a foil-lined 15x10x1-in. baking pan. Sprinkle with 1 tablespoon of brown sugar.
3. Place salmon on remaining half of pan. Mix cumin seeds, salt, pepper and remaining brown sugar; sprinkle over salmon.
4. Broil 3-4 in. from heat 8-10 minutes or until fish just begins to flake easily with a fork and grapefruit is lightly browned. Sprinkle salmon with parsley mixture; serve with grapefruit.

Tropical Pulled Pork Sliders

I used what I had in my cupboard to make this pork, and the results were fantastic! I enjoy transforming an inexpensive cut of meat into something extraordinary.
—**SHELLY MITCHELL** GRESHAM, OR

PREP: 15 MIN. • **COOK:** 8 HOURS
MAKES: 12 SERVINGS

- **1 boneless pork shoulder butt roast (3 pounds)**
- **2 garlic cloves, minced**
- **½ teaspoon lemon-pepper seasoning**
- **1 can (20 ounces) unsweetened crushed pineapple, undrained**
- **½ cup orange juice**
- **1 jar (16 ounces) mango salsa**
- **24 whole wheat dinner rolls, split**

1. Rub roast with garlic and lemon-pepper. Transfer to a 4-qt. slow cooker; top with pineapple and orange juice. Cook, covered, on low 8-10 hours or until meat is tender.

2. Remove roast; cool slightly. Skim fat from cooking juices. Shred pork with two forks. Return pork and cooking juices to slow cooker. Stir in salsa; heat through. Serve with rolls.

Apple Rice Salad with Sunflower Seeds

The possibilities for this salad are endless! Try wild or brown rice instead of white; scallions instead of sweet onions; or a four-ounce jar of pimientos instead of red bell pepper.

—**DIANN MAYER** AUSTIN, TX

START TO FINISH: 25 MIN. • **MAKES:** 6 SERVINGS

- **3 cups cooked long grain rice, cooled**
- **1 medium apple, chopped**
- **½ cup chopped sweet red pepper**
- **½ cup chopped carrot**
- **⅓ cup unsalted sunflower kernels**
- **⅓ cup finely chopped sweet onion**
- **5 pitted dates, chopped**
- **2 tablespoons minced fresh parsley**

DRESSING

- **⅓ cup apple cider or juice**
- **1 tablespoon lemon juice**
- **1 tablespoon olive oil**
- **1 teaspoon salt-free seasoning blend**
- **½ teaspoon salt**
- **¼ teaspoon pepper**

In a large bowl, combine the first eight ingredients. In a small bowl, whisk dressing ingredients until blended. Pour over salad and toss to coat.

Cardamom Yogurt Pudding with Honeyed Oranges

I live in Florida, and the holiday season ushers in the new citrus crop here. My favorite citrus is navel oranges, so I added them to pudding to create this special dessert.

—**LILY JULOW** LAWRENCEVILLE, GA

PREP: 25 MIN. + CHILLING • **COOK:** 15 MIN. + COOLING • **MAKES:** 4 SERVINGS

- **1 teaspoon unflavored gelatin**
- **2 tablespoons cold water**
- **2 cups reduced-fat plain Greek yogurt**
- **⅓ cup sugar**
- **1 teaspoon vanilla extract**
- **½ teaspoon ground cardamom**
- **4 medium navel oranges, divided**
- **¼ cup orange blossom honey**
- **¼ teaspoon ground cinnamon**

1. In a small saucepan, sprinkle gelatin over cold water; let stand 1 minute. Heat and stir over low heat until the gelatin is completely dissolved.

2. In a small bowl, whisk yogurt, sugar, vanilla and cardamom until sugar is dissolved. Whisk in gelatin mixture. Refrigerate, covered, for about 2 hours or until soft-set.

3. Meanwhile, place a small strainer over a bowl. Cut a thin slice from the top and bottom of two oranges; stand oranges upright on a cutting board. With a knife, cut off peel and outer membrane from each orange. Working over strainer, cut along the membrane of each segment to remove fruit. Place orange sections in strainer.

4. Squeeze juice from remaining oranges; transfer to a small saucepan. Stir in honey, cinnamon and juice drained from orange sections. Bring to a boil, stirring occasionally. Reduce heat; simmer, uncovered, 9-12 minutes or until syrupy. Remove from heat; gently stir in orange sections. Cool completely.

5. To serve, alternately layer the orange and yogurt mixtures into four dessert dishes.

giving*thanks*

If there's ever a time to pull out all the stops for a meal, it's Thanksgiving. But for families hosting out-of-towners, it's nice to have a few short-cut options, too. From down-home country cooking to quick and easy fixings, here you'll find a feast that works for you. And if apple-picking is on your list of autumn activities, you'll get bushels of inspiring recipes in our unique collection—there's so much more to be made than just pie....

If your closest neighbor is the farm three miles down the road, you're probably familiar with a good old-fashioned Thanksgiving. But you don't need a tractor parked out front to enjoy the kind of from-scratch feast that would make your grandmother proud. You just need a few helping hands and a collection of tried-and-true, down-home recipes—like she used to make—to experience the most gratifying meal of the year.

While this menu may seem ambitious, it's got plenty of room for a few sanity-saving tricks. Use the timeline on p. 96 to help you plan and get a jump start on the big day with a variety of make-ahead dishes. You'll be grateful you did.

A COUNTRY **THANKSGIVING**

givingthanks | MAKE-AHEAD TIPS

A FEW WEEKS BEFORE

- Prepare two grocery lists: one for nonperishable items to purchase now and one for perishable items to purchase a few days before Thanksgiving.
- Bake the cake portion of the Cranberry-Walnut Cake with Butter Sauce, cool completely, cover with plastic wrap and foil, then freeze.

TWO DAYS BEFORE

- Prepare the Sour Cream Pumpkin Pie and the Crunchy-Topped Chocolate Buttermilk Pie. Cool, cover and chill until ready to serve.

ONE DAY BEFORE

- Prepare Mom's Gelatin Fruit Salad, chill in mold until ready to serve.
- Prepare the Sweet Potato Salad with Orange Dressing. Cover and chill overnight.
- Bake the Bacon & Cheese Filled Loaves. Cool, wrap in plastic and store in fridge.
- If preparing the Sausage & Rice Stuffed Pumpkins or the Butternut Squash Gratin, follow the make-ahead suggestions as noted with either recipe.
- Cook the eggs for the Spinach Gorgonzola Salad.
- Prepare the Green Bean Salad with Bacon. Cover and store in fridge. Can be served chilled or reheated before serving.
- Prepare the Cranberry-Raisin Relish. Cover and chill until serving.

THANKSGIVING DAY

- In the morning, thaw the Cranberry-Walnut Cake (prepare Butter Sauce just before serving) and bake the Garden Herb Drop Biscuits.
- Prepare the Sage-Roasted Turkey & Corn Bread Stuffing.
- About an hour before the turkey is done, prepare the Herbed Corn Saute and Spinach Gorgonzola Salad (wait to dress the salad until just before serving).
- Start the Caramelized Onion & Garlic Smashed Potatoes and prep the broccoli for the Cheddar-Broccoli Casserole.
- When the turkey is done, increase oven temp to 350° and bake the Cheddar-Broccoli Casserole and finish the smashed potatoes.
- Remove the bread from the fridge and reheat before serving.

Caramelized Onion & Garlic Smashed Potatoes

Caramelized onions add a sweet, rich taste to these potatoes—along with garlic, bacon and chives. A perfect side for Thanksgiving or any other large family meal, it comes together on the stove top, freeing up your oven for the main dish.

—CRYSTAL HOLSINGER SURPRISE, AZ

PREP: 10 MIN. • **COOK:** 40 MIN. • **MAKES:** 10 SERVINGS

- **6 tablespoons butter, divided**
- **1 large sweet onion, chopped**
- **8 garlic cloves, peeled and halved**
- **1 tablespoon minced fresh thyme or 1 teaspoon dried thyme**
- **1¼ teaspoons salt**
- **¾ teaspoon pepper**
- **3 pounds red potatoes, cubed (about 8 cups)**
- **1 cup whole milk, warmed**
- **2 bacon strips, cooked and crumbled**
- **1 tablespoon minced fresh chives**

1. In a large skillet, heat 4 tablespoons of butter over medium heat. Add onion; cook and stir 8-10 minutes or until softened. Reduce heat to medium-low; stir in garlic halves, thyme, salt and pepper. Cook 25-30 minutes or until golden brown, stirring occasionally.

2. Meanwhile, place potatoes in a Dutch oven; add water to cover. Bring to a boil. Reduce heat; cook, uncovered, 10-15 minutes or until tender. Drain, then shake potatoes over low heat for 1 minute to dry.

3. Mash potatoes slightly, gradually adding milk and remaining butter. Stir in onion mixture. Top with the bacon and chives.

Mom's Gelatin Fruit Salad

My mom found this recipe many years ago and has since handed it down to me and my sisters. It makes an appearance every Thanksgiving.

—LINDA STEMEN MONROEVILLE, IN

PREP: 15 MIN. • **COOK:** 10 MIN. + CHILLING • **MAKES:** 12 SERVINGS

- **2 envelopes unflavored gelatin**
- **½ cup cold water**
- **2 cups sugar**
- **2 cups orange juice**
- **½ cup lemon juice**
- **6 medium oranges, peeled and sectioned**
- **1 cup green grapes, halved**
- **12 maraschino cherries, halved**
- **½ cup chopped dates, optional**

1. In a small saucepan, sprinkle gelatin over cold water; let stand 1 minute. Heat and stir over low heat until gelatin is completely dissolved. Stir in sugar, orange juice and lemon juice; cook and stir 6-8 minutes or until sugar is dissolved.

2. Transfer to a bowl; refrigerate, covered, until slightly thickened, about 1½ hours. Fold in fruit. Pour into a 6-cup ring mold coated with cooking spray or a 2-qt. serving bowl. Refrigerate until firm. If using a ring mold, unmold onto a serving plate.

Creamy Turkey Gravy

PICTURED ON PAGE 94

You'll never reach for store-bought gravy again after making this. It's so simple, you'll be amazed!

—PHYLLIS SCHMALZ KANSAS CITY, KS

START TO FINISH: 15 MIN. • **MAKES:** 2⅓ CUPS

- **2 tablespoons cornstarch**
- **2 tablespoons turkey drippings**
- **⅛ teaspoon salt**
- **⅛ teaspoon pepper**
- **2 cups chicken broth**
- **¼ cup whole milk**

In a small saucepan, mix the cornstarch, drippings, salt and pepper until smooth. Gradually whisk in broth and milk. Bring to a boil, stirring constantly; cook and stir for 2 minutes or until thickened.

Herbed Corn Saute

PICTURED ON PAGE 94

We always make this side dish for our holiday celebrations, especially since it's so easy to double. Fresh herbs really dress up the corn.

—PAT DAZIS CHARLOTTE, NC

START TO FINISH: 20 MIN. • **MAKES:** 4 SERVINGS

- **1 tablespoon butter**
- **1 tablespoon olive oil**
- **1 package (16 ounces) frozen corn, thawed**
- **2 large sweet red peppers, chopped**
- **2 tablespoons minced fresh chives**
- **1 teaspoon minced fresh sage or ¼ teaspoon dried sage leaves**
- **1 teaspoon minced fresh thyme or ½ teaspoon dried thyme**
- **½ teaspoon salt**
- **¼ teaspoon pepper**
- **2 garlic cloves, minced**

In a large skillet, heat butter and oil over medium-high heat. Add corn, peppers, herbs, salt and pepper; cook and stir until peppers are crisp-tender. Add garlic; cook 1 minute longer.

Spinach Gorgonzola Salad

PICTURED ON PAGE 94

You can serve the vinaigrette warm if you prefer—before drizzling over the salad, heat it in the microwave on high for about 30 seconds.

—TRISHA KRUSE EAGLE, ID

START TO FINISH: 15 MIN. • **MAKES:** 12 SERVINGS (1 CUP EACH)

- **¼ cup olive oil**
- **3 tablespoons balsamic vinegar**
- **2 tablespoons honey mustard**
- **1 tablespoon reduced-sodium soy sauce**
- **2 teaspoons ketchup**
- **1 teaspoon sugar**
- **½ teaspoon garlic salt**

SALAD

- **2 packages (6 ounces each) fresh baby spinach**
- **1 medium red onion, thinly sliced**
- **6 hard-cooked eggs, sliced**
- **1½ cups (6 ounces) crumbled Gorgonzola cheese**

In a small bowl, whisk the first seven ingredients until blended. In a large bowl, combine spinach and onion. Add dressing; toss to coat. Top with eggs and cheese. Serve immediately.

Sour Cream Pumpkin Pie

This is traditional pumpkin pie...with a twist! I like the zesty orange taste of the sour cream topping paired with the pumpkin custard. When I serve this pie, there's never any left, so you might want to make two!
—JOAN BINGHAM CORNWALL, VERMONT

PREP: 15 MIN.
BAKE: 45 MIN. + COOLING
MAKES: 8 SERVINGS

Pastry for single-crust pie (9 inches)
2 eggs
1 can (15 ounces) solid-pack pumpkin
1 can (14 ounces) sweetened condensed milk
2½ teaspoons grated orange peel, divided
2 teaspoons pumpkin pie spice
½ teaspoon salt
1¼ cups sour cream
2 tablespoons sugar
2 teaspoons thawed orange juice concentrate

1. Preheat oven to 425°. On a lightly floured surface, roll pastry dough to a ⅛-in.-thick circle; transfer to a 9-in. pie plate. Trim pastry to ½ in. beyond rim of plate; flute edge. Refrigerate while preparing filling.
2. In a large bowl, whisk eggs, pumpkin, milk, 2 teaspoons orange peel, pie spice and salt until well blended. Pour into pastry. Bake on a lower oven rack 15 minutes. Reduce oven setting to 350°; bake 25-30 minutes longer or until a knife inserted near the center comes out clean.
3. In a small bowl, mix the sour cream, sugar, orange juice concentrate and remaining orange peel; spread evenly over the filling. Bake 5 minutes longer or until set. Cool on a wire rack; serve or refrigerate within 2 hours.

PASTRY FOR SINGLE-CRUST PIE (9 INCHES) *Combine 1¼ cups all-purpose flour and ¼ teaspoon salt; cut in ½ cup cold butter until crumbly. Gradually add 3-5 tablespoons ice water, tossing with a fork until dough holds together when pressed. Wrap in plastic wrap; refrigerate 1 hour.*

Sage-Roasted Turkey & Corn Bread Stuffing

This is the best turkey stuffing I have ever eaten. It's slightly sweet and crumbly, and the fresh sage comes through in every bite.
—BETTY FULKS ONIA, AR

PREP: 45 MIN. • **BAKE:** 3¾ HOURS + STANDING • **MAKES:** 16 SERVINGS (8 CUPS STUFFING)

- **½ cup butter, softened**
- **¼ cup finely chopped fresh sage**
- **½ teaspoon pepper, divided**
- **1 turkey (14 to 16 pounds)**
- **¼ cup olive oil**
- **½ teaspoon salt**

STUFFING

- **2 tablespoons butter**
- **2 large onions, chopped**
- **½ teaspoon salt**
- **½ teaspoon pepper**
- **8 cups cubed corn bread**
- **3 tablespoons thinly sliced fresh sage leaves**
- **1 egg**
- **¼ cup chicken broth**
- **¼ cup heavy whipping cream**

1. Preheat oven to 325°. In a small bowl, mix butter, sage and 1/4 teaspoon pepper. Place turkey on a rack in a shallow roasting pan, breast side up. With fingers, loosen skin from turkey breast; rub butter mixture under the skin. Secure skin to underside of breast with toothpicks. Tuck wings under turkey; tie drumsticks together.

2. Brush turkey with oil; sprinkle with salt and remaining pepper. Roast, uncovered, 3¾ to 4¼ hours or until a thermometer inserted in thigh reads 180°. Baste occasionally with pan drippings. (Cover loosely with foil if turkey browns too quickly.)

3. For stuffing, in a large skillet, heat butter over medium heat. Add onions, salt and pepper; cook 15-20 minutes or until the onions are golden brown, stirring occasionally. Add corn bread and sage; toss to combine.

4. In a small bowl, whisk egg, broth and cream; stir into stuffing mixture. Transfer to a greased 11x7-in. baking dish. Bake, covered, 45 minutes. Uncover and bake 10 minutes longer or until lightly browned and a thermometer reads 165°.

5. Remove turkey from oven; tent with foil. Let stand for 20 minutes before carving.

Cheddar-Broccoli Casserole

PICTURED AT LEFT

I've added my own twists to this casserole over the years, such as using sharp cheddar cheese, cheese crackers and Parmesan. My family and friends can't seem to get enough of it!

—JAMES PELLERIN BRADENTON, FL

PREP: 30 MIN. • **BAKE:** 45 MIN. • **MAKES:** 12 SERVINGS

- **3½ cups half-and-half cream, divided**
- **2 tablespoons butter**
- **½ teaspoon garlic powder**
- **½ teaspoon salt**
- **½ teaspoon pepper**
- **3 tablespoons cornstarch**
- **1 package (8 ounces) cream cheese, softened**
- **2 bunches broccoli, cut into florets (about 9 cups)**
- **2 cups (8 ounces) shredded cheddar cheese**

TOPPING

- **1 cup crushed cheese crackers**
- **¼ cup shredded Parmesan cheese**
- **¼ cup butter, melted**

1. Preheat oven to 350°. In a large saucepan, combine 3 cups cream, butter and seasonings; bring to a boil. Mix cornstarch and remaining cream until smooth; gradually stir into the cream mixture. Return to a boil, stirring constantly; cook and stir 2 minutes or until thickened. Stir in cream cheese until melted. Stir in broccoli.

2. Transfer to a greased 2½-qt. baking dish. Sprinkle with cheddar cheese. Bake, covered, 30 minutes.

3. In a small bowl, mix topping ingredients; sprinkle over casserole. Bake, uncovered, for 15-20 minutes longer or until broccoli is tender and topping is lightly browned.

Garden Herb Drop Biscuits

PICTURED AT LEFT

Since we live in military housing, we usually don't have much yard space for a garden. So we decided to purchase our own 5th-wheel travel trailer that stays in a park, and now I have herbs and vegetables growing anywhere I can put them! I like using them in recipes like this.

—DREAMA CRUMP HEPHZIBAH, GA

PREP: 20 MIN. • **BAKE:** 15 MIN. • **MAKES:** 1 DOZEN

- **2¼ cups biscuit/baking mix**
- **1 cup (4 ounces) shredded cheddar cheese**
- **2 green onions, finely chopped**
- **1 tablespoon minced fresh parsley or 1 teaspoon dried parsley flakes**
- **1 tablespoon minced fresh basil or 1 teaspoon dried basil**
- **2 teaspoons minced fresh oregano or ½ teaspoon dried oregano**
- **½ teaspoon sugar**
- **¼ teaspoon garlic powder**
- **⅔ cup plus 1 tablespoon 2% milk, divided**
- **⅓ cup sour cream**
- **2 teaspoons spicy brown mustard**
- **1 egg**

1. Preheat oven to 425°. In a large bowl, mix the first eight ingredients. In a small bowl, whisk ⅔ cup milk, sour cream and mustard until blended. Add to baking mix mixture; stir just until moistened.

2. Drop by ¼ cupfuls 2 in. apart onto a greased baking sheet. In a small bowl, whisk the egg with remaining milk; brush over tops. Bake 12-14 minutes or until golden brown. Serve warm.

Sweet Potato Salad with Orange Dressing

For a lovely side dish that goes well with almost any entree, try this delightful sweet potato salad. The potatoes, fruit and nuts tossed in a citrus dressing are a favorite in my home.

—MARIE RIZZIO INTERLOCHEN, MI

PREP: 25 MIN.
COOK: 15 MIN.
MAKES: 10 SERVINGS

- **2 pounds medium sweet potatoes, peeled and cubed (about 6 cups)**
- **1 cup fat-free mayonnaise**
- **2 tablespoons orange juice**
- **1 tablespoon honey**
- **1½ teaspoons grated orange peel**
- **1½ teaspoons minced fresh gingerroot**
- **¼ teaspoon salt**
- **¼ teaspoon pepper**
- **1 medium Granny Smith apple, peeled and chopped**
- **1 cup finely chopped fennel bulb**
- **½ cup dried cranberries**
- **½ cup chopped pecans, toasted**
- **¼ cup chopped walnuts, toasted**

1. Place sweet potatoes in a Dutch oven; cover with water. Bring to a boil. Reduce heat; cook, covered, 8-10 minutes or just until tender. Drain.

2. Meanwhile, in a large bowl, mix mayonnaise, orange juice, honey, orange peel, ginger, salt and pepper. Stir in apple, fennel, cranberries, pecans and walnuts. Add sweet potatoes; toss gently to coat. Serve warm or refrigerate, covered, and serve cold.

Bacon & Cheese Filled Loaves

When I entered this bread for a Los Angeles County Fair contest, I won third place! The braided, soft bread is also wonderful served with a hot bowl of soup.

—**MARINA CASTLE** CANYON COUNTRY, CA

PREP: 30 MIN. + RISING • **BAKE:** 25 MIN. • **MAKES:** 2 LOAVES (8 SERVINGS EACH)

10 bacon strips, chopped
¼ cup finely chopped onion
⅔ cup sour cream
⅔ cup shredded cheddar cheese
2 loaves (1 pound each) frozen bread dough, thawed
1 egg, lightly beaten
½ teaspoon dried parsley flakes
⅛ teaspoon poppy seeds

1. In a large skillet, cook bacon and onion over medium heat until bacon is crisp. Remove with a slotted spoon; drain on paper towels. Cool slightly.

2. In a small bowl, mix sour cream, cheese and bacon mixture. On two greased baking sheets, roll each loaf of dough into a 16x10-in. rectangle. Spoon half of the filling lengthwise down center third of each rectangle.

3. On each long side, cut ¾-in.-wide strips about 2½ in. into the center. Starting at one end, fold alternating strips at an angle across filling. Pinch both ends to seal.

4. Cover with kitchen towels; let rise in a warm place until doubled, about 1 hour. Preheat oven to 350°.

5. Brush loaves with egg; sprinkle with parsley and poppy seeds. Bake 25-30 minutes or until golden brown. Remove from pans to wire racks.

Butternut Squash Gratin

Squash finds its way into many of my recipes, but my favorite is butternut because I love the richness and sweetness it adds to a dish. After sharing it with my sisters, they now all make this side for their own Thanksgiving dinners.

—**CHERYL SNAVELY** HAGERSTOWN, MD

PREP: 20 MIN. • **BAKE:** 1 HOUR • **MAKES:** 12 SERVINGS

1 large butternut squash (about 5 pounds), peeled and cut into ¼-inch slices
4 shallots, chopped
2½ cups (10 ounces) shredded Gruyere or Swiss cheese, divided
½ cup spreadable pineapple cream cheese
1 cup heavy whipping cream
½ teaspoon salt
½ teaspoon pepper
1 cup crushed seasoned salad croutons

1. Preheat oven to 375°. In a greased 13x9-in. baking dish, layer half the squash, all the shallots and 1 cup of cheese. Top with remaining squash and 1 cup of cheese.

2. In a small bowl, beat cream cheese, cream, salt and pepper until smooth; pour over top. Sprinkle with remaining cheese; top with croutons. Bake, covered, 30 minutes. Bake, uncovered, 30-40 minutes longer or until the top is golden brown and the squash is tender.

THE NIGHT BEFORE THANKSGIVING

When planning a large holiday menu, look for recipes that can be prepped ahead of time. For example, the butternut squash for this gratin can be peeled and sliced; the shallots can be chopped; and the gratin can be layered into the dish the night before. Then cover and refrigerate over night. The next day, all you have to do is whip up the cream sauce, pour it over the top and bake.

Sausage & Rice Stuffed Pumpkins

My children often request this dish. It also adds a great "wow" factor to a festive buffet table.
—ANDRIA PECKHAM LOWELL, MI

PREP: 30 MIN. • **BAKE:** 55 MIN. • **MAKES:** 12 SERVINGS

- **3 small pie pumpkins (about 2 pounds each)**
- **½ pound bulk sweet Italian sausage**
- **1 pound fresh mushrooms, chopped**
- **2 medium onions, chopped**
- **1 medium green pepper, chopped**
- **2 garlic cloves, minced**
- **4 cups cooked long grain rice**
- **1 cup grated Parmesan cheese, divided**
- **2 eggs, lightly beaten**
- **¼ cup minced fresh parsley**
- **1 teaspoon salt**
- **½ teaspoon dried thyme**

1. Preheat oven to 450°. Cut a 3-in. circle around each pumpkin stem. Remove tops and set aside. Remove strings and seeds from pumpkins; discard seeds or save for toasting.

2. In a large skillet, cook sausage, vegetables and garlic over medium heat 6-8 minutes or until sausage is no longer pink, breaking up sausage into crumbles; drain. Remove from heat; stir in rice, ¾ cup cheese, eggs, parsley, salt and thyme.

3. Place the pumpkins in a 15x10x1-in. baking pan; fill with rice mixture. Replace pumpkin tops. Bake 30 minutes.

4. Reduce oven setting to 350°. Bake 25-35 minutes longer or until pumpkins are tender when pierced with a knife and a thermometer inserted in filling reads 160°. Sprinkle remaining cheese over filling.

5. To serve, remove rice. Scoop out pumpkins and serve with the rice.

PUMPKIN PREP

What a fun dish to make with the family! Kids will love doing the dirty work, scooping out the pumpkin guts and seeds to help you prepare for the big meal. To get a head start, clean out the pumpkins the night before and wrap them tightly in plastic wrap, along with the tops. Store them in the refrigerator overnight so they're fresh and ready to be stuffed the next day.

Green Bean Salad with Bacon

Serve it warm or chilled—this salad is versatile and ready for any occasion.
—**CYNTHIA BENT** NEWARK, DE

START TO FINISH: 30 MIN.
MAKES: 8 SERVINGS

- **1½ pounds fresh green beans, trimmed**
- **4 bacon strips, chopped**
- **2 medium onions, thinly sliced**
- **¼ cup cider vinegar**
- **2 tablespoons sugar**
- **2 tablespoons brown sugar**
- **1 teaspoon salt**

1. Place beans in a large saucepan; add water to cover. Bring to a boil. Cook, uncovered, 4-7 minutes or until crisp-tender. Drain.
2. In a large skillet, cook bacon over medium heat until crisp, stirring occasionally. Remove with a slotted spoon; drain on paper towels. Discard drippings, reserving 2 tablespoons drippings in pan.
3. Add onions to drippings; cook and stir until tender. In a small bowl, mix vinegar, sugars and salt until blended; stir into onions. Add beans; heat through, tossing to combine. Top with bacon.

Cranberry-Walnut Cake with Butter Sauce

Tired of plain ol' cakes? Give this recipe a shot! Cranberry lovers will definitely like it because the cake is tart, but the warm butter sauce creates the ideal balance of sweet and sour. Pour the sauce over the cake just before serving.

—**KATIE KAHRE** DULUTH, MN

PREP: 25 MIN.
BAKE: 30 MIN. + COOLING
MAKES: 15 SERVINGS (2 CUPS SAUCE)

- **3 tablespoons butter, softened**
- **1 cup sugar**
- **½ cup water**
- **2 cups all-purpose flour**
- **3 teaspoons baking powder**
- **1 teaspoon salt**
- **½ cup evaporated milk**
- **1 package (12 ounces) fresh or frozen cranberries**
- **1 cup chopped walnuts**

SAUCE

- **2 cups sugar**
- **1 cup butter, cubed**
- **¼ cup evaporated milk**
- **1 teaspoon vanilla extract**

1. Preheat oven to 375°. Grease a 13x9-in. baking pan.

2. In a large bowl, beat butter and sugar until crumbly, about 2 minutes. Gradually beat in water. In another bowl, whisk flour, baking powder and salt; add to creamed mixture alternately with milk, beating well after each addition. Fold in cranberries and walnuts (batter will be thick).

3. Spread into prepared pan. Bake 30-35 minutes or until a toothpick inserted in center comes out clean. Cool in pan on a wire rack.

4. Meanwhile, in a small saucepan, combine sauce ingredients; bring to a boil over medium heat, stirring constantly to dissolve sugar. Serve cake with warm sauce.

Cranberry-Raisin Relish

This is the only cranberry relish my kids will eat. It can be made up to one week ahead of time, and I personally think it gets better after it sits for a day or two. If you have leftovers after a big meal, spoon it over turkey sandwiches the next day.

—**SHEILA TATE** HARTSELLE, AL

PREP: 10 MIN. • **COOK:** 15 MIN. + CHILLING • **MAKES:** 20 SERVINGS (¼ CUP EACH)

- **1 pound fresh or frozen cranberries**
- **1 package (10 ounces) dried cranberries**
- **2½ cups water**
- **1 cup sugar**
- **1 cup raisins**
- **1 teaspoon ground cinnamon**

1. In a large saucepan, combine all ingredients. Bring to a boil, stirring to dissolve sugar. Reduce heat to medium; cook, uncovered, 10-15 minutes or until berries pop, stirring occasionally. Remove from heat.

2. Transfer to a large bowl; refrigerate, covered, until cold.

Crunchy-Topped Chocolate Buttermilk Pie

I took my love of buttermilk pie and chocolate and combined them to make this special pie. I have had grown men lick the bottom of the pie pan and ask, "When can you make this again?"

—**BRENDA HOFFMAN** STANTON, MI

PREP: 20 MIN. • **BAKE:** 1 HOUR + COOLING • **MAKES:** 10 SERVINGS

- **Pastry for single-crust pie (9 inches)**
- **1½ cups sugar**
- **3 eggs**
- **½ cup buttermilk**
- **⅓ cup butter, melted**
- **¼ cup all-purpose flour**
- **1 teaspoon vanilla extract**
- **½ cup semisweet chocolate chips**

TOPPING

- **¼ cup all-purpose flour**
- **¼ cup quick-cooking oats**
- **¼ cup flaked coconut**
- **¼ cup packed brown sugar**
- **¼ cup chopped pecans**
- **¼ cup cold butter**

1. Preheat oven to 350°. On a lightly floured surface, roll pastry dough to a ⅛-in.-thick circle; transfer to a 9-in. pie plate. Trim pastry to ½ in. beyond rim of plate; flute edge. Refrigerate while preparing filling.

2. In a large bowl, beat sugar, eggs, buttermilk, melted butter, flour and vanilla until blended. Pour into pastry; sprinkle with chocolate chips. Bake 35 minutes.

3. In a small bowl, mix the first five topping ingredients; cut in butter until crumbly. Sprinkle over pie. Bake 25-30 minutes longer or until center of pie is set. Cool on a wire rack; serve or refrigerate within 2 hours.

PASTRY FOR SINGLE-CRUST PIE (9 INCHES) *Combine 1¼ cups all-purpose flour and ¼ teaspoon salt; cut in ½ cup cold butter until crumbly. Gradually add 3-5 tablespoons ice water, tossing with a fork until dough holds together when pressed. Wrap in plastic wrap and refrigerate for 1 hour.*

It's okay if spending weeks preparing for a single meal isn't really your thing. You can still enjoy juicy turkey (with leftovers) and all the trimmings. In this quick-fix menu, the turkey is done in less than an hour, the beans in less than 30 minutes, the mashed potatoes can be made ahead, and half a dozen pumpkin parfaits can be whipped up before you finish counting your blessings.

With all that extra time on your hands, you can look forward to curling up on the couch for a traditional post-turkey nap. Happy Thanksgiving!

Easy Yeast Rolls (p. 116)
Maple-Glazed Green Beans (p. 110)
Creamy Make-Ahead Mashed Potatoes (p. 115)
Turkey Tenderloins with Shallot Berry Sauce (p. 112)

QUICK & EASY
THANKSGIVING

Sourdough Almond Stuffing

Rosemary, artichoke hearts and sun-dried tomatoes give this stuffing a sophisticated feel that's perfect for an elegant Thanksgiving dinner.

—**HANNAH THOMPSON** SCOTTS VALLEY, CA

PREP: 25 MIN. • **BAKE:** 30 MIN. • **MAKES:** 16 SERVINGS

- **¾ cup butter, cubed**
- **2 cups sliced baby portobello mushrooms**
- **1 medium onion, chopped**
- **4 garlic cloves, minced**
- **1 teaspoon salt**
- **1 teaspoon dried rosemary, crushed**
- **½ teaspoon pepper**
- **11 cups cubed day-old sourdough bread**
- **1 can (14 ounces) water-packed artichoke hearts, rinsed, drained and chopped**
- **¾ cup slivered almonds**
- **¾ cup oil-packed sun-dried tomatoes, chopped**
- **½ cup minced fresh basil**
- **2 eggs**
- **1 can (14½ ounces) chicken broth**

1. Preheat oven to 350°. In a large skillet, heat butter over medium-high heat; add mushrooms and onion; cook and stir until tender. Add garlic; cook 1 minute longer. Stir in salt, rosemary and pepper.

2. In a large bowl, combine bread cubes, artichokes, almonds, tomatoes, basil and mushroom mixture. In a small bowl, whisk eggs and broth. Gradually stir into bread mixture.

3. Transfer to a greased 13x9-in. baking dish. Bake, covered, for 25 minutes. Uncover; bake 5-10 minutes longer or until lightly browned.

Maple-Glazed Green Beans

PICTURED ON PAGE 109

After picking green beans for the first time, I decided to create a robust side dish to highlight them. I couldn't stop eating my creation, so the next day I went back to pick more beans so I could make this again!

—**MERRY GRAHAM** NEWHALL, CA

START TO FINISH: 25 MIN. • **MAKES:** 4 SERVINGS

- **3 cups cut fresh green beans**
- **1 large onion, chopped**
- **4 bacon strips, cut into 1-inch pieces**
- **½ cup dried cranberries**
- **¼ cup maple syrup**
- **¼ teaspoon salt**
- **¼ teaspoon pepper**
- **1 tablespoon bourbon, optional**

1. In a large saucepan, place steamer basket over 1 in. of water. Place beans in basket. Bring water to a boil. Reduce heat to maintain a low boil; steam, covered, 4-5 minutes or until crisp-tender.

2. Meanwhile, in a large skillet, cook onion and bacon over medium heat until bacon is crisp; drain. Stir cranberries, syrup, salt, pepper and, if desired, bourbon into the onion mixture. Add beans; heat through, tossing to combine.

Caramel Heavenlies

My mom made these treats for cookie exchanges when I was little, letting me sprinkle on the almonds and coconut. They're so easy to fix, making them perfect when you're crunched for time during the holidays.

—**DAWN BURNS** LAKE ST. LOUIS, MO

PREP: 20 MIN.
BAKE: 15 MIN. + COOLING
MAKES: ABOUT 6 DOZEN

- **12 whole graham crackers**
- **2 cups miniature marshmallows**
- **¾ cup butter, cubed**
- **¾ cup packed brown sugar**
- **1 teaspoon ground cinnamon**
- **1 teaspoon vanilla extract**
- **1 cup sliced almonds**
- **1 cup flaked coconut**

1. Preheat oven to 350°. Line a 15x10x1-in. baking pan with foil, letting foil extend over sides by 1 in.; lightly coat foil with cooking spray. Arrange graham crackers in prepared pan; sprinkle with marshmallows.

2. In a small saucepan, combine butter, brown sugar and cinnamon; cook and stir over medium heat until butter is melted and sugar is dissolved. Remove from heat; stir in vanilla.

3. Spoon butter mixture over marshmallows. Sprinkle with almonds and coconut. Bake 14-16 minutes or until browned. Cool completely in pan on wire rack.

4. Using the foil, lift the cookies out of the pan. Cut into triangles; discard foil.

USE A PIZZA CUTTER

To quickly cut the whole sheet of cookies into little triangles, after they have cooled completely, use the foil to lift the cookies out of the pan and place on a cutting board. Then use a pizza cutter to cut horizontal strips, then vertical strips so you have squares. Then make diagonal cuts across the sheet to make triangles. Transfer the cookies to a platter and discard foil.

Turkey Tenderloins with Shallot Berry Sauce

This original recipe used chicken and apricot, but I switched that to turkey and berry jam to use up some Thanksgiving leftovers. I was thrilled with how well it turned out.

—**KENDRA DOSS** COLORADO SPRINGS, CO

PREP: 15 MIN. • **COOK:** 25 MIN. • **MAKES:** 8 SERVINGS

- **4 turkey breast tenderloins (12 ounces each)**
- **½ teaspoon salt**
- **½ teaspoon pepper**
- **1 tablespoon olive oil**
- **¼ cup chicken broth**

SAUCE

- **1 tablespoon olive oil**
- **5 shallots, thinly sliced**
- **¼ teaspoon salt**
- **¼ teaspoon pepper**
- **½ cup chicken broth**
- **¼ cup balsamic vinegar**
- **3 tablespoons seedless raspberry jam**

1. Sprinkle turkey with salt and pepper. In a large skillet, heat oil over medium heat. Brown tenderloins on all sides in batches. Cook, covered, 8-10 minutes longer or until a thermometer reads 165°. Remove from pan; keep warm. Add broth to skillet; increase heat to medium-high. Cook, stirring to loosen browned bits from pan; remove from heat.

2. Meanwhile, in another skillet, heat oil over medium-high heat. Add shallots, salt and pepper; cook and stir until shallots are tender. Add broth, stirring to loosen browned bits from pan. Stir in vinegar and jam. Bring to a boil; cook 4-5 minutes or until slightly thickened, stirring occasionally.

3. Slice tenderloins; drizzle with pan juices. Serve with sauce.

KEEP TURKEY WARM

If you need to keep cooked turkey warm while you prepare other dishes or wait for guests to arrive, cover it with foil and place it in a 200° oven with a pan of water on the bottom. This will prevent the meat from getting dry. Also, wait to slice or carve the turkey until just before serving, and remember, cooked turkey should not be left at room temperature for longer than two hours.

Gorgonzola Phyllo Cups

You need only a few minutes to put these bites together. The richness of Gorgonzola, apples and dried cranberries is perfect any time of year, but it's especially good in the colder months.

—TRISHA KRUSE EAGLE, ID

START TO FINISH: 20 MIN.
MAKES: 2½ DOZEN

- **2 packages (1.9 ounces each) frozen miniature phyllo tart shells**
- **1⅓ cups crumbled Gorgonzola cheese**
- **½ cup chopped apple**
- **⅓ cup dried cranberries**
- **⅓ cup chopped walnuts**

1. Preheat oven to 350°. Place tart shells on a 15x10x1-in. baking pan. In a small bowl, mix remaining ingredients; spoon into tart shells.

2. Bake 6-8 minutes or until lightly browned. Serve warm or at room temperature. Refrigerate leftovers.

FREEZE OPTION *Freeze cooled pastries in a freezer container, separating layers with waxed paper. To use, reheat pastries on a greased baking sheet in a preheated 350° oven until crisp and heated through.*

Pumpkin Crunch Parfaits

Have your little ones lend a hand with this dessert! It's a great treat for Thanksgiving or Halloween.

—LORRAINE DAROCHA BERKSHIRE, MA

START TO FINISH: 20 MIN.
MAKES: 6 SERVINGS

- **¾ cup cold whole milk**
- **1 package (3.4 ounces) instant vanilla pudding mix**
- **2 cups whipped topping**
- **1 cup canned pumpkin**
- **½ teaspoon pumpkin pie spice**
- **1 cup chopped pecans**
- **32 gingersnap cookies, crushed (about 1½ cups)**
- **Additional whipped topping**

1. In a large bowl, beat milk and pudding mix on low speed for 2 minutes. Stir in whipped topping, pumpkin and pie spice. Fold in pecans.

2. Spoon half of the mixture into six parfait glasses; top with half of the gingersnap crumbs. Repeat layers. Top with additional whipped topping. Refrigerate leftovers.

Crunchy Broccoli Salad

I never liked broccoli when I was younger, but now I'm hooked on this salad's light, sweet taste. It gives broccoli a whole new look and flavor, in my opinion.

—JESSICA CONREY CEDAR RAPIDS, IA

START TO FINISH: 25 MIN. • **MAKES:** 10 SERVINGS

- **8 cups fresh broccoli florets (about 1 pound)**
- **1 bunch green onions, thinly sliced**
- **½ cup dried cranberries**
- **3 tablespoons canola oil**
- **3 tablespoons seasoned rice vinegar**
- **2 tablespoons sugar**
- **¼ cup sunflower kernels**
- **3 bacon strips, cooked and crumbled**

In a large bowl, combine broccoli, green onions and cranberries. In a small bowl, whisk oil, vinegar and sugar until blended; drizzle over broccoli mixture and toss to coat. Refrigerate until serving. Sprinkle with sunflower kernels and bacon before serving.

Creamy Make-Ahead Mashed Potatoes

PICTURED ON PAGE 109

Can mashed potatoes get any better? My answer is yes—when you top them with a savory trio of cheese, onions and bacon.

—JOANN KOERKENMEIER DAMIANSVILLE, IL

PREP: 35 MIN. + CHILLING • **BAKE:** 40 MIN. • **MAKES:** 10 SERVINGS

- **3 pounds potatoes (about 9 medium), peeled and cubed**
- **6 bacon strips, chopped**
- **1 package (8 ounces) cream cheese, softened**
- **½ cup sour cream**
- **½ cup butter, cubed**
- **¼ cup 2% milk**
- **1½ teaspoons onion powder**
- **1 teaspoon salt**
- **1 teaspoon garlic powder**
- **½ teaspoon pepper**
- **1 cup (4 ounces) shredded cheddar cheese**
- **3 green onions, chopped**

1. Place potatoes in a Dutch oven; add water to cover. Bring to a boil. Reduce heat; cook, uncovered, 10-15 minutes or until tender.

2. Meanwhile, in a skillet, cook bacon over medium heat until crisp. Remove to paper towels with a slotted spoon; drain.

3. Drain potatoes; return to pan. Mash potatoes, gradually adding cream cheese, sour cream and butter. Stir in milk and seasonings. Transfer to a greased 13x9-in. baking dish; sprinkle with cheese, green onions and bacon. Refrigerate, covered, up to 1 day.

4. Preheat oven to 350°. Remove potatoes from refrigerator and let stand while oven heats. Bake, uncovered, 40-50 minutes or until heated through.

Pantry Mushroom Gravy

This quick and easy gravy is excellent served with turkey, meat loaf, Salisbury steak, hamburgers and just about anything you'd find on your Thanksgiving dinner table.

—TASTE OF HOME TEST KITCHEN

START TO FINISH: 20 MIN. • **MAKES:** 1¾ CUPS

- **1 can (4 ounces) mushroom stems and pieces**
- **3 tablespoons butter**
- **¼ cup finely chopped onion or 1 tablespoon dried minced onion**
- **3 tablespoons all-purpose flour**
- **1 teaspoon beef bouillon granules**
- **⅛ teaspoon pepper**
- **¼ to ½ teaspoon browning sauce, optional**

1. Drain mushrooms, reserving liquid. Add enough water to mushroom liquid to measure 1¼ cups.

2. In a small saucepan, heat butter over medium-high heat. Add onion; cook and stir until tender. Stir in flour, bouillon and pepper until blended. Add mushrooms. Gradually stir in mushroom liquid mixture. Bring to a boil, stirring constantly; cook and stir for 2 minutes or until gravy is thickened. If desired, stir in browning sauce.

Butterscotch-Toffee Cheesecake Bars

I took a cheesecake bar recipe and added a new flavor combo to transform it! The butterscotch and toffee really taste divine here.
—PAMELA SHANK PARKERSBURG, WV

PREP: 15 MIN. • **BAKE:** 30 MIN. + CHILLING • **MAKES:** 2 DOZEN

- **1 package yellow cake mix (regular size)**
- **1 package (3.4 ounces) instant butterscotch pudding mix**
- **⅓ cup canola oil**
- **2 eggs**
- **1 package (8 ounces) cream cheese, softened**
- **⅓ cup sugar**
- **1 cup brickle toffee bits, divided**
- **½ cup butterscotch chips**

1. Preheat oven to 350°. In a large bowl, combine cake mix, pudding mix, oil and 1 egg; mix until crumbly. Reserve 1 cup for topping. Press remaining mixture into an ungreased 13x9-in. baking pan. Bake 10 minutes. Cool completely on a wire rack.
2. In a small bowl, beat cream cheese and sugar until smooth. Add remaining egg; beat on low speed just until combined. Fold in ½ cup toffee bits. Spread over crust. Sprinkle with reserved crumb mixture. Bake 15-20 minutes or until filling is set.
3. Sprinkle with butterscotch chips and remaining toffee bits. Return to oven; bake 1 minute longer. Cool on a wire rack for 1 hour. Refrigerate 2 hours or until cold. Cut into bars.

Easy Yeast Rolls

PICTURED ON PAGE 108

Bake these simple, tender rolls to a golden brown, and they will disappear in no time. If you've never baked with yeast before, these rolls are the perfect starting point.
—WILMA HARTER WITTEN, SD

PREP: 45 MIN. + RISING • **BAKE:** 15 MIN. • **MAKES:** 4 DOZEN

- **2 packages (¼ ounce each) active dry yeast**
- **2 cups warm water (110° to 115°)**
- **½ cup sugar**
- **1 egg**
- **¼ cup canola oil**
- **2 teaspoons salt**
- **6 to 6½ cups all-purpose flour**

1. In a small bowl, dissolve yeast in warm water. In a large bowl, combine sugar, egg, oil, salt, yeast mixture and 4 cups flour; beat on medium speed until smooth. Stir in enough remaining flour to form a stiff dough.
2. Turn dough onto a floured surface; knead until smooth and elastic, about 6-8 minutes. Place in a greased bowl, turning once to grease the top. Cover with plastic wrap and let rise in a warm place until doubled, about 1 hour.
3. Punch down dough. Turn onto a lightly floured surface; divide into four portions. Divide and shape each portion into 12 balls. Roll each ball into an 8-in. rope; tie into a loose knot. Tuck ends under. Place 2 in. apart on greased baking sheets. Cover with kitchen towels; let rise in a warm place until doubled, about 30 minutes. Preheat the oven to 350°.
4. Bake 15-20 minutes or until golden brown. Remove from pans to wire racks.

Candied Pumpkin Spice Pecans

You'll be tempted to eat up an entire bowl of these sweet and spicy nuts, so grab a handful before you put them out. They'll be gone in a flash!

—JULIE PUDERBAUGH
BERWICK, PA

PREP: 15 MIN. + COOLING
MAKES: 2 CUPS

- **3 tablespoons butter**
- **½ cup sugar**
- **1 teaspoon pumpkin pie spice**
- **1 teaspoon vanilla extract**
- **2 cups pecan halves**

1. In a large heavy non-stick skillet, melt butter over medium heat. Stir in sugar. Cook until mixture turns an amber color, about 3-4 minutes, stirring occasionally (the mixture will separate).

2. Stir in pie spice and vanilla; add pecans. Reduce heat; cook and stir 3-4 minutes longer or until pecans are toasted. Spread onto foil to cool. Store in an airtight container.

PUMPKIN PIE SPICE

Combine 4 teaspoons ground cinnamon, 2 teaspoons ground ginger, 1 teaspoon ground cloves and ½ teaspoon ground nutmeg. Store in airtight container for 6 months.

Warm Cranberry Spread

My family loves all the cranberry recipes I make. But this one is also good made with the Door County cherries we purchase on our summer trips to Wisconsin.

—JENNIFER CHRISTENSON LITTLE CANADA, MN

START TO FINISH: 25 MIN. • **MAKES:** ABOUT 2¼ CUPS

- **1 package (8 ounces) cream cheese, softened**
- **1 package (4 ounces) crumbled feta cheese**
- **¾ cup whole-berry cranberry sauce**
- **⅓ cup slivered almonds, toasted**
- **⅓ cup sliced green onions**
- **Assorted crackers**

Preheat oven to 350°. In a small bowl, mix cream cheese and feta cheese until blended. Spread into an ungreased 9-in. pie plate. Spread with cranberry sauce. Bake, uncovered, 15-20 minutes or until heated through. Top with almonds and green onions. Serve with crackers.

NOTE *To toast nuts, spread in a 15x10x1-in. baking pan. Bake at 350° for 5-10 minutes or until lightly browned, stirring occasionally. Or, spread in a dry nonstick skillet and heat over low heat until lightly browned, stirring occasionally.*

German Chocolate Pie

Thanksgiving dinner at our house averages 25 guests and a dozen different pies. This particular pie resembles a luscious German chocolate cake.
—DEBBIE CLAY FARMINGTON, NM

PREP: 40 MIN. + CHILLING **BAKE:** 30 MIN. + COOLING • **MAKES:** 8 SERVINGS

Pastry for single-crust pie (9 inches)

FILLING

- **4 ounces German sweet chocolate, chopped**
- **1 tablespoon butter**
- **1 teaspoon vanilla extract**
- **⅓ cup sugar**
- **3 tablespoons cornstarch**
- **1½ cups whole milk**
- **2 egg yolks**

TOPPING

- **⅔ cup evaporated milk**
- **½ cup sugar**
- **¼ cup butter, cubed**
- **1 egg, lightly beaten**
- **1⅓ cups flaked coconut, toasted**
- **½ cup chopped pecans, toasted**

1. Preheat oven to 400°. On a lightly floured surface, roll pastry dough to a 1/8-in.-thick circle; transfer to a 9-in. pie plate. Trim pastry to 1/2 in. beyond rim of plate; flute edge.

2. Line unpricked pastry with a double thickness of foil. Fill with pie weights, dried beans or uncooked rice. Bake for 25 minutes. Remove foil and weights; bake 4-6 minutes longer or until golden brown. Cool on a wire rack.

3. For filling, in a microwave, melt chocolate and butter; stir until smooth. Stir in vanilla. In a small heavy saucepan, mix sugar and cornstarch. Whisk in whole milk. Cook and stir over medium heat until thickened and bubbly. Reduce heat to low; cook and stir for 2 minutes longer. Remove from heat.

4. In a small bowl, whisk a small amount of hot mixture into egg yolks; return all to pan, whisking constantly. Bring to a gentle boil; cook and stir 2 minutes. Remove from heat. Stir in the chocolate mixture. Pour into crust.

5. For topping, in a small saucepan, combine evaporated milk, sugar and butter. Cook and stir until butter is melted and mixture just comes to a boil. Remove from heat.

6. In a small bowl, whisk a small amount of hot mixture into egg; return all to pan, whisking constantly. Bring to a gentle boil; cook and stir 2 minutes. Remove from heat. Stir in coconut and pecans. Pour over filling.

7. Cool pie 30 minutes on a wire rack. Refrigerate, covered, until cold, at least 3 hours.

PASTRY FOR SINGLE-CRUST PIE (9 INCHES) *Combine 1 1/4 cups all-purpose flour and 1/4 teaspoon salt; cut in 1/2 cup cold butter until crumbly. Gradually add 3-5 tablespoons ice water, tossing with a fork until dough holds together when pressed. Wrap in plastic wrap and refrigerate for 1 hour.*

Raspberry Cranberry Relish

My friend just suggested cooking cranberries in honey. I played with this recipe, and this is now my family's favorite version of cranberries at Thanksgiving.

—ANITA DOUGHTY
WEST DES MOINES, IA

PREP: 10 MIN.
COOK: 15 MIN. + CHILLING
MAKES: 5 CUPS

- **1 package (12 ounces) fresh or frozen cranberries, thawed**
- **¾ cup cherry-flavored dried cranberries**
- **½ cup honey**
- **¼ cup cranberry-raspberry juice**
- **2 tablespoons orange marmalade**
- **½ teaspoon Chinese five-spice powder**
- **1 package (12 ounces) frozen unsweetened raspberries, thawed and drained**

1. In a large saucepan, combine the first six ingredients. Cook, uncovered, over medium heat until berries pop, about 15 minutes, stirring occasionally.
2. Remove from heat; gently stir in raspberries. Transfer to a small bowl; refrigerate, covered, until cold, at least 2 hours.

If a pair of rubber boots and a stroll through the apple orchards aren't part of your autumn ritual, it's time for a fall field trip. Apple-picking is an all-ages adventure that ends in bushels of sweet-crisp fruit just waiting to test your culinary boundaries. While it's expected that a good percentage of your harvest will inevitably end up in a pie or dipped in hot caramel for a festive treat, don't sell your cooking creations short.

From relish and stews to cakes and bars, an apple recipe a day is all it takes to break you out of your pie shell and introduce you to some fresh-picked recipes.

Apple & Sweet Pepper Relish (p. 126)
Caramel-Apple Skillet Buckle (p. 123)

APPLE **HARVEST**

Apple Salad with Tzatziki Dressing

A vegetarian friend inspired me to create this dish when she was longing for a great gyro with lots of cucumber. I made this salad instead, with some pita bread for scooping, and it turned out to be a real treat.
—AYSHA SCHURMAN AMMON, ID

START TO FINISH: 25 MIN. • **MAKES:** 6 SERVINGS

- **1 medium Granny Smith apple, sliced and halved**
- **1 medium Jonagold or other sweet apple, sliced and halved**
- **1 medium red onion, chopped**
- **½ cup finely chopped leek (white portion only)**
- **½ cup chopped English cucumber**
- **½ cup dry roasted peanuts, chopped**

DRESSING

- **⅓ cup plain yogurt**
- **3 tablespoons grated peeled English cucumber, patted dry**
- **2 teaspoons minced fresh mint**
- **2 teaspoons lemon juice**
- **1 garlic clove, minced**
- **½ teaspoon sugar**
- **¼ teaspoon salt**
- **⅛ teaspoon white pepper**

In a large bowl, combine the first six ingredients. In a small bowl, mix dressing ingredients. Add to apple mixture; toss to coat.

Caramel-Apple Skillet Buckle

PICTURED ON PAGE 121

My grandma used to make a version of this for me when I was a little girl. She would use fresh apples from the tree in her backyard. I've adapted her recipe because I love the combination of apples, pecans and caramel.

—**EMILY HOBBS** SPRINGFIELD, MO

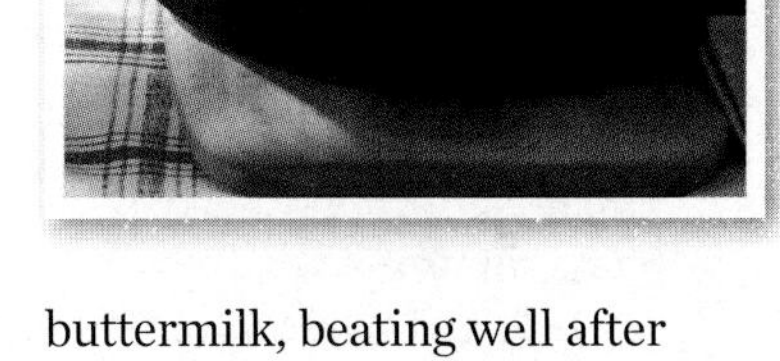

PREP: 35 MIN. • **BAKE:** 1 HOUR + STANDING • **MAKES:** 12 SERVINGS

- **½ cup butter, softened**
- **¾ cup sugar**
- **2 eggs**
- **1 teaspoon vanilla extract**
- **2 cups all-purpose flour**
- **2½ teaspoons baking powder**
- **1¾ teaspoons ground cinnamon**
- **½ teaspoon ground ginger**
- **¼ teaspoon salt**
- **1½ cups buttermilk**

TOPPING

- **⅔ cup packed brown sugar**
- **½ cup all-purpose flour**
- **¼ cup cold butter**
- **¾ cup finely chopped pecans**
- **½ cup old-fashioned oats**
- **6 cups thinly sliced peeled Gala or other sweet apples (about 6 medium)**
- **18 caramels, unwrapped**
- **1 tablespoon buttermilk**
- **Vanilla ice cream, optional**

1. Preheat oven to 350°. In a large bowl, cream butter and sugar until light and fluffy. Add eggs, one at a time, beating well after each addition. Beat in vanilla. In another bowl, whisk flour, baking powder, cinnamon, ginger and salt; add to creamed mixture alternately with buttermilk, beating well after each addition. Pour into a greased 12-in. ovenproof skillet.

2. For topping, in a small bowl, mix brown sugar and flour; cut in butter until crumbly. Stir in the pecans and oats; sprinkle over batter. Top with apples. Bake 60-70 minutes or until the apples are golden brown. Cool in pan on a wire rack.

3. In a microwave, melt caramels with buttermilk; stir until smooth. Drizzle over cake. Let stand until set. If desired, serve with ice cream.

Herbed Apple & Vegetable Saute

I made this side dish for the first time on a cold, snowy night, and it was the perfect comfort food. The apple cider adds just a hint of sweetness, and the rosemary and sage add a touch of wintery flavor we all love.

—**KEATON BUSTER** WAUCONDA, IL

START TO FINISH: 30 MIN. • **MAKES:** 4 SERVINGS

- **1 cup plus 2 tablespoons apple cider, divided**
- **2 fresh rosemary sprigs**
- **¼ teaspoon pepper, divided**
- **1 tablespoon olive oil**
- **3 medium carrots, chopped**
- **1 medium parsnip, peeled and chopped**
- **2 large Cortland or other apples, peeled and chopped**
- **¾ teaspoon dried sage leaves**
- **¼ teaspoon salt**
- **¼ teaspoon dried thyme**

1. In a large saucepan, combine 1 cup cider, the rosemary and ⅛ teaspoon pepper. Bring to a boil; cook 13-15 minutes or until liquid is reduced to ¼ cup.

2. Meanwhile, in a large skillet, heat oil over medium heat. Add carrots; cook and stir 4 minutes. Stir in parsnip and remaining cider; cook 4-6 minutes longer or until vegetables are crisp-tender, stirring occasionally. Add the apples, sage, salt, thyme and remaining pepper; cook and stir 6-8 minutes or until apples are slightly softened.

3. Remove rosemary from cider reduction. Serve drizzled over vegetable mixture.

Moroccan Beef and Apple Stew

I like to cook various dishes from around the world, so when I found a recipe for Moroccan tagine, I adapted it to our family's tastes. It starts off a bit sweet and ends with a spicy bite!

—DAWN ELLIOTT GREENVILLE, MI

PREP: 25 MIN. + CHILLING • **COOK:** 2½ HOURS • **MAKES:** 8 SERVINGS

- **1¾ pounds beef stew meat**
- **5 tablespoons Mrs. Dash Caribbean Citrus seasoning blend, divided**
- **½ cup butter, cubed, divided**
- **4 medium onions, coarsely chopped**
- **2 celery ribs, cut into ⅛-inch slices**
- **4 garlic cloves, minced**
- **2 cups beef broth**
- **3 medium sweet potatoes, peeled and cubed (about 5 cups)**
- **4 medium Granny Smith apples, peeled and cut into 1½-inch pieces**
- **4 medium carrots, cut into ½-inch slices**
- **1 cup apple butter**
- **¼ cup minced fresh cilantro**
- **Hot cooked couscous**

1. In a large bowl, toss beef with 4 tablespoons seasoning blend. Refrigerate, covered, 30 minutes.

2. In a Dutch oven, heat 1/4 cup butter over medium heat. Brown beef in batches. Remove with a slotted spoon.

3. In same pan, melt remaining butter. Add onions, celery and remaining seasoning blend; cook and stir 6-8 minutes or until vegetables are tender. Add garlic; cook 1 minute longer. Stir in broth. Return beef to pan; bring to a boil. Reduce heat; simmer, covered, 1½ hours.

4. Stir in sweet potatoes, apples, carrots and apple butter. Cook, covered, 30-40 minutes longer or until meat and vegetables are tender. Sprinkle with cilantro. Serve with couscous.

Bavarian Apple Bars

My husband and I were engaged at the time I first tasted these bars, while volunteering in the kitchen at Christian camp. Since his favorite desserts are apple pie and cheesecake, I knew the recipe needed to come home with me!

—CRYSTAL STANLEY ANCHOR, IL

PREP: 30 MIN. • **BAKE:** 50 MIN. + CHILLING • **MAKES:** 2 DOZEN

- **1 cup butter, softened**
- **⅔ cup sugar**
- **½ teaspoon vanilla extract**
- **2 cups all-purpose flour**

FILLING

- **2 packages (8 ounces each) cream cheese, softened**
- **½ cup plus ⅔ cup sugar, divided**
- **1 teaspoon vanilla extract**
- **2 eggs**
- **8 cups thinly sliced peeled Golden Delicious or Fuji apples (about 8 medium)**
- **1 teaspoon ground cinnamon**
- **½ cup slivered almonds**

1. Preheat oven to 375°. In a large bowl, cream butter and sugar until light and fluffy. Beat in vanilla. Gradually beat in flour. Press onto bottom and 1 in. up sides of a greased 13x9-in. baking pan.

2. For filling, in a large bowl, beat cream cheese and 1/2 cup sugar until smooth. Beat in vanilla. Add eggs; beat on low speed just until blended. Pour into crust.

3. In a large bowl, toss apples with cinnamon and remaining sugar. Arrange over cream cheese layer; sprinkle with almonds. Bake 50-60 minutes or until cream cheese layer is set and edges of crust are golden brown.

4. Cool in pan on a wire rack for 1 hour. Refrigerate for at least 2 hours. Cut into bars.

Apple Red-Hot Slab Pie

The color alone from the Red Hots candy makes this slab pie an instant hit. It's my absolute favorite because it holds so many family memories for us.

—LINDA MORTEN
SOMERVILLE, TX

PREP: 45 MIN. + CHILLING
BAKE: 50 MIN.
MAKES: 24 SERVINGS

- **5 cups all-purpose flour**
- **2 tablespoons sugar**
- **2 teaspoons salt**
- **2 cups cold butter, cubed**
- **1 to 1¼ cups ice water**

FILLING

- **⅔ cup sugar**
- **⅔ cup all-purpose flour**
- **½ teaspoon salt**
- **6 cups thinly sliced peeled Granny Smith apples (about 6 medium)**
- **6 cups thinly sliced peeled Gala or Jonathan apples (about 6 medium)**
- **1 cup Red Hots candies**
- **¼ cup cold butter**
- **Vanilla ice cream, optional**

1. In a large bowl, mix flour, sugar and salt; cut in butter until crumbly. Gradually add ice water, tossing with a fork until dough holds together when pressed. Divide dough in two portions so that one portion is slightly larger than the other. Shape each into a rectangle; wrap in plastic wrap. Refrigerate 1 hour or overnight.

2. Preheat oven to 375°. For filling, in a large bowl, mix sugar, flour and salt. Add apples and Red Hots; toss to coat.

3. On a lightly floured surface, roll out larger portion of dough into an 18x13-in. rectangle. Transfer to an ungreased 15x10x1-in. baking pan. Press onto the bottom and up sides of pan. Add filling; dot with butter.

4. Roll out remaining dough; place over filling. Fold bottom pastry over edge of top pastry; seal and flute or press with a fork to seal. Prick top with a fork.

5. Bake 50-55 minutes or until golden brown and filling is bubbly. Cool on a wire rack. Serve warm. If desired, top with ice cream.

Apple & Sweet Pepper Relish

Before you turn your apples into cobbler or pie, consider this unique relish. On burgers, brats or served alongside pork, this sweet and savory condiment will be a game-changer at your next cookout.
—JANETTE SCHULZ
MCDONOUGH, GA

PREP: 10 MIN.
COOK: 20 MIN. + CHILLING
MAKES: ABOUT 7 CUPS

- **2 cups cider vinegar**
- **2 cups sugar**
- **¾ teaspoon salt**
- **4 cups chopped peeled Braeburn or other apples (about 4 medium)**
- **2 large onions, chopped**
- **1 medium sweet red pepper, chopped**
- **1 medium green pepper, chopped**

1. In a nonreactive Dutch oven, combine all ingredients; bring to a boil. Reduce heat; simmer, uncovered, 10-15 minutes or until onions are crisp-tender, stirring occasionally. Transfer to a large bowl; cool to room temperature.
2. Refrigerate, covered, at least 6-8 hours before serving. If desired, transfer to covered jars and refrigerate up to 2 weeks.

Thyme-Baked Apple Slices

PICTURED ABOVE

My children love this healthy apple side dish along with chicken fingers for lunch. It's also a wonderful alternative to potatoes when serving meat. My family even asks for seconds!
—CONSTANCE HENRY HIBBING, MN

PREP: 15 MIN. • **BAKE:** 25 MIN. • **MAKES:** 6 SERVINGS

- **4 cups apple cider**
- **¼ cup butter, cubed**
- **8 large Braeburn apples (about 4 pounds)**
- **3½ teaspoons minced fresh thyme, divided**

1. Place cider in a large saucepan. Bring to a boil; cook 18-20 minutes or until liquid is reduced to ⅔ cup. Remove from heat; stir in butter.
2. Peel and cut each apple into eight wedges. In a large bowl, toss apples with ¼ cup of the reduced cider and 3 teaspoons thyme. Transfer to foil-lined 15x10x1-in. baking pan. Bake 10 minutes.
3. Drizzle with remaining reduced cider. Bake 12-15 minutes longer or until tender. Sprinkle with remaining thyme.

Warm Apple-Cinnamon Pastry Twists

For a simple twist on dessert, these fun, tender pastries have all the flavors and spices of apple pie rolled into handheld servings.

—PATRICIA QUINN OMAHA, NE

PREP: 35 MIN. + CHILLING • **BAKE:** 20 MIN. • **MAKES:** 16 SERVINGS

- **1½ cups all-purpose flour**
- **½ teaspoon salt**
- **½ cup shortening**
- **4 to 5 tablespoons ice water**
- **¼ cup sugar**
- **¾ teaspoon ground cinnamon**
- **⅛ teaspoon ground nutmeg**
- **2 large Granny Smith apples**
- **2 tablespoons butter, softened**
- **2 tablespoons butter, melted**
- **Vanilla ice cream**

1. In a large bowl, mix flour and salt; cut in shortening until crumbly. Gradually add ice water, tossing with a fork until dough holds together when pressed. Shape into a disk; wrap in plastic wrap. Refrigerate 1 hour or overnight.

2. Preheat oven to 400°. In a shallow bowl, mix sugar, cinnamon and nutmeg. Cut each apple into eight wedges.

3. On a lightly floured surface, roll dough into a 12-in.-square; spread with softened butter. Fold dough into thirds. Roll folded dough into a 16x10-in. rectangle; cut crosswise into sixteen 1-in. wide strips. Wrap each strip around an apple wedge.

4. Brush tops with melted butter; roll in sugar mixture. Place on a parchment paper-lined baking sheet. Bake 20-25 minutes or until pastry is golden brown and apples are tender. Serve warm with ice cream.

Apple Caramel Bread Pudding

I've made this bread pudding for years, and everyone loves it. You can prepare it the night before, cover it with plastic wrap and then bake it in the morning. After it's cooked, it can sit out for a couple hours without getting soggy.

—JAN BRADFORD WEST VALLEY CITY, UT

PREP: 35 MIN. + CHILLING • **BAKE:** 35 MIN. • **MAKES:** 15 SERVINGS

- **1 cup plus 2 tablespoons packed brown sugar, divided**
- **½ cup butter, cubed**
- **2 tablespoons light corn syrup**
- **¾ teaspoon ground cinnamon**
- **4 cups sliced peeled Granny Smith apples (about 4 medium)**
- **4 eggs**
- **1 cup 2% milk**
- **1 teaspoon vanilla extract**
- **½ teaspoon salt**
- **1 loaf (1 pound) egg bread, cut into 1½-inch cubes**

1. In a small saucepan, combine 1 cup brown sugar, butter, corn syrup and cinnamon; cook and stir 4-6 minutes over medium heat until blended. Pour into a greased 13x9-in. baking dish; top evenly with apples. Cool slightly.

2. In a large bowl, whisk eggs, milk, vanilla, salt and remaining brown sugar until blended; stir in bread. Pour over apples. Refrigerate, covered, several hours or overnight.

3. Preheat oven to 350°. Remove bread pudding from refrigerator; uncover and let stand while oven heats. Bake 35-40 minutes or until bubbly and top is golden. Serve warm.

Spiced Apple Cake with Caramel Icing

Easy to prepare and popular with my friends and family, this apple cake is one of my all-time favorite autumn recipes. A slice of this soft treat is delicious with a hot cup of coffee or tea.

—MONICA BURNS LUSBY, MD

PREP: 45 MIN. • **BAKE:** 1¼ HOURS + COOLING • **MAKES:** 12 SERVINGS

- **3 cups chopped peeled Gala or Braeburn apples (about 3 medium)**
- **½ cup bourbon**
- **2 cups sugar**
- **1½ cups canola oil**
- **3 eggs**
- **2 teaspoons vanilla extract**
- **3 cups all-purpose flour**
- **2 teaspoons apple pie spice**
- **1 teaspoon salt**
- **1 teaspoon baking soda**
- **1 cup chopped walnuts, toasted**

ICING

- **¼ cup butter, cubed**
- **½ cup packed brown sugar**
- **1 tablespoon 2% milk**
- **1 tablespoon bourbon**
- **Dash salt**
- **⅛ teaspoon vanilla extract**

1. Preheat oven to 350°. Grease and flour a 10-in. tube pan. In a large bowl, toss apples with bourbon.

2. In a large bowl, beat sugar, oil, eggs and vanilla until well blended. In another bowl, whisk flour, pie spice, salt and baking soda; gradually beat into sugar mixture. Stir in apple mixture and walnuts.

3. Transfer to prepared pan. Bake 1¼ to 1½ hours or until a toothpick inserted in center comes out clean. Cool in the pan 10 minutes before removing to a wire rack.

4. In a small heavy saucepan, combine butter, brown sugar, milk, bourbon and salt. Bring to a boil over medium heat, stirring occasionally; cook and stir for 3 minutes. Remove from heat; stir in vanilla. Drizzle over warm cake. Cool completely.

NOTES *To remove cakes easily, use solid shortening to grease plain and fluted tube pans. To toast nuts, spread in 15x10x1-in. baking pan. Bake at 350° for 5-10 minutes or until lightly browned, stirring occasionally.*

Roasted Sweet Potato & Apple Soup

Savory with just a touch of sweetness, this fall soup is sure to keep the chill away. Serve it as a starter or paired with a grilled sandwich for lunch or a light dinner.

—LISA KALMBACH PAPILLION, NE

PREP: 20 MIN. • **BAKE:** 40 MIN. • **MAKES:** 4 SERVINGS

- **2 medium sweet potatoes, peeled and cubed**
- **1 large onion, cut into 1-inch pieces**
- **1 large Gala or other apple, peeled and cubed**
- **3 garlic cloves**
- **2 tablespoons olive oil**
- **3 cups vegetable or chicken broth**
- **¾ teaspoon salt**
- **¼ teaspoon pepper**
- **Reduced-fat sour cream, optional**

1. Preheat oven to 400°. Place sweet potatoes, onion, apple and garlic cloves in a greased 15x10x1-in. baking pan; drizzle with oil and toss to coat. Roast 40-45 minutes or until very tender, stirring occasionally.

2. Cool slightly. Process in batches in a blender with broth until smooth. Transfer to a large saucepan. Stir in salt and pepper; heat through, stirring occasionally. If desired, serve with sour cream.

Crafty Pie-Making Kit

Share your favorite pie recipe with all the apples of your eye.

MATERIALS

- **10x14-inch burlap sacks**
- **Apples or ingredients of your choice**
- **Recipe card**
- **Ribbon or twine**

DIRECTIONS

1. Order 10x14-inch burlap sacks.
2. Fill sacks with the baking goods and attach the recipe with ribbon or twine.
3. You could also include nuts and spices for a little something extra.

PARTY FAVOR PROBLEM SOLVED

Looking for a simple gift idea for a fall bridal shower or a ladies luncheon? These DIY baking kits are perfect for sharing your favorite recipe.

easter*g*atherings

As the flowers begin to peek out from beneath the newly thawed ground, a host of springtime celebrations awaits on the horizon. From Easter dinners and brunches to garden luncheons, here you'll find entertaining ideas that will awaken the senses and capture spring's freshest picks.

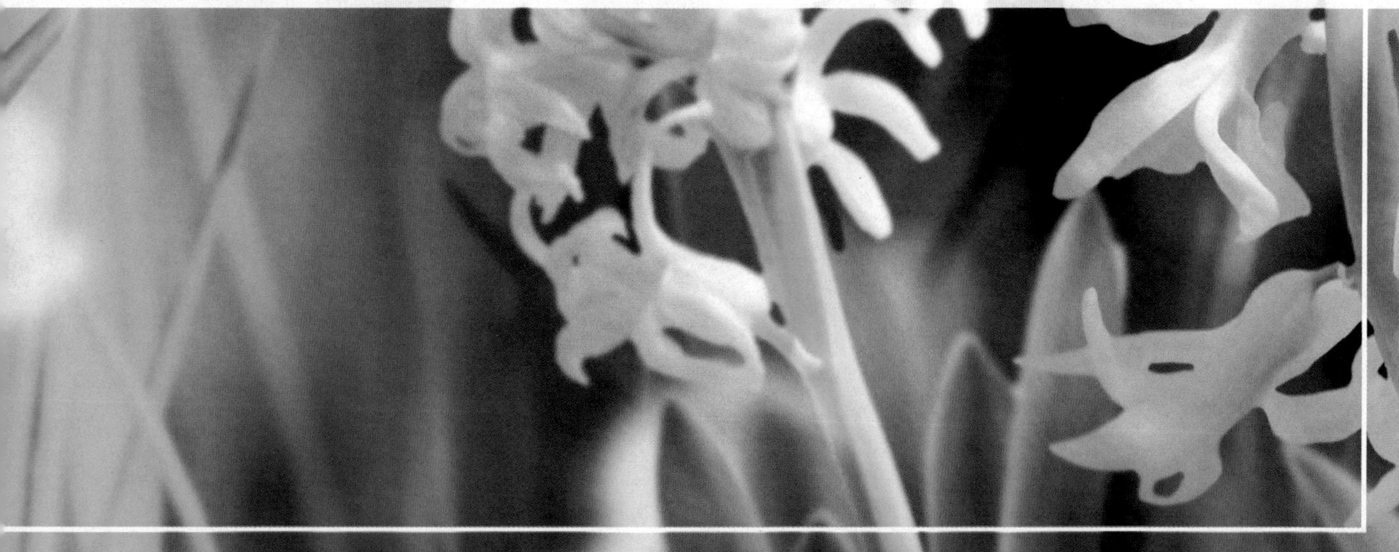

Asparagus grows wild in Greece, where an Easter dinner would not be complete without the presence of spring's finest produce and fresh aromatic herbs to round out a traditional roasted lamb. Accompanying this Mediterranean-inspired menu is a festive Tsoureki Paschalino (Easter Bread, with nestled dyed eggs), typically made on Holy Thursday and often served with cheese. With a collection of recipes this vibrant and rich, you might consider replacing your annual ham with an elegant Greek feast for four.

FORMAL **GREEK EASTER**

Garlic-Herb Cornish Hens

I grow basil and mint in my garden and love stepping outside to pick what I need for this recipe. The hens make a nice alternative to lamb for a family Easter dinner.

—BEE ENGELHART
BLOOMFIELD TOWNSHIP, MI

PREP: 15 MIN. + MARINATING
BAKE: 40 MIN. + STANDING
MAKES: 4 SERVINGS

- **3 tablespoons lemon juice**
- **3 garlic cloves, minced**
- **1 tablespoon minced fresh basil**
- **1 tablespoon minced fresh mint**
- **½ teaspoon salt**
- **2 tablespoons olive oil, divided**
- **2 Cornish game hens (20 to 24 ounces each)**

1. In a small bowl, mix the first five ingredients; stir in 1 tablespoon oil. With fingers, carefully loosen the skin from the Cornish hen breasts; rub herb mixture under the skin, over the skin and inside cavities. Tuck wings under hens; tie drumsticks together. Refrigerate, covered, at least 4 hours or overnight.
2. Preheat oven to 375°. Place on a rack in a shallow roasting pan, breast side up. Brush hens with remaining oil.
3. Roast 40-50 minutes or until a thermometer inserted in thigh reads 180°. Remove from oven; tent with foil. Let stand for 10 minutes before splitting the hens in half.

Roasted Asparagus & Tomatoes

It seems I have a habit of buying too much asparagus when it's in season, but it doesn't go to waste! I toss the spears with cherry tomatoes and goat cheese for this side. Be sure to use good quality goat cheese because it makes all the difference.

—HOLLY BATTISTE BARRINGTON, NJ

START TO FINISH: 30 MIN. • **MAKES:** 4 SERVINGS

- **1 pound fresh asparagus, trimmed**
- **1 cup grape tomatoes**
- **¼ cup coarsely chopped walnuts**
- **1 tablespoon olive oil**
- **¼ teaspoon dried oregano**
- **¼ teaspoon salt**
- **¼ teaspoon pepper**
- **2 tablespoons crumbled goat cheese**
- **1 tablespoon minced fresh basil**

1. Preheat oven to 400°. Place asparagus, tomatoes and walnuts in a greased 15x10x1-in. baking pan. Mix oil, oregano, salt and pepper; add to asparagus mixture and toss to coat.
2. Roast 15-20 minutes or until asparagus is crisp-tender, turning vegetables occasionally. Sprinkle with the cheese. Top with basil before serving.

Baklava Bites

I love anything baked in phyllo dough. I find these little bundles are easier to make than traditional baklava, but taste just as good!

—**BARB TEMPLIN** NORWOOD, MN

PREP: 1 HOUR • **BAKE:** 20 MIN. • **MAKES:** 3 DOZEN

- **⅓ cup pistachios**
- **⅓ cup chopped walnuts**
- **¼ cup unblanched almonds**
- **2 tablespoons sugar**
- **2 tablespoons dry bread crumbs**
- **1½ teaspoons ground cinnamon**
- **1 teaspoon grated orange peel**
- **2 tablespoons honey**
- **1 cup butter, melted, divided**
- **1 ounce semisweet chocolate, finely chopped**
- **15 sheets phyllo dough (14x9 inch size)**

SYRUP

- **¼ cup honey**
- **2 tablespoons sugar**
- **2 tablespoons water**
- **1 tablespoon orange juice**

1. Place the first seven ingredients in a food processor; process until finely chopped. Transfer to a small bowl; stir in honey and 2 tablespoons melted butter. Stir in chocolate.
2. Preheat oven to 350°. Place one sheet of phyllo dough on a work surface; brush with butter. Layer with four additional phyllo sheets, brushing each layer. (Keep the remaining phyllo covered with plastic wrap and a damp towel to prevent it from drying out.)
3. Using a sharp knife, cut the layered sheets into 12 squares. Carefully press each stack into a greased miniature muffin cup; fill each with a rounded teaspoonful of filling. Form into bundles by gathering edges of phyllo squares and twisting centers to close. Repeat twice with remaining ingredients.
4. Brush tops with remaining melted butter. Bake 18-20 minutes or until golden brown.
5. Meanwhile, in a small saucepan, combine the syrup ingredients; bring to a boil. Reduce heat; cook and stir until sugar is completely dissolved.
6. Remove baklava bites from oven; drizzle immediately with syrup. Remove from the pans to wire racks; cool. Store in an airtight container.

Chickpea & Feta Salad

This fresh, colorful salad displays the best of the Mediterranean cuisine that I love—feta cheese, crisp vegetables and a nice lemony flavor. Though wonderful any time of the year, it's especially enjoyable in the spring.

—**PAULA ALTHOUSE** HAMBURG, PA

START TO FINISH: 20 MIN. • **MAKES:** 12 SERVINGS (¾ CUP EACH)

- **½ cup olive oil**
- **¼ cup minced fresh chives**
- **4 garlic cloves, minced**
- **2 tablespoons minced fresh oregano or 2 teaspoons dried oregano**
- **2 teaspoons grated lemon peel**
- **3 tablespoons lemon juice**
- **½ teaspoon salt**
- **½ teaspoon pepper**
- **2 cans (15 ounces each) chickpeas or garbanzo beans, rinsed and drained**
- **2 cups (8 ounces) crumbled feta cheese**
- **2 celery ribs, finely chopped**
- **1 large red onion, finely chopped**
- **1 medium cucumber, peeled and chopped**

In a small bowl, whisk the first eight ingredients. In a large bowl, combine the remaining ingredients. Add dressing; toss lightly to combine.

Roast Rack of Lamb with Herb Sauce

This sauce uses eight of my favorite herbs, but making it is a cinch. The aroma of the lamb while it roasts is amazing!
—MYA ZERONIS PITTSBURGH, PA

PREP: 30 MIN. + MARINATING • **BAKE:** 35 MIN. + STANDING
MAKES: 4 SERVINGS (1¾ CUPS SAUCE)

- **¼ cup minced fresh rosemary**
- **1½ teaspoons coarsely ground pepper**
- **1½ teaspoons salt**
- **2 racks of lamb (1½ pounds each)**
- **1 tablespoon olive oil**

SAUCE

- **¾ cup fresh parsley leaves**
- **⅔ cup fresh basil leaves**
- **⅓ cup each fresh cilantro leaves, mint leaves, oregano leaves and thyme leaves**
- **⅓ cup coarsely chopped fresh chives**
- **⅓ cup chopped shallots**
- **2 garlic cloves, crushed**
- **3 tablespoons grated lemon peel**
- **½ cup lemon juice**
- **2 tablespoons Dijon mustard**
- **¾ teaspoon salt**
- **½ teaspoon pepper**
- **⅓ cup olive oil**

1. Mix rosemary, pepper and salt; rub over lamb. Refrigerate, covered, 8 hours or overnight.
2. Preheat oven to 375°. Place lamb in a shallow roasting pan, fat side up; drizzle with oil.
3. Roast 35-45 minutes or until meat reaches desired doneness (for medium-rare, a thermometer should read 145°; medium, 160°; well-done, 170°). Remove lamb from oven; tent with foil. Let stand 10 minutes before serving.
4. Meanwhile, place herbs, shallots and garlic in a food processor; pulse until herbs are chopped. Add lemon peel, lemon juice, mustard, salt and pepper; process until blended. Continue processing while gradually adding oil in a steady stream. Serve lamb with the sauce.

UPGRADE FROM HAM TO LAMB

Do you avoid lamb because you think it has a "gamey" flavor? Look for leaner cuts of lamb, which have a delicate, mild flavor. Also remember that mutton, a sheep that is older than 1 year, has a stronger taste than lamb. In fact, lamb can be a great change of pace from beef, chicken or pork and is not as expensive as you might think. According to the Natural Lamb Co-op, a 3-ounce portion of lamb is comparable in price to the finer cuts of beef and pork.

Couscous Salad with Olives & Raisins

PICTURED AT LEFT

There's plenty to like in this Mediterranean side dish, and it pairs well with just about any meat or poultry entree.
—MYA ZERONIS PITTSBURGH, PA

PREP: 15 MIN.
COOK: 5 MIN. + COOLING
MAKES: 8 SERVINGS

- **2 cups vegetable stock**
- **1 package (10 ounces) couscous**
- **2 tablespoons olive oil**
- **1 teaspoon grated lemon peel**
- **2 tablespoons lemon juice**
- **½ teaspoon salt**
- **¼ teaspoon pepper**
- **2 plum tomatoes, seeded and chopped**
- **¾ cup sliced Greek olives**
- **⅔ cup raisins**
- **1½ tablespoons finely chopped fresh mint**

1. In a large saucepan, bring stock to a boil. Stir in couscous. Remove from heat; let stand, covered, 5-10 minutes or until stock is absorbed. Fluff with a fork. Cool completely.
2. In a small bowl, whisk oil, lemon peel, lemon juice, salt and pepper until blended; stir into couscous. Stir in remaining ingredients.

Lemony Yogurt Cream Pie

I developed this recipe when my sister gave me a box of lemons from her tree. The addition of yogurt in the filling tempers the lemony tartness slightly.
—**KAREN SCHREINER** KINGMAN, AZ

PREP: 45 MIN. + CHILLING • **BAKE:** 25 MIN. + COOLING • **MAKES:** 8 SERVINGS

- **1¼ cups all-purpose flour**
- **¼ teaspoon salt**
- **½ cup cold butter, cubed**
- **4 to 6 tablespoons ice water**

FILLING

- **¼ cup cornstarch**
- **1 cup 2% milk**
- **1 cup sugar**
- **3 egg yolks**
- **1 teaspoon grated lemon peel**
- **⅓ cup lemon juice**
- **¼ cup butter, cubed**
- **1 cup plain Greek yogurt**

TOPPING

- **1½ cups heavy whipping cream**
- **5 tablespoons confectioners' sugar**
- **1 tablespoon lemon juice**
- **1 teaspoon grated lemon peel**

1. In a small bowl, mix flour and salt; cut in butter until crumbly. Gradually add ice water, tossing with a fork until dough holds together when pressed. Shape into a disk; wrap in plastic wrap. Refrigerate 1 hour or overnight.
2. On a lightly floured surface, roll dough to a ⅛-in.-thick circle; transfer to a 9-in. pie plate. Trim pastry to ½ in. beyond rim of plate; flute edge. Refrigerate for 30 minutes. Preheat the oven to 425°.
3. Line pastry with a double thickness of foil. Fill with pie weights, dried beans or uncooked rice. Bake on a lower oven rack 20-25 minutes or until edges are golden brown. Remove foil and weights; bake 3-6 minutes longer or until bottom is golden brown. Cool completely on a wire rack.
4. In a large heavy saucepan, whisk cornstarch, milk, sugar, egg yolks, lemon peel and lemon juice until blended; cook and stir over medium heat until thickened and bubbly. Cook and stir 2 minutes longer. Remove from heat; stir in butter until melted. Cool for 10 minutes or until lukewarm (mixture will be thick). Stir in the yogurt until smooth; transfer to crust. Refrigerate, covered, until cold.
5. In a large bowl, beat cream until it begins to thicken. Add confectioners' sugar, lemon juice and peel; beat until stiff peaks form. Spread over pie.

NOTE *Let pie weights cool before storing. Beans and rice may be reused for pie weights, but not for cooking.*

Rosemary Goat Cheese Bites

My mom makes her own goat cheese and I wanted to show it off for a party. Once everyone tried it for the first time, I knew I had created a winning recipe.
—**CRYSTAL BRUNS** ILIFF, CO

START TO FINISH: 25 MIN. • **MAKES:** 1 DOZEN

- **¼ cup finely chopped pecans**
- **¼ teaspoon ground cinnamon**
- **1 log (4 ounces) fresh goat cheese**
- **1½ teaspoons minced fresh rosemary, divided**
- **Toasted French bread baguette slices, optional**
- **1 tablespoon honey**

1. In a shallow bowl, toss pecans with cinnamon. In a small bowl, mix cheese and ¾ teaspoon rosemary until blended. Shape mixture into 12 balls; roll in pecan mixture to coat. Flatten slightly into patties.
2. If desired, serve patties with toasted baguette slices. Drizzle with honey and sprinkle with remaining rosemary.

Easter Egg Bread

I've made this treat for 20 years, and it goes especially well with baked ham. Colored hard-cooked eggs baked in the dough give the sweet bread an Easter appearance, but you can leave the eggs out to enjoy the bread anytime.

—HEATHER DURANTE WELLSBURG, WV

PREP: 55 MIN. + RISING
BAKE: 25 MIN. + COOLING
MAKES: 1 LOAF (16 SLICES)

- **½ cup sugar**
- **2 packages (¼ ounce each) active dry yeast**
- **1 to 2 teaspoons ground cardamom**
- **1 teaspoon salt**
- **6 to 6½ cups all-purpose flour**
- **1½ cups whole milk**
- **6 tablespoons butter, cubed**
- **4 eggs**
- **3 to 6 hard-cooked eggs, unpeeled**
- **Assorted food coloring**
- **Canola oil**
- **2 tablespoons water**

1. In a large bowl, mix sugar, yeast, cardamom, salt and 2 cups flour. In a small saucepan, heat milk and butter to 120°-130°. Add to dry ingredients; beat on medium speed 2 minutes. Add 3 eggs; beat 2 minutes longer. Stir in enough remaining flour to form a soft dough (dough will be sticky).
2. Turn dough onto a floured surface; knead until smooth and elastic, about 6-8 minutes. Place in a greased bowl, turning once to grease the top. Cover with plastic wrap and let rise in a warm place until doubled, about 45 minutes.
3. Meanwhile, dye hard-cooked eggs with food coloring following food coloring package directions. Let stand until completely dry.
4. Punch down dough. Turn onto a lightly floured surface; divide into thirds. Roll each portion into a 24-in. rope. Place ropes on a greased baking sheet and braid. Bring ends together to form a ring. Pinch ends to seal. Lightly coat dyed eggs with oil; arrange on braid, tucking them carefully between ropes.
5. Cover with a kitchen towel; let rise in a warm place until doubled, about 20 minutes. Preheat oven to 375°.
6. In a bowl, whisk remaining egg and water; gently brush over dough, avoiding eggs. Bake 25-30 minutes or until golden brown. Remove from pan to a wire rack to cool. Refrigerate leftovers.

Spanakopita Bites

For an easy spanakopita, try this appetizer that is made in a pan, then cut into squares. You'll enjoy the taste of the classic version without all the hassle.
—**BARBARA SMITH** CHIPLEY, FL

PREP: 20 MIN. + FREEZING • **BAKE:** 35 MIN. • **MAKES:** 10½ DOZEN

- **1 egg, lightly beaten**
- **1 package (10 ounces) frozen chopped spinach, thawed and squeezed dry**
- **2 cups (8 ounces) crumbled feta cheese**
- **1 cup (8 ounces) 4% small-curd cottage cheese**
- **¾ cup butter, melted**
- **16 sheets phyllo dough (14x9-inch size)**

1. Preheat oven to 350°. In a large bowl, mix egg, spinach and cheeses. Brush a 15x10x1-in. baking pan with some of the butter.
2. Place one sheet of phyllo dough in prepared pan; brush with butter. Layer with seven additional phyllo sheets, brushing each layer. (Keep remaining phyllo covered with plastic wrap and a damp towel to prevent it from drying out.) Spread top with spinach mixture. Top with remaining phyllo dough, brushing each sheet with butter.
3. Freeze, covered, 30 minutes. Using a sharp knife, cut into 1-in. squares. Bake 35-45 minutes or until golden brown. Refrigerate leftovers.

Golden Greek Baby Potatoes

This recipe was inspired by a tiny Greek restaurant we used to go to during grad school. To make the potatoes extra delicious, use a high-quality olive oil and a nice kosher or sea salt.

—KAROL CHANDLER-EZELL NACOGDOCHES, TX

START TO FINISH: 40 MIN. • **MAKES:** 4 SERVINGS

- **2 tablespoons olive oil**
- **1 tablespoon butter**
- **¼ cup chopped onion**
- **1¼ pounds baby Yukon Gold potatoes**
- **¼ cup water**
- **3 tablespoons minced fresh chives or 2 green onions, thinly sliced**
- **1½ teaspoons Greek seasoning**
- **1 to 1½ teaspoons grated lemon peel**
- **1 garlic clove, minced**
- **½ teaspoon pepper**
- **¼ teaspoon kosher salt**
- **1 to 2 tablespoons lemon juice**
- **1 tablespoon minced fresh parsley**

1. In a small skillet, heat oil and butter over medium heat. Add onion; cook and stir 1-2 minutes or until softened. Reduce heat to medium-low; cook 12-15 minutes or until deep golden brown, stirring occasionally.

2. Meanwhile, place potatoes and water in a large microwave-safe dish. Microwave, covered, on high 6-8 minutes or until tender.

3. Add chives, Greek seasoning, lemon peel, garlic, pepper and salt to onion mixture; cook and stir 1 minute longer. Drain potatoes; add onion mixture. Flatten potatoes with a fork, tossing them to coat with onion mixture. Add lemon juice and parsley; toss to combine.

NOTE *This recipe was tested in a 1,100-watt microwave.*

Greek Salad with Lemon Dressing

I love salads and Greek food, so I decided to create a Greek salad. I based my recipe on a salad from one of my favorite restaurants. My husband and kids were the taste-testers, and now this is one of my most-requested dishes for family get-togethers and holidays.

—PATTI LEAKE COLUMBIA, MO

START TO FINISH: 30 MIN. • **MAKES:** 12 SERVINGS (¾ CUP EACH)

- **¼ cup lemon juice**
- **¼ cup olive oil**
- **1 teaspoon sugar**
- **½ teaspoon Greek seasoning**
- **½ teaspoon minced fresh oregano**
- **¼ teaspoon minced fresh rosemary**
- **¼ teaspoon pepper**

SALAD

- **8 cups torn mixed salad greens**
- **1 medium cucumber, seeded and chopped**
- **1 medium sweet red pepper, thinly sliced**
- **1 medium sweet orange or yellow pepper, thinly sliced**
- **1 medium tomato, halved and sliced**
- **1 package (4 ounces) crumbled tomato and basil feta cheese**
- **6 green onions, chopped**
- **1 jar (12 ounces) pepperoncini, drained**
- **1 cup pitted Greek olives**

1. In a small bowl, whisk the first seven ingredients until blended.

2. In a large bowl, combine the first seven salad ingredients. Drizzle dressing over salad; toss to coat. Top with pepperoncini and olives. Serve immediately.

DIY SEASONING

To make Greek seasoning, combine 1½ teaspoons dried oregano; 1 teaspoon each of dried mint and dried thyme; ½ teaspoon each dried basil, dried marjoram, and dried onion, and ¼ teaspoon dried minced garlic.

Greek Zucchini & Feta Bake

Looking to highlight your meal with something light, indulgent and golden on top? Turn to this Greek-style egg bake.
—GABRIELA STEFANESCU WEBSTER, TX

PREP: 40 MIN. • **BAKE:** 30 MIN. + STANDING • **MAKES:** 12 SERVINGS

- **2 tablespoons olive oil, divided**
- **5 medium zucchini, cut into ½-in. cubes (about 6 cups)**
- **2 large onions, chopped (about 4 cups)**
- **1 teaspoon dried oregano, divided**
- **½ teaspoon salt**
- **¼ teaspoon pepper**
- **6 eggs**
- **2 teaspoons baking powder**
- **1 cup (8 ounces) reduced-fat plain yogurt**
- **1 cup all-purpose flour**
- **2 packages (8 ounces each) feta cheese, cubed**
- **¼ cup minced fresh parsley**
- **1 teaspoon paprika**

1. Preheat oven to 350°. In a Dutch oven, heat 1 tablespoon oil over medium-high heat. Add half of the zucchini, half of the onions and ½ teaspoon oregano; cook and stir 8-10 minutes or until zucchini is crisp-tender. Remove from pan. Repeat with remaining vegetables. Stir in salt and pepper. Cool slightly.
2. In a large bowl, whisk eggs and baking powder until blended; whisk in the yogurt and flour just until blended. Stir in the cheese, parsley and zucchini mixture. Transfer to a greased 13x9-in. baking dish. Sprinkle with paprika.
3. Bake, uncovered, 30-35 minutes or until golden brown and set. Let stand 10 minutes before cutting.

NOTE *If desired, thinly slice 1 medium zucchini and toss with 2 teaspoons olive oil; arrange over casserole before sprinkling with paprika. Bake as directed.*

Citrus Spiced Olives

PICTURED ON PAGE 132

Lemon, lime and orange bring a burst of sunny citrus flavor to marinated olives, and you can even blend the olives and spread the mixture onto baguette slices.

—**ANN SHEEHY** LAWRENCE, MA

PREP: 20 MIN. + CHILLING
MAKES: 4 CUPS

- **½ cup white wine**
- **¼ cup canola oil**
- **3 tablespoons salt-free seasoning blend**
- **4 garlic cloves, minced**
- **½ teaspoon crushed red pepper flakes**
- **2 teaspoons each grated orange, lemon and lime peels**
- **3 tablespoons each orange, lemon and lime juices**
- **4 cups mixed pitted olives**

In a large bowl, combine the first five ingredients. Add citrus peels and juices; whisk until blended. Add olives and toss to coat. Refrigerate, covered, at least 4 hours before serving.

The Easter Bunny isn't the only one who will be bright-eyed and bushy-tailed come Sunday morning. Just wait 'til your guests see what's in store for your celebratory brunch

Whether you're making strata for a small gathering or stuffed French toast for the family, each one of these recipes offers a fresh taste of spring and a fanciful twist on your favorite breakfast items—no reservation required.

Ham & Cheese Breakfast Muffins (p. 147)
Spring Strawberry Sangria (p. 149)
Herbed Vegetable Strata (p. 153)
Fresh Fruit Salad with Honey-Orange Dressing (p. 151)

EASTER **BRUNCH**

Spinach Potato Pie

When we have breakfast with relatives, I like to make this crustless quiche with hash browns and spinach. With a side of fruit, we think it makes a great weekend brunch.
—**DEANNA PHILLIPS** FERNDALE, WA

PREP: 25 MIN. • **BAKE:** 55 MIN.
MAKES: 6 SERVINGS

- **5 eggs, lightly beaten**
- **4 cups frozen shredded hash brown potatoes**
- **2 cups chopped fresh spinach**
- **¾ cup chopped red onion**
- **½ cup 2% cottage cheese**
- **7 bacon strips, cooked and crumbled**
- **3 green onions, chopped**
- **4 garlic cloves, minced**
- **½ teaspoon salt**
- **¼ teaspoon pepper**
- **⅛ teaspoon hot pepper sauce**
- **3 plum tomatoes, sliced**
- **½ cup shredded Parmesan cheese**

1. Preheat oven to 350°. In a large bowl, combine the first 11 ingredients. Pour into a greased 9-in. pie plate.
2. Bake 40 minutes. Arrange tomatoes over top; sprinkle with Parmesan cheese. Bake 15-20 minutes longer or until a knife inserted near the edge comes out clean. Let stand 5 minutes before cutting.

San Diego Succotash

I brought home some summer squash from my job at a plant nursery, decided to put it in succotash and this recipe was born. I decided to name it after my hometown because the yellow and green colors of the dish remind me of the sunny days here in beautiful San Diego.
—**PAT SALLUME** SAN DIEGO, CA

START TO FINISH: 20 MIN. • **MAKES:** 6 SERVINGS

- **2 tablespoons butter**
- **1 medium zucchini, halved and sliced**
- **1 small yellow summer squash, halved and sliced**
- **1 package (10 ounces) frozen corn**
- **1½ cups frozen lima beans**
- **1 shallot, chopped**
- **1 garlic clove, minced**
- **¼ teaspoon salt**
- **¼ teaspoon pepper**

In a large skillet, heat butter over medium-high heat. Add zucchini, summer squash, corn, lima beans and shallot; cook and stir for 6-8 minutes or until vegetables are crisp-tender. Add garlic, salt and pepper; cook 1 minute longer.

Banana-Oatmeal Pancakes with Blueberry Maple Syrup

Breakfast is generally the only meal I'm able to share with my boyfriend, so I like to make a delicious healthy morning meal for us to enjoy. He's a pancake fanatic, so these banana pancakes make a regular appearance at our table.

—JENNIFER WALKER DENVER, CO

PREP: 20 MIN. • **COOK:** 5 MIN./BATCH • **MAKES:** 18 PANCAKES (2 CUPS SYRUP)

- **1½ cups quick-cooking oats**
- **½ cup all-purpose flour**
- **½ cup whole wheat flour**
- **2 tablespoons baking powder**
- **2 tablespoons packed brown sugar**
- **¾ teaspoon salt**
- **¼ teaspoon ground cinnamon**
- **3 eggs**
- **2 cups 2% milk**
- **¼ cup unsweetened applesauce**
- **½ teaspoon vanilla extract**
- **⅔ cup mashed ripe bananas (about 2 medium)**
- **3 cups fresh or frozen blueberries, divided**
- **1 cup maple syrup**
- **Sliced ripe banana, optional**

1. In a large bowl, whisk oats, flours, baking powder, brown sugar, salt and cinnamon. In a another bowl, whisk eggs, milk, applesauce and vanilla until blended. Add to dry ingredients, stirring just until moistened. Fold in bananas. Let stand 5 minutes.
2. Lightly grease a griddle; heat over medium heat. Pour batter by 1/4 cupfuls onto griddle. Cook until bubbles on top begin to pop and bottoms are golden brown. Turn; cook until second side is golden brown.
3. In a small saucepan, combine 1½ cups blueberries and syrup. Bring to a boil; cook and stir 4-5 minutes or until berries are softened. Mash blueberries. Press through a fine-mesh strainer into a bowl; discard pulp. Stir in remaining blueberries. Serve pancakes with syrup and banana slices if desired.

Ham & Cheese Breakfast Muffins

PICTURED ON PAGE 144

Ever since we began making these muffins, they have been a huge hit with family and friends. They are simple to make, tasty warm or cold and never stay around for long.

—LAURA NEWCOMER BOWDOIN, ME

PREP: 15 MIN. • **BAKE:** 20 MIN. • **MAKES:** 20 MUFFINS

- **3 cups all-purpose flour**
- **3 teaspoons baking powder**
- **½ teaspoon baking soda**
- **¼ teaspoon salt**
- **Dash pepper**
- **2 eggs**
- **1⅓ cups buttermilk**
- **⅓ cup canola oil**
- **1 cup finely chopped fully cooked ham**
- **1 cup (4 ounces) shredded cheddar cheese**
- **¾ cup finely chopped onion**

1. Preheat oven to 400°. In a large bowl, whisk flour, baking powder, baking soda, salt and pepper. In another bowl, whisk eggs, buttermilk and oil until blended. Add to flour mixture; stir just until moistened. Fold in ham, cheese and onion.
2. Fill greased or foil-lined muffin cups three-fourths full. Bake 18-22 minutes or until a toothpick inserted in center comes out clean. Cool 5 minutes before removing from pans to wire racks. Serve warm.

Southwestern Eggs Benedict with Avocado Sauce

I frequently make this spicy spin-off of classic Eggs Benedict for my husband, who loves breakfast. I like the heat from the jalapenos and also that the avocado sauce is a healthier substitute for the usual Hollandaise sauce.

—KARA SCOW MCKINNEY, TX

START TO FINISH: 30 MIN. • **MAKES:** 6 SERVINGS

- **1 medium ripe avocado, peeled and cubed**
- **½ cup water**
- **½ cup reduced-fat sour cream**
- **¼ cup fresh cilantro leaves**
- **2 tablespoons ranch salad dressing mix**
- **2 tablespoons lime juice**
- **2 tablespoons pickled jalapeno slices**
- **1 garlic clove, chopped**
- **¼ teaspoon salt**
- **⅛ teaspoon pepper**
- **6 slices whole wheat bread, toasted**
- **12 slices deli ham**
- **6 slices Monterey Jack cheese**
- **2 teaspoons white vinegar**
- **6 eggs**

1. Preheat oven to 425°. Place first 10 ingredients in a blender; cover and process until smooth.
2. Place toast on a baking sheet. Top each with two slices ham and one slice cheese. Bake 6-8 minutes or until cheese is melted.
3. Meanwhile, place 2-3 in. of water in a large saucepan or skillet with high sides; add vinegar. Bring to a boil; adjust heat to maintain a gentle simmer. Break cold eggs, one at a time, into a small bowl; holding bowl close to surface of water, slip egg into pan.
4. Cook, uncovered, 3-5 minutes or until whites are completely set and yolks begin to thicken but are not hard. Using a slotted spoon, lift eggs out of water. Serve immediately with ham and cheese toasts and avocado mixture.

NEED A LITTLE COACHING ON POACHING?

When poaching eggs, it's important to make sure the water is at a gentle simmer; otherwise the egg whites will tear apart. Adding vinegar to the water helps the egg whites set quicker, but make sure your eggs are as fresh as possible. The whites in fresh eggs hold together tighter—near-expired eggs have looser whites and may fall apart in the water.

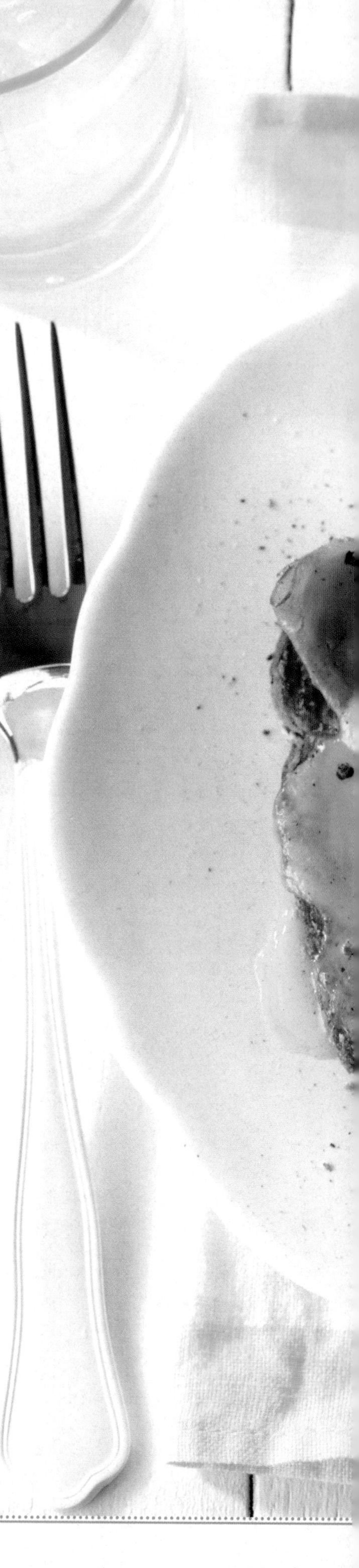

Spring Strawberry Sangria

PICTURED ON PAGE 145

Wine-infused berries make a lovely addition to this special-occasion drink. I love serving this during the beginning of Spring to celebrate the new season.

—GINA QUARTERMAINE
ALEXANDRIA, VA

PREP: 10 MIN. + CHILLING
MAKES: 10 SERVINGS (ABOUT 2 QUARTS)

- **4 cups dry white wine, chilled**
- **½ pound fresh strawberries, hulled and sliced**
- **¼ cup sugar**
- **2 cups club soda, chilled**
- **2 cups Champagne, chilled**

1. In a large pitcher, combine wine, strawberries and sugar. Refrigerate at least 1 hour.
2. Just before serving, stir in club soda and Champagne.

Mascarpone-Stuffed French Toast with Triple Berry Topping

My family loves it when I make this rich and delicious French toast. With a warm, creamy filling of mascarpone cheese and a sauce of mixed berries, it's a very easy-to-make breakfast treat that looks like you spent all morning preparing it.

—**PAMELA SHANK** PARKERSBURG, WV

PREP: 20 MIN. • **COOK:** 10 MIN./BATCH • **MAKES:** 6 SERVINGS (4 CUPS SAUCE)

- **½ cup sugar**
- **3 tablespoons cornstarch**
- **¼ teaspoon salt**
- **½ cup water**
- **1 package (12 ounces) frozen unsweetened mixed berries**
- **2 cups coarsely chopped fresh strawberries or blueberries**
- **1 loaf (1 pound) challah or egg bread, cut into 12 slices**
- **6 tablespoons mascarpone cheese**
- **6 eggs**
- **1½ cups heavy whipping cream**
- **¾ cup 2% milk**
- **3 teaspoons ground cinnamon**
- **¾ teaspoon vanilla extract**
- **4 tablespoons butter**

1. In a large saucepan, combine sugar, cornstarch and salt. Whisk in water. Stir in frozen berries. Bring to a boil; cook and stir 1-2 minutes or until thickened. Remove from heat; stir in the fresh berries.
2. Spread half of the bread slices with 1 tablespoon mascarpone to within ½ in. of edges. Top with remaining bread. In a shallow bowl, whisk eggs, cream, milk, cinnamon and vanilla.
3. In a large skillet, heat 2 tablespoons butter over medium heat. Dip both sides of sandwiches in egg mixture, allowing each side to soak 2 minutes. Place in skillet; toast 4-5 minutes on each side or until golden brown. Repeat with remaining butter and sandwiches. Serve with warm berry sauce.

Fresh Fruit Salad with Honey-Orange Dressing

PICTURED ON PAGE 145

This fruit salad was a first-time endeavor for my husband's 73rd surprise birthday party. It's been a hit ever since. The night before serving, I combine the oranges, pineapple, grapes and strawberries in a large plastic bag and refrigerate until ready to serve. I also make the dressing the night before.

—LEA ANN SCHALK GARFIELD, AR

START TO FINISH: 30 MIN. • **MAKES:** 16 SERVINGS (¾ CUP EACH)

- **½ cup honey**
- **⅓ cup thawed orange juice concentrate**
- **1 tablespoon canola oil**
- **1 teaspoon poppy seeds**

SALAD

- **3 cups sliced fresh strawberries**
- **2 cups seedless red grapes, halved**
- **2 cups cubed fresh pineapple**
- **2 medium navel oranges, peeled and coarsely chopped**
- **2 medium apples, chopped**
- **2 ripe medium bananas, sliced**

1. In a small bowl, whisk honey, orange juice concentrate, oil and poppy seeds until blended. In a large bowl, combine strawberries, grapes, pineapple and oranges.
2. Just before serving, stir in apples and bananas. Pour dressing over salad; toss to coat.

Apricot Coffee Cake with Coconut Topping

Several years ago, I found my niche writing coffee cake recipes to enter into the New York State Fair. I have developed several recipes over the course of my 25-year marriage. My husband is a tough critic, so I knew I had a hit when he labeled this one a winner.

—SUZANNE KATKO SYRACUSE, NY

PREP: 25 MIN. • **BAKE:** 25 MIN. • **MAKES:** 8 SERVINGS

- **1 can (8½ ounces) apricot halves**
- **¼ cup shortening**
- **¾ cup sugar**
- **1 egg**
- **¼ cup 2% milk**
- **1¼ cups all-purpose flour**
- **¼ cup graham cracker crumbs**
- **2 teaspoons baking powder**
- **½ teaspoon salt**

TOPPING

- **3 tablespoons butter, softened**
- **½ cup packed brown sugar**
- **1 cup flaked coconut**
- **2 tablespoons 2% milk**

1. Preheat oven to 350°. Grease a 9-in. round baking pan. Drain apricot halves, reserving ¼ cup juice. Cut each piece in half.
2. In a large bowl, beat shortening and sugar until crumbly. Beat in egg, milk and reserved juice. In another bowl, whisk flour, cracker crumbs, baking powder and salt; gradually beat into creamed mixture.
3. Transfer to prepared pan; arrange apricots over batter. Bake 25-30 minutes or until a toothpick inserted in center comes out clean.
4. Preheat broiler. For topping, in a small bowl, beat butter and brown sugar until crumbly. Beat in coconut and milk. Spread over warm cake. Broil 4-5 in. from heat for 4-6 minutes or until golden brown. Serve warm.

Strawberry-Rhubarb Cream Cheese Tarts

I created these tarts for a recipe contest featuring dairy products, which, as a dairy farmer's daughter and former county dairy princess, I am always happy to promote. The tarts were awarded first place. They're a little time-consuming, but worth it for rehearsal dinners, luncheons, brunches or bridal showers.

—**MAREL RAUB** DUNCANNON, PA

PREP: 25 MIN. • **BAKE:** 30 MIN. + CHILLING • **MAKES:** 5 TARTS

- **1½ cups all-purpose flour**
- **½ teaspoon salt**
- **¼ cup cold butter**
- **¼ cup shortening**
- **3 to 4 tablespoons ice water**

CREAM CHEESE FILLING

- **1 package (8 ounces) cream cheese, softened**
- **½ cup sugar**
- **1 teaspoon vanilla extract**
- **1 egg, lightly beaten**

STRAWBERRY-RHUBARB FILLING

- **½ cup sugar**
- **2 tablespoons plus 1 teaspoon cornstarch**
- **2 cups sliced fresh strawberries**
- **2 cups diced fresh or frozen rhubarb**

DRIZZLE

- **4½ teaspoons sugar**
- **¾ teaspoon cornstarch**
- **½ cup heavy whipping cream**
- **1 tablespoon rum**
- **½ cup sliced almonds, toasted**

1. Preheat oven to 350°. In a small bowl, mix flour and salt; cut in butter and shortening until crumbly. Gradually add ice water, tossing with a fork until dough holds together when pressed. Divide into five portions. Press dough onto bottom and up sides of five ungreased 4-in. fluted tart pans with removable bottoms; place on a baking sheet.
2. For cream cheese filling, in a small bowl, beat cream cheese and sugar until smooth. Beat in vanilla. Add egg; beat on low speed just until blended. Divide evenly among pastries.
3. For strawberry-rhubarb filling, in a large saucepan, mix sugar and cornstarch. Stir in strawberries and rhubarb; bring to a boil. Cook and stir 2 minutes or until thickened; spoon over cream cheese mixture. Bake 25-30 minutes or until filling is set. Cool on a wire rack 1 hour.
4. For drizzle, in a small saucepan, mix sugar and cornstarch. Whisk in cream. Cook and stir over medium heat until thickened and bubbly. Reduce heat to low; cook and stir 2 minutes longer. Remove from heat and transfer to a small bowl; stir in rum. Press waxed paper onto surface of cream mixture. Cool to room temperature.
5. Sprinkle almonds over tarts; drizzle with cream mixture. Refrigerate for at least 1 hour before serving.

NOTE *If using frozen rhubarb, measure rhubarb while still frozen, then thaw completely. Drain in a colander, but do not press liquid out. To toast nuts, spread in a 15x10x1-in. baking pan. Bake at 350° for 5-10 minutes or until lightly browned, stirring occasionally. Or, spread in a dry nonstick skillet and heat over low heat until lightly browned, stirring occasionally.*

SHORTENING OR BUTTER

Using shortening in your dough contributes to a flaky crust, whereas butter gives the pastry a rich flavor. While you can use all butter (½ cup) or all shortening in the recipe above, the combination of both is recommended for best results. If you prefer, you can use store-bought pie dough instead. Enough for a single 9-inch pie will make five 4-inch tart crusts.

Herbed Vegetable Strata

We always serve food at our Bunco games, and since one of us is a vegetarian, we're always coming up with fun meatless dishes we can all enjoy. This strata can easily be doubled and tastes fantastic hot or at room temperature.

—DORIS MANCINI PORT ORCHARD, WA

PREP: 40 MIN. + CHILLING
BAKE: 40 MIN. + STANDING
MAKES: 12 SERVINGS

- **3 teaspoons olive oil, divided**
- **1 pound fresh asparagus, trimmed and cut into 2-inch pieces**
- **2 medium zucchini, quartered and sliced**
- **1 cup fresh or frozen corn**
- **2 shallots, chopped**
- **3 garlic cloves, minced**
- **4 teaspoons each minced fresh sage, basil and parsley**
- **½ teaspoon salt**
- **½ teaspoon pepper**
- **1 loaf (1 pound) Italian bread, cut into 1-inch cubes**
- **3 cups (12 ounces) shredded Gruyere or Swiss cheese**
- **5 eggs**
- **1¾ cups 2% milk**
- **½ cup chopped pecans**

1. Preheat oven to 350°. In a large skillet, heat 1 teaspoon oil over medium-high heat. Add asparagus; cook and stir until crisp-tender. Transfer to a large bowl.

2. Repeat with an additional 1 teaspoon oil and zucchini; add to asparagus. In same pan, cook and stir corn, shallots and garlic in remaining oil until shallots are tender; stir in herbs, salt and pepper. Add to asparagus mixture; stir in bread cubes.

3. Place half of mixture in a greased 13x9-in. baking dish. Sprinkle with 1½ cups cheese. Repeat layers. In another bowl, whisk eggs and milk; pour over casserole. Sprinkle with the pecans. Refrigerate, covered, for at least 1 hour.

4. Bake, uncovered, for 40-50 minutes or until a knife inserted near center comes out clean. Let stand 10 minutes before serving.

FREEZE OPTION *After assembling; cover and freeze. To use, partially thaw in refrigerator overnight. Remove from the refrigerator 30 minutes before baking. Preheat oven to 350°. Bake strata, covered, 45 minutes. Uncover; bake 10-15 minutes longer or until a knife inserted near the center comes out clean. Let stand 10 minutes before serving.*

Strawberry Bliss

An easy-to-make puff pastry crust is topped with a soft-set pudding layer with a hint of strawberry flavor. Because this dessert needs to chill for at least an hour, it's an ideal dish for a make-ahead brunch.

—CANDACE RICHTER STEVENS POINT, WI

PREP: 30 MIN. • **BAKE:** 20 MIN. + CHILLING • **MAKES:** 12 SERVINGS

- **1 cup water**
- **½ cup butter, cubed**
- **1 cup all-purpose flour**
- **4 eggs**
- **1 package (8 ounces) cream cheese, softened**
- **½ cup sugar**
- **5 tablespoons seedless strawberry jam**
- **3 cups cold milk**
- **1 package (5.1 ounces) instant vanilla pudding mix**
- **½ cup heavy whipping cream**
- **3 cups chopped fresh strawberries**

1. Preheat oven to 400°. In a large saucepan, bring water and butter to a rolling boil. Add flour all at once and beat until blended. Cook over medium heat, stirring vigorously until mixture pulls away from sides of pan and forms a ball. Remove from heat; let stand 5 minutes.
2. Add eggs, one at a time, beating well after each addition. Continue beating until mixture is smooth and shiny.
3. Spread into a greased 15x10x1-in. baking pan. Bake 20-25 minutes or until puffed and golden brown. Cool completely in pan on a wire rack.
4. In a large bowl, beat cream cheese, sugar and jam until smooth. Beat in milk and pudding mix until smooth. In a small bowl, beat cream until stiff peaks form; fold into pudding mixture. Spread over crust. Refrigerate at least 1 hour.
5. Just before serving, top with the strawberries.

Orange Dream Smoothies

This is such an easy way to brighten up a breakfast or brunch. Bursting with orange flavor, it's cool and frothy—and you may never want just plain OJ again!

—PHYLLIS SCHMALZ KANSAS CITY, KS

START TO FINISH: 5 MIN. • **MAKES:** 6 SERVINGS

- **1 can (6 ounces) frozen orange juice concentrate, thawed**
- **2 cups fat-free frozen yogurt**
- **½ teaspoon orange extract**
- **1 bottle (1 liter) club soda, chilled**
- **Ice cubes**
- **1 medium orange, thinly sliced**

1. Place orange juice concentrate, yogurt and extract in a blender; cover and process until blended.
2. Transfer to a pitcher; stir in club soda. Serve immediately over ice. Serve with orange slices.

Creamy Baked Eggs

My husband loves eggs prepared in any way. This recipe is simple but special, and the eggs come out just as he likes them every time. If you like soft yolks, cook the eggs for 10 minutes; for firmer yolks, cook for about 12 minutes.

—**MACEY ALLEN** GREEN FOREST, AR

START TO FINISH: 25 MIN.
MAKES: 8 SERVINGS

- **¼ cup half-and-half cream**
- **8 eggs**
- **1 cup (4 ounces) shredded Jarlsberg cheese**
- **2 tablespoons grated Parmesan cheese**
- **¼ teaspoon salt**
- **⅛ teaspoon pepper**
- **2 green onions, chopped**

1. Preheat oven to 400°. Pour cream into a greased 9-in. pie plate or ovenproof skillet. Gently break an egg into a small bowl; slip egg into pie plate. Repeat with remaining eggs. Sprinkle with cheeses, salt and pepper.
2. Bake 10-12 minutes or until egg whites are completely set and yolks begin to thicken but are not hard. Top with green onions; serve immediately.

When the fragrance of fresh flowers alone is enough to brighten your day, it's time to welcome spring's arrival with a celebration of all things vibrant, crisp and new—including recipes that let you experience fresh produce like never before. Celebrate the season's offerings with appetizers such as Sweet Pea and Asparagus Guacamole (p. 165), and an entree that will change the way you prepare chicken for good (p. 166). But remember, dishes like these were born to be shared, so invite the girls over for a fashionable foodie fling—this spring luncheon menu is ready for its debut.

Chilled Avocado Soup Appetizers with Crab (p. 162)
Zucchini & Cheese Roulades (p. 165)
Mini Mixed Salads in Crispy Wontons (p. 159)

SPRING **GARDEN PARTY**

Asparagus & Snap Pea Salad

Perfect for when you're expecting a large number of guests for dinner, this salad boasts springtime flavors and freshness. It's usually the first empty bowl at a potluck.
—MICHELLE BOTTRALL GRAND RAPIDS, MI

PREP: 25 MIN. + CHILLING
MAKES: 14 SERVINGS (¾ CUP EACH)

2 pounds fresh asparagus, trimmed and cut into 1-inch pieces

DRESSING

⅓ cup rice vinegar
2 tablespoons olive oil
1 tablespoon Dijon mustard
2 teaspoons sugar
½ teaspoon salt
¼ teaspoon pepper

SALAD

2 cups cherry tomatoes, halved
2 cups fresh sugar snap peas, cut into thirds
1 small sweet red pepper, finely chopped
1 small red onion, finely chopped
1 cup (4 ounces) crumbled feta or Gorgonzola cheese
1 cup glazed walnuts, coarsely chopped
⅔ cup dried cherries

1. In a Dutch oven, bring 8 cups water to a boil. Add asparagus in batches; cook, uncovered, 2-4 minutes or just until crisp-tender. Remove asparagus and immediately drop into ice water. Drain and pat dry.
2. In a small bowl, whisk the dressing ingredients until blended. In a large bowl, combine asparagus, tomatoes, snap peas, red pepper and onion. Drizzle dressing over asparagus mixture; toss to coat. Refrigerate until serving.
3. Just before serving, stir in cheese, walnuts and cherries.

Mini Mixed Salads in Crispy Wontons

PICTURED ON PAGE 157

It's a salad and an appetizer all tucked into one bite-sized offering! This is about to be your new favorite party food.

—SHEYNA LAIDLEY BROOKLYN, NY

PREP: 40 MIN. • **BAKE:** 10 MIN. • **MAKES:** 3 DOZEN

- **36 wonton wrappers**
- **2 tablespoons canola oil**

DRESSING

- **2 tablespoons grated onion**
- **2 tablespoons raspberry vinegar**
- **2 tablespoons honey Dijon mustard**
- **½ teaspoon salt**
- **⅓ cup canola oil**

SALAD

- **1 package (5 ounces) spring mix salad greens, torn**
- **1 medium cucumber, peeled and finely chopped**
- **¾ cup finely chopped fresh broccoli florets**
- **1 medium carrot, shredded**
- **2 green onions, chopped**
- **1½ cups cherry tomatoes, halved**

1. Preheat oven to 375°. Brush each side of wonton wrappers with oil; gently press into miniature muffin cups. Bake 6-8 minutes or until golden brown. Remove to wire racks to cool.
2. In a small bowl, whisk onion, vinegar, mustard and salt. Gradually whisk in oil until blended. In a large bowl, mix salad greens, cucumber, broccoli, carrot and green onions. Drizzle dressing over salad; toss to coat.
3. Place about 2 tablespoons salad into each wonton cup; top with a tomato half. Serve immediately.

Pear-Blueberry Ambrosia with Creamy Lime Dressing

You can offer this creamy and decadent ambrosia as either a side salad or a dessert. It's such a refreshing combination—and the blueberries provide a lovely pop of color.

—LAURA MURPHY COLUMBUS, MS

START TO FINISH: 20 MIN. • **MAKES:** 10 SERVINGS

- **1 carton (8 ounces) mascarpone cheese**
- **2 tablespoons sugar**
- **2 teaspoons grated lime peel**
- **2 tablespoons lime juice**
- **3 medium ripe pears, peeled and chopped**
- **3 medium ripe bananas, sliced**
- **1½ cups fresh blueberries**
- **½ cup chopped hazelnuts**

In a small bowl, mix mascarpone cheese, sugar, lime peel and lime juice. In a large bowl, combine pears, bananas and blueberries. Spoon cheese mixture over fruit; gently toss to coat. Sprinkle with hazelnuts. Refrigerate until serving.

Strawberry Blitz Torte

I really love baking my mom's German torte. Don't be intimidated by this dessert—it's much easier to put together than you might think!
—**LINDA KAY HENDERSON** SCHAUMBURG, IL

PREP: 45 MIN. • **BAKE:** 30 MIN. + COOLING • **MAKES:** 12 SERVINGS

- **4 egg whites**
- **½ cup butter, softened**
- **½ cup sugar**
- **3 egg yolks**
- **1 teaspoon almond extract**
- **1 cup all-purpose flour**
- **1 teaspoon baking powder**
- **⅛ teaspoon salt**
- **⅓ cup 2% milk**

MERINGUE

- **½ teaspoon vanilla extract**
- **¼ teaspoon cream of tartar**
- **1 cup sugar**
- **½ cup sliced almonds**

FILLING

- **2 tablespoons sugar**
- **1 tablespoon cornstarch**
- **1 cup 2% milk**
- **2 egg yolks**
- **1 tablespoon butter**
- **½ teaspoon vanilla or almond extract**
- **2½ cups sliced fresh strawberries**
- **Sweetened whipped cream, optional**

1. Place egg whites in a large bowl; let stand at room temperature 30 minutes. Preheat oven to 325°. Line bottoms of two greased 8-in. round baking pans with parchment paper; grease paper.
2. In a large bowl, cream butter and sugar until light and fluffy. Add egg yolks, one at a time, beating well after each addition. Beat in extract.
3. In another bowl, whisk flour, baking powder and salt; add to creamed mixture alternately with milk, beating well after each addition. Transfer to prepared pans.
4. For meringue, with clean beaters, beat egg whites with vanilla and cream of tartar on medium speed until foamy. Gradually add sugar, 1 tablespoon at a time, beating on high after each addition until sugar is dissolved. Continue beating until stiff glossy peaks form. Spread over batter in pans; sprinkle with almonds.
5. Bake 28-32 minutes or until meringue is lightly browned. Cool completely in pans on wire racks (meringue will crack).
6. Meanwhile, for filling, in a small heavy saucepan, mix sugar and cornstarch. Whisk in milk. Cook and stir over medium heat until thickened and bubbly. Reduce heat to low; cook and stir 2 minutes longer. Remove from the heat.
7. In a small bowl, whisk a small amount of hot mixture into egg yolks; return all to pan, whisking constantly. Bring to a gentle boil; cook and stir 2 minutes. Remove from heat; stir in butter and vanilla. Cool completely.
8. Loosen edges of cakes from pans with a knife. Using two large spatulas, carefully remove one cake to a serving plate, meringue side up. Gently spread with filling. Arrange strawberries over filling. Top with remaining cake layer, meringue side up. If desired, serve with whipped cream. Refrigerate leftovers.

MERINGUE—WHAT YOU NEED TO KNOW

For best results when making meringue, make sure the egg whites come to room temperature. Many cooks prefer using copper bowls because the acidity stabilizes the whites and produces a fluffier foam, but you can also use glass or stainless-steel bowls. Avoid using wood, aluminum or plastic as these materials may contain fat residue that will interfere with the structure of the whites. Finally, if working in a humid environment, add 1 teaspoon of cornstarch to the sugar. This will prevent the meringue from absorbing excess liquid.

Basmati Rice Confetti Salad

My step-mom passed this recipe to me, and it's so simple to put together. We like this salad served cold, so I let it sit in the fridge for about half an hour, but it's also good served warm.
—AMANDA BIRD GRANTSVILLE, UT

PREP: 35 MIN. + CHILLING • **MAKES:** 12 SERVINGS (¾ CUP EACH)

- **1½ cups uncooked basmati rice**
- **1 can (15¼ ounces) whole kernel corn, drained**
- **8 green onions, chopped**
- **1 medium tomato, chopped**
- **1 medium green pepper, chopped**
- **1 medium red onion, chopped**
- **¼ cup slivered almonds**
- **¼ cup golden raisins**
- **¼ cup dried cranberries**
- **¼ cup minced fresh parsley**

DRESSING

- **½ cup olive oil**
- **⅓ cup white vinegar**
- **2 tablespoons sugar**
- **1 tablespoon lemon juice**
- **½ teaspoon curry powder**
- **¼ teaspoon salt**
- **⅛ teaspoon pepper**

1. Cook rice according to package directions. Remove from the heat; cool completely.

2. In a large bowl, combine vegetables, almonds, raisins, cranberries and parsley; stir in rice. In a small bowl, whisk dressing ingredients until blended. Pour dressing over rice mixture; toss to coat. Refrigerate at least 30 minutes before serving to allow flavors to blend.

Chilled Avocado Soup Appetizers with Crab

PICTURED ON PAGE 157

We have a large avocado tree outside our house, so I like to put the fruit to good use in recipes like this. To give the soup an elegant touch, top it with edible flowers.
—DORI GRASSKA PACIFIC PALISADES, CA

PREP: 15 MIN. + CHILLING • **MAKES:** 28 SERVINGS

- **2 cups chicken or vegetable stock**
- **1 cup (8 ounces) plain yogurt**
- **2 medium ripe avocados, peeled and pitted**
- **1 medium apple, peeled and cubed**
- **1 tablespoon lime juice**
- **½ teaspoon salt**
- **½ teaspoon crushed red pepper flakes**
- **¼ teaspoon pepper**
- **⅔ cup creme fraiche or sour cream**
- **8 ounces lump crabmeat, drained**
- **Minced fresh cilantro and lime slices**

1. Place first eight ingredients in a blender; cover and process until smooth. Transfer to a pitcher; refrigerate 1 hour to allow flavors to blend.

2. To serve, pour soup into shot glasses; top with creme fraiche, crab, cilantro and lime slices.

Ginger-Grapefruit Fizz

Sometimes it's hard to find a special, non-alcoholic beverage for parties that isn't a punch. That's why I love this grown-up bubbly drink that offers a little tartness from the grapefruit and spice from the ginger.

—DAWN VIOLA CLERMONT, FL

PREP: 25 MIN. + CHILLING
MAKES: 8 SERVINGS

- **1 cup sugar**
- **1 cup water**
- **½ cup sliced fresh gingerroot**
- **½ teaspoon whole peppercorns**
- **¼ teaspoon vanilla extract**
- **⅛ teaspoon salt**
- **¼ cup coarse sugar**
- **3 cups fresh grapefruit juice, chilled**
- **Ice cubes**
- **4 cups sparkling water, chilled**

1. In a small saucepan, bring the first six ingredients to a boil. Reduce heat; simmer 10 minutes. Refrigerate until cold. Strain syrup, discarding ginger and peppercorns.
2. Using water, moisten rims of eight cocktail glasses. Sprinkle coarse sugar on a plate; hold each glass upside down and dip rims into sugar. Discard remaining sugar on plate.
3. In a pitcher, combine the grapefruit juice and syrup. Pour 1/2 cup into prepared glasses over ice; top with 1/2 cup of sparkling water.

Creamy Spinach & Rigatoni Bake

You can easily make this a vegetarian entree by leaving out the pancetta. It's sometimes nice to have an alternative option for guests.
—TAMMY REX NEW TRIPOLI, PA

PREP: 25 MIN.
BAKE: 20 MIN.
MAKES: 10 SERVINGS

- **1 package (16 ounces) rigatoni**
- **8 ounces sliced pancetta, chopped**
- **¾ cup butter, cubed**
- **½ cup chopped onion**
- **¾ cup all-purpose flour**
- **1½ teaspoons salt**
- **¾ teaspoon pepper**
- **5¼ cups 2% milk**
- **4 cups (16 ounces) shredded Italian cheese blend**
- **1 can (14 ounces) water-packed artichoke hearts, rinsed, drained and chopped**
- **1 package (10 ounces) frozen chopped spinach, thawed and squeezed dry**
- **¼ cup shredded Parmesan cheese**

1. Preheat oven to 375°. Cook rigatoni according to package directions.
2. Meanwhile, in a large skillet, cook pancetta over medium heat until crisp, stirring occasionally. Remove with a slotted spoon; drain on paper towels. Discard the drippings.
3. In same pan, heat butter over medium-high heat. Add onion; cook and stir until tender. Stir in flour, salt and pepper until blended; gradually whisk in milk. Bring to a boil, stirring constantly; cook and stir 2-3 minutes or until thickened. Remove from the heat. Stir in cheese blend until melted.
4. Stir in artichokes, spinach and pancetta. Drain rigatoni; add to cheese sauce. Transfer to a greased 13x9-in. baking dish; sprinkle with Parmesan cheese.
5. Bake, uncovered, for 20-25 minutes or until golden brown and bubbly.

Sweet Pea and Asparagus Guacamole

I decided it was time to switch up my guacamole, so I got creative for this recipe. My local farmers market had beautiful snow peas and asparagus that I incorporated. When squash blossoms are in season, I like to add those, too.

—AMIE VALPONE NEW YORK, NY

START TO FINISH: 30 MIN. • **MAKES:** 2½ CUPS

- **1 medium onion, chopped**
- **3 garlic cloves, minced**
- **⅓ cup vegetable broth**
- **2 cups fresh snow peas**
- **1½ cups cut fresh asparagus (1-inch pieces)**
- **¼ cup sunflower kernels**
- **Dash of saffron threads or ¼ teaspoon ground turmeric**
- **2 medium ripe avocados, peeled and cubed**
- **3 tablespoons minced fresh parsley**
- **3 tablespoons grated lemon peel**
- **3 tablespoons lemon juice**
- **1 teaspoon white balsamic vinegar**
- **½ teaspoon salt**
- **⅛ teaspoon white pepper**
- **⅛ teaspoon chili powder**
- **Tortilla chips or pita wedges, optional**

1. In a large skillet, cook onion and garlic in broth over medium-high heat until tender. Add snow peas, asparagus, sunflower kernels and saffron; cook 4-6 minutes longer or until vegetables are tender.
2. Transfer to a food processor. Add avocados, parsley, lemon peel, lemon juice, vinegar, salt, white pepper and chili powder; process until blended. Refrigerate until serving. If desired, serve with tortilla chips.

Zucchini & Cheese Roulades

PICTURED ON PAGE 157

My husband enjoys this recipe so much that he even helps me roll up the roulades! You can change the filling any way you like—I have used feta instead of Parmesan, or try sun-dried tomatoes in place of the olives.

—APRIL MCKINNEY MURFREESBORO, TN

START TO FINISH: 25 MIN. • **MAKES:** 2 DOZEN

- **1 cup part-skim ricotta cheese**
- **¼ cup grated Parmesan cheese**
- **2 tablespoons minced fresh basil or 2 teaspoons dried basil**
- **1 tablespoon capers, drained**
- **1 tablespoon chopped Greek olives**
- **1 teaspoon grated lemon peel**
- **1 tablespoon lemon juice**
- **⅛ teaspoon salt**
- **⅛ teaspoon pepper**
- **4 medium zucchini**

1. In a small bowl, mix the first nine ingredients.
2. Slice zucchini lengthwise into twenty-four ⅛-in.-thick slices. Moisten a paper towel with cooking oil; using long-handled tongs, rub on grill rack to coat lightly. Grill zucchini slices in batches, covered, over medium heat 2-3 minutes on each side or until tender.
3. Place 1 tablespoon ricotta mixture on the end of each zucchini slice. Roll up and secure each with a toothpick.

Lemon & Thyme Roasted Chicken

I love lemon and thyme together, so I decided to roast a chicken with that combo. The seasoning is simple, and the meat comes out juicy and tender.
—PAM NELSON BEAVERTON, OR

PREP: 25 MIN. • **BAKE:** 1½ HOURS + STANDING • **MAKES:** 6 SERVINGS

- **1 tablespoon minced fresh thyme or 1 teaspoon dried thyme**
- **1 teaspoon sea salt**
- **¼ teaspoon garlic powder**
- **¼ teaspoon coarsely ground pepper**
- **1 roasting chicken (5 to 6 pounds)**
- **1 medium lemon, halved**
- **¼ large sweet onion**
- **¼ cup fresh thyme sprigs**
- **6 garlic cloves, peeled**
- **Lemon wedges**

1. Preheat oven to 350°. Mix minced thyme, salt, garlic powder and pepper. Place chicken on a rack in a shallow roasting pan, breast side up. Tuck wings under chicken; tie drumsticks together. Squeeze juice from lemon halves over chicken; sprinkle with thyme mixture.
2. Loosely stuff chicken with squeezed lemon halves, onion, thyme sprigs and garlic. Roast 1½ to 2 hours or until a thermometer inserted in thickest part of thigh reads 170°-175°. (Cover loosely with foil if chicken browns too quickly.)
3. Remove chicken from oven; tent with foil. Let stand for 15 minutes before carving. Serve with lemon wedges.

WHEN LEMONS GO ON SALE...

Next time lemon or limes go on sale, stock up. When you get home, juice the fruit and store it in the freezer. You can also freeze whole lemons or limes in a freezer bag. That way, when you need just a small amount of juice, you can remove one lemon at a time. You can quickly defrost them in the microwave so they're ready to be squeezed. Note: The fruit might be a little soft after it's been frozen, but the juice will still be good.

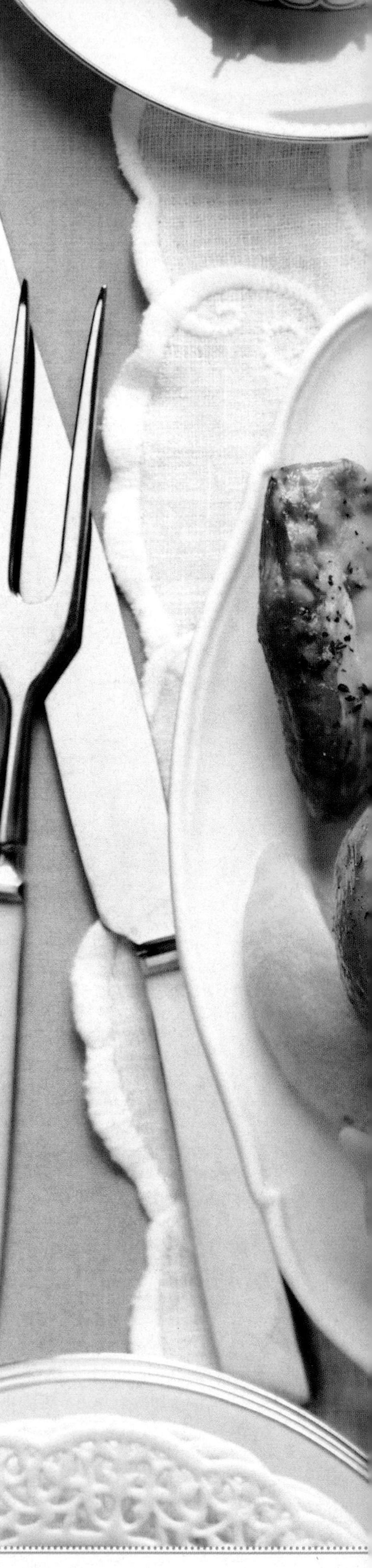

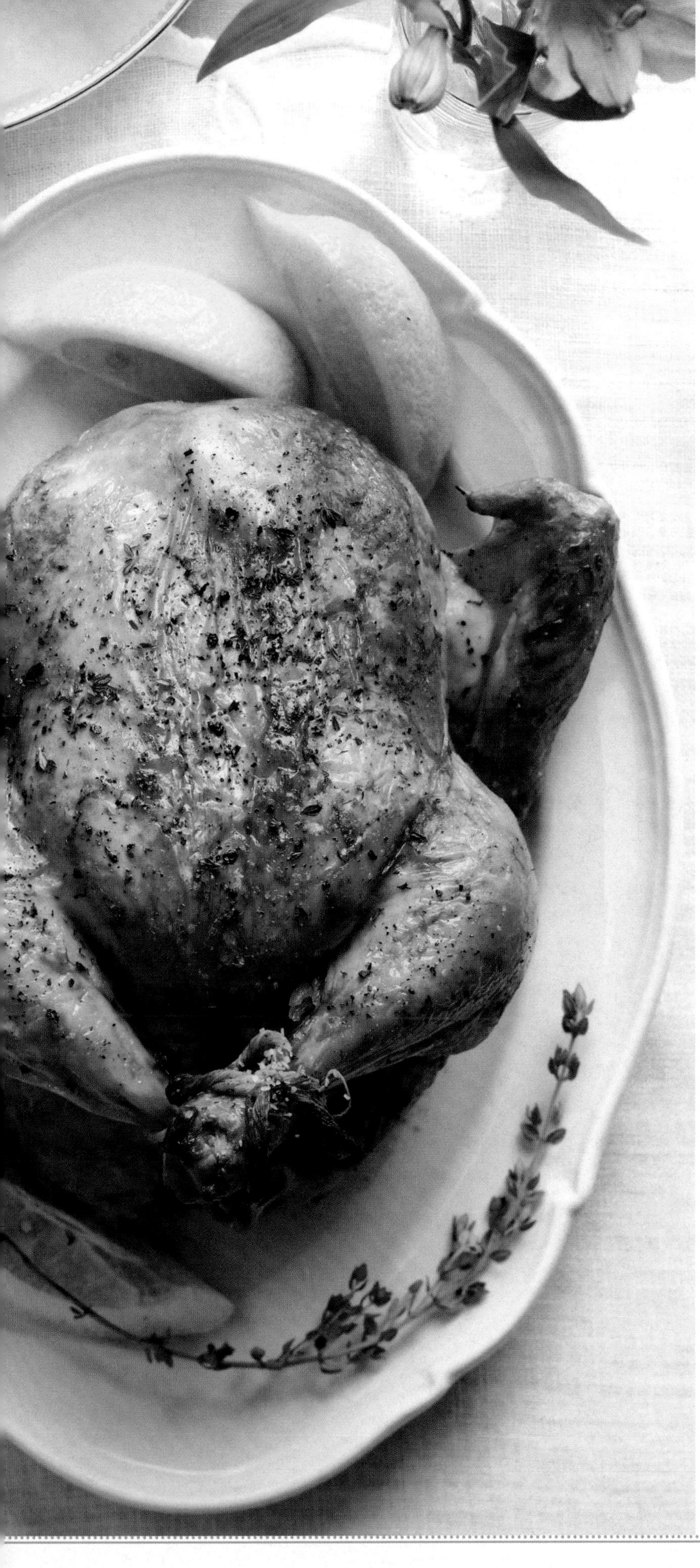

Herb-Garden Potato Salad

Switch up the herbs combination if you desire—I sometimes swap out the dill for fresh tarragon.
—DEBRA KEIL OWASSO, OK

PREP: 45 MIN. + CHILLING
MAKES: 6 SERVINGS

- **2 pounds red potatoes, cubed (about 5 cups)**
- **1 cup reduced-fat mayonnaise**
- **2 tablespoons white wine vinegar**
- **2 garlic cloves, minced**
- **¾ teaspoon pepper**
- **½ teaspoon salt**
- **¼ cup minced fresh chives**
- **2 tablespoons snipped fresh dill**
- **1 tablespoon minced fresh basil**
- **1 teaspoon minced fresh oregano**
- **1 tablespoon capers, drained**

1. Place potatoes in a large saucepan; add water to cover. Bring to a boil. Reduce heat; cook, uncovered, 10-15 minutes or until tender. Drain; cool completely.
2. In a large bowl, whisk mayonnaise, vinegar, garlic, pepper and salt until blended. Stir in herbs and capers. Add potatoes; toss to coat. Refrigerate, covered, until cold.

special*c*elebrations

Who has a birthday coming up? Here you can browse through a collection of cakes that will make anyone feel like the most special person on the planet. In fact, with eight fun themes for celebrations in this section, you'll be able to pick your favorite frosty treat for the Fourth of July, nail down a cookout menu for Father's Day and thumb through an assortment of sweet treats and crafts for a Vintage Halloween. It's party time!

On this special day in history, you stood before the love of your life and whispered "I do." Whether it's been 12 months or 50 years, to celebrate such an occasion, an ordinary dinner simply will not do.

You need a menu that reflects your shared tastes—and one that's worthy of a loving toast. If buttery scallops resting on a bed of wine-infused fettuccini doesn't appeal to your senses, perhaps the Steak au Poivre for 2 (p. 172) is the better choice for you.

Both menus here are custom-built for two, complete with a celebratory cocktail and a dessert so good, you'll fall in love with every bite.

In need of a special gift to put the final touches on your romantic evening? Turn to p. 177 for some anniversary inspiration. Here's to another year!

Buttery Sour Cream Muffins (p. 176)
French 75 (p. 178)
Sea Scallops and Fettuccine (p. 176)

ANNIVERSARY **FOR TWO**

Steak au Poivre for Two

With the punch of peppercorns and a smooth, beefy sauce, this steak is everything you could want in a celebratory meal. You'll love the hint of sweetness the bittersweet chocolate adds to the meat.

—CRYSTAL BRUNS ILIFF, CO

START TO FINISH: 30 MIN. • **MAKES:** 2 SERVINGS

- **2 beef tenderloin steaks (1 inch thick and 5 ounces each)**
- **2 tablespoons olive oil, divided**
- **1 tablespoon whole white or black peppercorns, crushed**
- **¼ teaspoon salt**
- **1 tablespoon finely chopped shallot**
- **¼ cup port wine**
- **1 tablespoon balsamic vinegar**
- **¼ cup condensed beef consomme, undiluted**
- **1 teaspoon minced fresh rosemary or ¼ teaspoon dried rosemary, crushed**
- **½ ounce bittersweet chocolate, chopped**

1. Rub steaks with 1 tablespoon oil; sprinkle with peppercorns and salt. In a skillet, heat 2 teaspoons oil over medium heat. Add steaks; cook 5-7 minutes on each side or until meat reaches desired doneness (for medium-rare, a thermometer should read 145°; medium, 160°; well-done, 170°). Remove and keep warm.

2. In same pan, heat remaining oil over medium-high heat. Add shallot; cook and stir 1 minute or until tender. Add wine and vinegar, stirring to loosen browned bits from pan. Bring to a boil; cook and stir 2-3 minutes or until slightly thickened.

3. Stir in consomme and rosemary; bring to a boil. Add chocolate; cook and stir until melted and sauce is slightly thickened. Serve with steaks.

CHOOSE YOUR MENU

Skip the fancy steak house and set your dining room table for two. You're about to wow your sweetie with a meal worthy of your best linens. The first menu you see here features Steak au Poivre; Lemon & Garlic New Potatoes; Apple, Blue Cheese and Bibb Salad; Pomegranate Martinis; and Cherry Bombs for dessert. Beginning on p. 176, you'll find a menu featuring Sea Scallops and Fettuccine, Buttery Sour Cream Muffins, Bacon Clam Chowder, French 75 cocktails, and Irish Cream Cheesecake to satisfy any sweet tooth. Enjoy!

Lemon & Garlic New Potatoes for Two

PICTURED AT LEFT

This is a simplified version of a dish my Costa Rican host sister used to make when I was in the Peace Corps. It has become a favorite side dish at my house and is easily made for two.

—**KATIE BARTLE** PARKVILLE, MO

START TO FINISH: 25 MIN.
MAKES: 2 SERVINGS

- **½ pound baby red potatoes (1¾-inch wide, about 6), halved**
- **1 tablespoon olive oil**
- **1 garlic clove, minced**
- **2 tablespoons shredded Parmesan cheese**
- **1 tablespoon lemon juice**
- **⅛ teaspoon salt**
- **⅛ teaspoon pepper**

1. Place potatoes in a saucepan; add water to cover. Bring to a boil. Reduce heat; cook, uncovered, 10-15 minutes or until tender. Drain; remove from pan.

2. In same pan, heat oil over medium-high heat. Return potatoes to pan; cook and stir 4-5 minutes or until lightly browned. Add garlic; cook 1 minute longer. Remove from heat. Add remaining ingredients; toss to combine.

Apple, Blue Cheese & Bibb Salad for Two

Red or Golden Delicious apples add a sweet crunch to this simple salad, while a homemade honey-mustard dressing gives it an extra-special touch.

—REBEKAH BEYER SABETHA, KS

START TO FINISH: 20 MIN. • **MAKES:** 2 SERVINGS

- **2 tablespoons olive oil**
- **¾ teaspoon white balsamic or white wine vinegar**
- **¾ teaspoon honey**
- **¾ teaspoon mayonnaise**
- **⅛ teaspoon mustard seed, toasted**
- **⅛ teaspoon stone-ground mustard (whole grain)**
- **Dash salt**
- **Dash coarsely ground pepper**

SALAD

- **1 cup torn Bibb or Boston lettuce**
- **¾ cup chopped Red and/or Golden Delicious apple**
- **¼ cup crumbled blue cheese**
- **3 tablespoons walnut halves, toasted**
- **2 tablespoons golden raisins**

In a small bowl, whisk the first eight ingredients until blended. In a bowl, combine lettuce, apple and cheese. Drizzle with dressing and toss to coat. Sprinkle with walnuts and raisins. Serve immediately.

NOTE *To toast nuts, spread in a 15x10x1-in. baking pan. Bake at 350° for 5-10 minutes or until lightly browned, stirring occasionally. Or, spread in a dry nonstick skillet and heat over low heat until lightly browned, stirring occasionally.*

BUTTERHEAD LETTUCE

Boston lettuce and Bibb lettuce are types of Butterhead known for their tender, creamy leaves and mild sweet flavor. Because the leaves are more delicate than most lettuces, they're best for salads with lighter dressings.

Pomegranate Martini

We've got the perfect anniversary cocktail for you to shake up for your better half. Not too strong and not too sweet, this no-fail recipe is worth a toast!

—TASTE OF HOME TEST KITCHEN

START TO FINISH: 5 MIN. • **MAKES:** 1 SERVING

- **Ice cubes**
- **2 ounces pomegranate juice**
- **1 ounce vodka**
- **½ ounce triple sec**
- **½ ounce club soda**
- **½ teaspoon lemon juice**
- **Pomegranate seeds**

Fill a shaker three-fourths full with ice. Add pomegranate juice, vodka, triple sec, club soda and lemon juice. Cover and shake 10-15 seconds or until condensation forms on outside of shaker. Strain into a chilled cocktail glass. Add pomegranate seeds.

NOTE *To quickly chill a martini glass, place in the freezer for 5 minutes, or fill the glass with ice while you prepare the drink. Remove ice before using.*

Cherry Bombs

I like to make as many of these bombs as I can and keep them in the freezer. After a special dinner, your guests will love breaking open the outer shell to get to the chocolate-covered cherry center. It's like an inside-out sundae.
—LINDA TRIPLETT RENTON, WA

PREP: 15 MIN. + FREEZING • **MAKES:** 2 SERVINGS

- **1 cup vanilla ice cream, softened if necessary**
- **2 chocolate-covered cherries**
- **2 tablespoons seedless raspberry jam**
- **⅓ cup chocolate hard-shell ice cream topping**
- **¼ cup whipped cream**
- **2 tablespoons chocolate syrup**

1. Line two muffin cups with plastic wrap. Divide ice cream between cups. Press a chocolate-covered cherry into each; smooth ice cream over cherries. Freeze overnight or until firm.

2. Invert ice cream onto a waxed paper-lined plate; remove and discard plastic wrap. Spread jam over ice cream; freeze until firm.

3. Place a wire rack over a sheet of waxed paper. Using a fork, transfer ice cream to rack. Pour ice cream topping over each to coat. Transfer to dessert plates; freeze until serving. Serve with the whipped cream and the chocolate syrup.

Sea Scallops and Fettuccine

PICTURED ON PAGE 171

When my husband and I decided to lose some weight, we found this recipe and loved it so much we had it every Tuesday. It's so easy, he could fix it on nights when I was running late.

—**DONNA THOMPSON** LARAMIE, WY

START TO FINISH: 30 MIN.
MAKES: 2 SERVINGS

- **4 ounces uncooked fettuccine**
- **1 tablespoon olive oil**
- **½ medium sweet red pepper, julienned**
- **1 garlic clove, minced**
- **½ teaspoon grated lemon peel**
- **¼ teaspoon crushed red pepper flakes**
- **½ cup reduced-sodium chicken broth**
- **¼ cup white wine or additional reduced-sodium chicken broth**
- **1 tablespoon lemon juice**
- **6 sea scallops (about 12 ounces)**
- **2 teaspoons grated Parmesan cheese**

1. Cook fettuccine according to package directions; drain. Meanwhile, in a large skillet, heat oil over medium-high heat. Add red pepper, garlic, lemon peel and pepper flakes; cook and stir for 2 minutes.

2. Stir in broth, wine and lemon juice. Bring to a boil. Reduce heat; simmer, uncovered, 5-6 minutes or until liquid is reduced by about half.

3. Cut each scallop horizontally in half; add to red pepper mixture. Simmer, covered, 4-5 minutes or until scallops are firm and opaque. Serve over the fettuccine. Sprinkle with cheese.

Buttery Sour Cream Muffins

PICTURED ON PAGE 170

With just three ingredients you can round out a lovely meal for two with these buttery muffins. They taste like old-fashioned biscuits and practically melt in your mouth.

—**MARY CLECKLEY** SLATON, TX

START TO FINISH: 30 MIN. • **MAKES:** 3 SERVINGS

- **½ cup self-rising flour**
- **¼ cup butter, melted**
- **¼ cup sour cream**
- **1 tablespoon water**

Preheat oven to 350°. In a small bowl, mix all ingredients just until moistened. Coat muffin cups with cooking spray; fill three-fourths full. Bake 18-20 minutes or until a toothpick inserted in center comes out clean. Cool 5 minutes before removing from pan to a wire rack. Serve warm.

NOTE *As a substitute for the self-rising flour, place 3/4 teaspoon baking powder and 1/4 teaspoon salt in a 1/2 cup measuring cup. Add all-purpose flour to measure 1/2 cup.*

Special Gift Ideas

Traditional anniversary themes and thoughtful ideas to celebrate your years together.

1 YEAR
The theme is paper: Write love letters to each other.

5 YEARS
The theme is wood: Have dinner by the fire.

10 YEARS
The theme is tin: Fill a canister with homemade candies and other treats.

15 YEARS
The theme is crystal: Give a crystal vase with flowers.

20 YEARS
The theme is china: Prepare a special meal and set the table with your wedding china.

25 YEARS
The theme is silver: Have a silver frame engraved with a secret message on the back.

30 YEARS
The theme is pearls: Relax with a bucket of oysters.

35 YEARS
The theme is coral: Plan a trip to a seaside destination.

40 YEARS
The theme is ruby: Get out the little red dress and toast with a glass of red wine.

45 YEARS
The theme is sapphire: Listen to your favorite blues album.

50 YEARS
The theme is gold: Splurge on tickets to a special event and wrap the tickets in gold paper.

Bacon Clam Chowder

Chopping the clams into tiny pieces adds big flavor to every bite of this full-bodied chowder. Everyone says it's the best they've ever tasted.
—**BETTY LINEAWEAVER** PARADISE, CA

START TO FINISH: 30 MIN. • **MAKES:** 3 CUPS

- **1 cup reduced-sodium chicken broth**
- **1 medium potato, peeled and cubed**
- **½ cup chopped celery**
- **¼ cup chopped onion**
- **½ teaspoon chicken bouillon granules**
- **¼ teaspoon dried thyme**
- **1 can (6½ ounces) minced clams**
- **1 tablespoon cornstarch**
- **½ cup half-and-half cream**
- **1½ teaspoons butter**
- **Dash cayenne pepper**
- **2 bacon strips, cooked and crumbled**

1. In a small saucepan, combine the first six ingredients; bring to a boil. Reduce heat; simmer, uncovered, 10-12 minutes or until potato is tender.
2. Meanwhile, drain clams, reserving juice. Place clams in a small food processor; process until finely chopped.
3. In a small bowl, mix cornstarch and cream until smooth; stir into pan. Add reserved clam juice. Bring to a boil; cook and stir 2 minutes or until soup is thickened. Stir in butter, cayenne and clams; heat through. Top servings with bacon.

FOR A COLORFULLY SWEET TOUCH

Give your toast a decorative touch by using colored sugar to rim the glass. Simply place about ¼ cup of granulated sugar in a small mason jar. Add a drop or two of food coloring. Place the lid on the jar and shake.

French 75

PICTURED AT RIGHT

Named after a WWI French field gun, this champagne cocktail is said to have a potent kick. The original recipe calls for nearly twice as much gin, but we prefer this more manageable sparkling version.
—**TASTE OF HOME TEST KITCHEN**

START TO FINISH: 5 MIN. • **MAKES:** 1 SERVING.

- **Coarse sugar**
- **Ice cubes**
- **¾ ounce gin**
- **1 tablespoon confectioners' sugar**
- **2 teaspoons lemon juice**
- **3 ounces chilled champagne**

1. Sprinkle a thin layer of sugar on a plate. Moisten the rim of a chilled champagne flute with water; hold glass upside down and dip rim into sugar.
2. Fill a shaker three-fourths full with ice. Add gin, confectioners' sugar and lemon juice; cover and shake 10-15 seconds or until condensation forms on outside of shaker. Strain into a prepared flute; top with champagne.

Irish Cream Cheesecake

If you have a 4-inch springform pan, this will be your new favorite dessert. The taste of the Irish cream liqueur comes through in every bite of this scaled-down cheesecake. It's perfect for splitting with someone special.

—JUDY FERRIL SHOREWOOD, MN

PREP: 25 MIN. + COOLING
BAKE: 20 MIN. + CHILLING
MAKES: 2 SERVINGS

- **2 tablespoons graham cracker crumbs**
- **½ teaspoon sugar**
- **¾ teaspoon unsalted butter, melted**

FILLING

- **3 ounces reduced-fat cream cheese**
- **2 tablespoons sugar**
- **1 tablespoon reduced-fat sour cream**
- **1¼ teaspoons Irish cream liqueur**
- **¾ teaspoon all-purpose flour**
- **¼ teaspoon vanilla extract**
- **Dash salt**
- **2 tablespoons beaten egg**
- **2 teaspoons miniature semisweet chocolate chips**

1. Preheat oven to 375°. Place a 4-in. springform pan coated with cooking spray on a double thickness of heavy-duty foil (about 12 in. square). Wrap foil securely around pan.

2. In a small bowl, mix cracker crumbs and sugar; stir in butter. Press onto bottom of prepared pan. Bake 5 minutes. Cool on a wire rack. Reduce oven setting to 325°.

3. In a small bowl, beat cream cheese and sugar until smooth. Beat in sour cream, liqueur, flour, vanilla and salt. Add beaten egg; beat on low speed just until blended. Pour into crust; sprinkle with chocolate chips. Place springform pan in a larger baking pan; add 1 in. of hot water to larger pan. Bake 18-20 minutes or until center is just set and the top appears dull.

4. Remove springform pan from water bath. Cool cheesecake on a wire rack for 10 minutes. Loosen sides from pan with a knife; remove foil. Cool 1 hour longer. Refrigerate overnight, covering when completely cooled. Remove rim from pan.

For a refreshing poolside snack or a sweet finish to your Fourth of July star-spangled cookout, these frozen goodies are proof that summer just got cooler.

So get ready to stock your freezer with frosty treats so fabulous, they'll put your gallon of ordinary ice cream to shame. Let this be the season you show off all the wild ways you can use your scoops—you'll soon discover that they're anything but vanilla. After all, why go out with a bang when you can go out with a Hazelnut Brownie Bombe (p. 187)?

Frozen Mini Berry Trifles (p. 186)
Raspberry Cheesecake Floats (p. 189)
Strawberry Ice Cream Charlotte (p. 186)
Mocha-Pecan Ice Cream Bonbons (p. 183)

FROSTY **TREATS**

Oatmeal Cookie Ice Cream Sandwiches

If you're tight on time, you can use store-bought cookies, but I highly recommend making these oatmeal chocolate cookies from scratch. There's just something about the homemade cookies with ice cream that makes these dessert sandwiches really memorable!
—**DIANE HALFERTY** CORPUS CHRISTI, TX

PREP: 35 MIN. • **BAKE:** 10 MIN. + FREEZING • **MAKES:** 10 SERVINGS

- **½ cup butter, softened**
- **⅓ cup sugar**
- **⅓ cup packed dark brown sugar**
- **1 egg**
- **2 teaspoons vanilla extract**
- **⅔ cup all-purpose flour**
- **½ teaspoon baking soda**
- **¼ teaspoon salt**
- **¼ teaspoon ground cinnamon**
- **1½ cups quick-cooking oats**
- **½ cup finely chopped semisweet chocolate**
- **3 cups dulce de leche ice cream, softened if necessary**
- **¼ cup brickle toffee bits**

1. Preheat oven to 350°. In a large bowl, cream butter and sugars until light and fluffy. Beat in egg and vanilla. In another bowl, whisk flour, baking soda, salt and cinnamon; gradually beat into creamed mixture. Stir in oats and chocolate.

2. Shape dough into twenty 1¼-in. balls. Place 2½ in. apart on ungreased baking sheets; flatten slightly with bottom of a glass dipped in sugar, smoothing edges if necessary. Bake 10-13 minutes or until golden brown. Transfer from pans to wire racks to cool completely.

3. To assemble, place about ¼ cup ice cream on bottom of a cookie; sprinkle with 1 teaspoon toffee bits. Top with a second cookie, pressing gently to flatten ice cream. Place on a baking sheet; freeze overnight or until firm. Repeat with remaining cookies and ice cream. For longer storage, wrap frozen sandwiches individually and return to freezer.

Tropical Cheesecake Freeze

You'll feel like you've escaped to the beach after one bite of this summer dessert. The coconutty, cheesecake-like crust can also be used for pies and ice cream cake fillings.
—DEBRA GOFORTH NEWPORT, TN

PREP: 30 MIN. + FREEZING • **MAKES:** 9 SERVINGS

- **½ cup macadamia nuts, toasted**
- **1 cup crushed gingersnap cookies (about 20 cookies)**
- **¼ cup flaked coconut, toasted**
- **2 tablespoons butter, melted**
- **1 package (8 ounces) cream cheese, softened**
- **½ cup sugar**
- **½ cup coconut milk**
- **1 teaspoon coconut extract**
- **1 carton (16 ounces) frozen whipped topping, thawed**
- **¾ cup chopped dried pineapple**
- **¾ cup chopped dried mango**
- **½ cup maraschino cherries, halved and patted dry**

1. Place nuts in a food processor; pulse until chopped. Add crushed cookies, coconut and butter; pulse just until blended. Reserve 1/2 cup mixture for topping; press remaining mixture onto the bottom of a greased 8-in.-square baking dish. Freeze 30 minutes or until firm.

2. In a large bowl, beat cream cheese, sugar, coconut milk and extract until blended. Fold in whipped topping, pineapple, mango and cherries. Spread over crust; sprinkle with reserved topping. Freeze, covered, for at least 6 hours or overnight.

3. Remove from freezer about 10 minutes before serving. Cut into squares.

NOTE *To toast nuts and coconut, place separately in a dry nonstick skillet and heat over low heat until lightly browned, stirring occasionally.*

Mocha-Pecan Ice Cream Bonbons

PICTURED ON PAGE 181

You might think bonbons are too tricky to put together, but these babies are a breeze!
—TASTE OF HOME TEST KITCHEN

PREP: 25 MIN. + FREEZING • **MAKES:** ABOUT 5 DOZEN

- **2 cups finely chopped toasted pecans**
- **1 quart vanilla ice cream or flavor of your choice**
- **2 cups (12 ounces) semisweet chocolate chips**
- **½ cup butter, cubed**
- **1 tablespoon instant coffee granules**

1. Line a 15x10x1-in. baking pan with waxed paper; place in freezer to keep cold. Place pecans in a shallow bowl.

2. Working quickly, scoop ice cream with a melon baller to make 3/4-in. balls; immediately roll in pecans. Place on the prepared pan; freeze for at least 1 hour or until firm.

3. In a microwave, melt the chocolate chips and butter; stir until smooth. Stir in coffee granules until dissolved; cool completely.

4. Working quickly and in batches, use a toothpick to dip ice cream balls in chocolate mixture; allow excess to drip off. Place on wax paper-lined pan; remove toothpick. Return to freezer; freeze until set. For longer storage, transfer bonbons to a covered freezer container and return to freezer.

Frosty Orange Cream Cheese Cups

PICTURED AT RIGHT

Citrusy and refreshing, these bite-sized frozen treats will cool you down during the dog days of summer.

—ROXANNE CHAN ALBANY, CA

PREP: 35 MIN. + FREEZING • **MAKES:** 2 DOZEN

- **1¼ cups crushed gingersnap cookies (about 25 cookies)**
- **5 tablespoons butter, melted**
- **4 ounces cream cheese, softened**
- **2 tablespoons confectioners' sugar**
- **2 tablespoons plus ½ cup heavy whipping cream, divided**
- **½ cup orange marmalade**
- **4 ounces white baking chocolate, chopped**
- **⅓ cup salted pistachios, chopped**

1. In a small bowl, mix cookie crumbs and butter; press onto bottoms and up sides of ungreased mini-muffin cups. Freeze 20 minutes.

2. In a small bowl, beat cream cheese, confectioners' sugar and 2 tablespoons cream until smooth. Stir in marmalade; drop by scant tablespoonfuls into cups. Freeze 2 hours or until set.

3. In a double boiler or metal bowl over hot water, melt white chocolate with remaining cream; stir until smooth. Cool slightly. Spoon or drizzle over cups. Sprinkle with pistachios. Freeze, covered, overnight or until firm. Serve frozen.

CRUMB AND COOKIE CRUSTS

Try the Frosty Orange Cream Cheese Cups with different crusts. If you prefer a graham crust, replace the cookie crumbs with graham cracker crumbs (about 24 squares). For a chocolate crust, replace with chocolate wafer crumbs (about 20 wafers). But for a truly sweet treat, process about 15 cream-filled cookies to get the amount of crumbs needed for this recipe. And don't stop there: Have fun trying different flavors of jam for the filling. The possibilities are as endless as they are delicious!

Berries & Chocolate Sauce for Ice Cream

PICTURED AT LEFT

It's about time someone created an ice cream sundae just for adults! I frequently make this dessert to use up juicy berries during peak summer months.

—**EMORY DOTY** JASPER, GA

PREP: 30 MIN. + STANDING
MAKES: 6 SERVINGS

- **4 cups fresh strawberries, sliced**
- **1 cup fresh blueberries**
- **⅓ cup vodka**
- **¼ cup sugar**
- **6 ounces dark chocolate candy bars, chopped**
- **4 teaspoons butter**
- **¾ cup heavy whipping cream**
- **Vanilla ice cream**
- **Slivered almonds**

1. In a large bowl, toss berries with vodka and sugar. Refrigerate, covered, overnight.

2. Place chocolate and butter in a small bowl. In a small saucepan, bring cream just to a boil. Pour over chocolate and butter; stir with a whisk until smooth. Cool 15 minutes.

3. Serve berry mixture over ice cream. Drizzle with chocolate sauce and sprinkle with almonds.

Strawberry Ice Cream Charlotte

PICTURED ON PAGE 181

My family loves ice cream cakes, so they were delighted when I first presented this dessert. It's light, delicious and has a festive presentation.

—**SCARLETT ELROD** NEWNAN, GA

PREP: 35 MIN. + FREEZING • **MAKES:** 12 SLICES

- **2 packages (3 ounces each) soft ladyfingers, split**
- **4 cups strawberry ice cream, softened if necessary**
- **1¾ cups strawberry sorbet, softened if necessary**
- **2 cups fresh strawberries, hulled**
- **2 tablespoons confectioners' sugar**
- **¾ cup marshmallow creme**
- **1 cup heavy whipping cream**

1. Line the sides and bottom of an ungreased 9-in. springform pan with ladyfingers, rounded sides out; trim to fit, if necessary. (Save remaining ladyfingers for another use.)

2. Quickly spread ice cream into prepared pan; freeze, covered, for 30 minutes. Spread sorbet over ice cream; freeze 30 minutes longer.

3. Meanwhile, place strawberries and confectioners' sugar in a food processor; process until pureed. Reserve 1/4 cup puree for swirling. Transfer remaining puree to a large bowl; whisk in the marshmallow creme.

4. In a small bowl, beat cream until soft peaks form. Fold into marshmallow mixture. Spread evenly over sorbet; drizzle with reserved puree. Cut through puree with a knife to swirl. Freeze, covered, overnight.

5. Remove from freezer; carefully loosen sides from pan with a knife. Remove rim from pan. Serve immediately.

Frozen Mini Berry Trifles

PICTURED ON PAGE 180

I developed this as a quick birthday dessert for a friend recovering from surgery. You can used shaped muffin pans to fit special occasions or regular muffin cups.

—**PHYLLIS KENDALL** HAZELWOOD, MO

PREP: 30 MIN. + FREEZING • **MAKES:** 24 SERVINGS

- **1 package (12 ounces) frozen unsweetened mixed berries, thawed**
- **1 cup boiling water**
- **1 package (3 ounces) cherry gelatin**
- **2 cups butter pecan ice cream, softened if necessary**
- **1 loaf (16 ounces) frozen pound cake, thawed and cut into ½-inch cubes**
- **Whipped topping**

1. Place berries in a blender; cover and process until pureed. In a small bowl, add boiling water to gelatin; stir 2 minutes to completely dissolve.

2. Stir in ice cream and pureed berries until blended. Fold in cake cubes. Fill 24 muffin cups two-thirds full. Freeze, covered, 4 hours or until firm.

3. Remove from freezer about 10 minutes before serving. Carefully run a knife around sides of cups to loosen. Invert onto serving plates; serve with whipped topping.

Hazelnut Brownie Bombe

I love making ice cream bombes—they look so elegant but are so simple to make!
—MELISSA MILLWOOD LYMAN, SC

PREP: 45 MIN.
BAKE: 55 MIN. + FREEZING
MAKES: 16 SERVINGS

- **2 cups (12 ounces) semisweet chocolate chips**
- **½ cup butter, cubed**
- **3 eggs**
- **1½ cups sugar**
- **½ teaspoon salt**
- **1 teaspoon vanilla extract**
- **¾ cup all-purpose flour**
- **3 cups whole hazelnuts, toasted and chopped, divided**
- **3 quarts chocolate ice cream, softened if necessary**
- **½ cup Nutella**

1. Preheat oven to 350°. Line bottom of a greased 9-in. springform pan with parchment paper; grease paper.

2. In a microwave, melt the chocolate chips and butter; stir until smooth. Cool slightly. In a large bowl, beat eggs, sugar and salt. Stir in vanilla and chocolate mixture. Add flour, mixing well. Stir in 1 cup of hazelnuts.

3. Spread into prepared pan. Bake 55-60 minutes or until a toothpick inserted in center comes out with moist crumbs (do not overbake). Cool completely in pan on a wire rack.

4. Meanwhile, line a 4-qt. bowl with a 9-in. diameter top with plastic wrap. Quickly spread ice cream into bowl. Freeze, covered, until firm.

5. Loosen sides of brownie with a knife; remove rim from pan. Transfer brownie to a serving plate and remove paper. Spread top with Nutella. Invert ice cream mold onto brownie; remove bowl and plastic wrap. Immediately press remaining hazelnuts onto ice cream. Freeze, covered, at least 1 hour before serving. Cut into wedges.

NOTE *To toast whole hazelnuts, spread hazelnuts in a 15x10x1-in. baking pan. Bake in a 350° oven 7-10 minutes or until fragrant and lightly browned, stirring occasionally. To remove skins, wrap hazelnuts in a tea towel; rub with towel to loosen skins.*

Chocolate-Cherry Ice Cream Cake

Oh, say can you see...this amazing dessert at your next gathering? I make it ahead of time and keep it in the freezer, wrapped in foil, for a week or so before serving.

—SCARLETT ELROD NEWNAN, GA

PREP: 30 MIN. + FREEZING
MAKES: 12 SERVINGS

- **1½ cups Oreo cookie crumbs (about 15 cookies)**
- **2 tablespoons butter, melted**
- **4 cups cherry ice cream, softened if necessary**
- **8 Oreo cookies, coarsely chopped**
- **1 cup (6 ounces) miniature semisweet chocolate chips, divided**
- **4 cups fudge ripple ice cream, softened if necessary**
- **Sweetened whipped cream, optional**
- **12 fresh sweet cherries**

1. Preheat oven to 350°. In a small bowl, mix cookie crumbs and butter. Press onto bottom and 1 in. up sides of a greased 9-in. springform pan. Bake 8-10 minutes or until firm. Cool on a wire rack.

2. Spread cherry ice cream into crust; freeze, covered, until firm. Layer with chopped cookies and ½ cup chocolate chips. Spread fudge ripple ice cream over chocolate chips. Sprinkle with remaining chocolate chips. Freeze, covered, 8 hours or until firm.

3. Remove cake from the freezer 10 minutes before serving; carefully loosen sides from pan with a knife. Remove rim from pan. If desired, serve with the whipped cream. Top with cherries.

Patriotic Pops

My kids love homemade ice pops, and I love knowing that they're enjoying frozen treats that are good for them. We whip up a big batch with multiple flavors so they have many choices, but these red, white and blue ones are a surefire hit!
—SHANNON CARINO FRISCO, TX

PREP: 15 MIN. + FREEZING • **MAKES:** 1 DOZEN

- **1¼ cups sliced fresh strawberries, divided**
- **1¾ cups (14 ounces) vanilla yogurt, divided**
- **1¼ cups fresh or frozen blueberries, divided**
- **12 freezer pop molds or 12 paper cups (3 ounces each) and wooden pop sticks**

1. In a blender, combine 1 cup strawberries and 2 tablespoons yogurt; cover and process until blended. Transfer to a small bowl. Chop remaining the strawberries; stir into strawberry mixture.

2. In same blender, combine 1 cup blueberries and 2 tablespoons yogurt; cover and process until blended. Stir in remaining blueberries.

3. Layer 1 tablespoon strawberry mixture, 2 tablespoons yogurt and 1 tablespoon blueberry mixture in each of 12 molds or paper cups. Top molds with holders. If using cups, top with foil and insert sticks through foil. Freeze until firm.

Raspberry Cheesecake Floats

PICTURED ON PAGE 181

I have yet to meet a cheesecake I didn't like! Here, the cream cheese and raspberries create an ideal combination. Although ice cream floats are summery, I like this treat so much that I whip it up during the winter, too.
—DEIRDRE DEE COX KANSAS CITY, KS

START TO FINISH: 15 MIN. • **MAKES:** 6 SERVINGS

- **2 cans (12 ounces each) cream soda, divided**
- **¼ teaspoon almond extract**
- **3 ounces cream cheese, softened**
- **1 package (12 ounces) frozen unsweetened raspberries**
- **4 cups vanilla ice cream, softened if necessary, divided**

TOPPINGS

- **Whipped cream**
- **Fresh blackberries and blueberries**

1. Place ½ cup cream soda, extract, cream cheese, raspberries and 2 cups ice cream in a blender; cover and process until smooth.

2. Divide among six tall glasses. Top with remaining ice cream and cream soda. Serve with whipped cream and berries. Serve immediately.

This June, invite the dads in your neighborhood for a kicked-back salute to what Father knows best—grilled meat. Since Dad is not about to step down from being king of the cookout—and because you never outgrow being Pop's sous chef—give a helping hand to round out the ribs, steaks, chicken and burgers by whipping up some scrumptious summer salads, sweet and savory sauces and a refreshing beer cocktail to keep everyone cool. If it's true what they say, "The quickest way to a man's heart is through his stomach," then this menu has love written all over it.

Lemon Vinaigrette Potato Salad (p. 195)
Heirloom Tomatoes with Balsamic Vinaigrette (p. 196)
Peppered T-Bone Steaks with Salsa (p. 198)

FATHER'S DAY GRILLING

Almond & Apple Wild Rice Salad

Try a mixture of red and green apples to give this unique salad a pop of color.
—DAN WELLBERG ELK RIVER, MN

PREP: 5 MIN. • **COOK:** 1 HOUR + CHILLING • **MAKES:** 10 SERVINGS

1½ cups uncooked wild rice
2 medium apples, chopped
2 tablespoons plus ½ cup orange juice
4 teaspoons olive oil
4 teaspoons red wine vinegar
1 tablespoon honey
¾ teaspoon salt
¼ teaspoon white pepper
2 celery ribs, chopped
½ cup unblanched almonds, coarsely chopped
Optional toppings: halved green grapes, cubed cheddar cheese and chopped red onion

1. Cook wild rice according to package directions. Transfer to a large bowl; cool completely.
2. Meanwhile, in a small bowl, toss apples with 2 tablespoons orange juice. In another bowl, whisk the remaining orange juice, oil, vinegar, honey, salt and pepper.
3. Add apples and celery to rice. Drizzle with dressing; toss to combine. Refrigerate, covered, until chilled. Sprinkle with almonds; serve with toppings if desired.

Linda's Best Marinated Chicken

I have been using this grilled chicken recipe since I was 12 years old. The chicken comes out so juicy and tender.
—LINDA PACE LEES SUMMIT, MO

PREP: 15 MIN. + MARINATING • **GRILL:** 40 MIN. • **MAKES:** 4 SERVINGS

1¼ cups olive oil
½ cup red wine vinegar
⅓ cup lemon juice
¼ cup reduced-sodium soy sauce
¼ cup Worcestershire sauce
2 tablespoons ground mustard
1 tablespoon pepper
3 garlic cloves, minced
1 broiler/fryer chicken (3 to 4 pounds), cut up

1. Place the first eight ingredients in a blender; cover and process until blended. Pour 2 cups marinade into a large resealable plastic bag.
Add chicken; seal bag and turn to coat. Refrigerate 4 hours or overnight. Cover and refrigerate remaining marinade.
2. Drain chicken, discarding marinade in bag. Grill chicken, covered, over medium heat 40-45 minutes or until juices run clear, turning occasionally and basting with reserved marinade during the last 15 minutes.

Honey Chipotle Ribs

Nothing's better than having a sauce with the perfect "slathering" consistency. Here's one that'll ensure a lip-smacking feast.
—CAITLIN HAWES WESTWOOD, MA

PREP: 5 MIN. • **COOK:** 1½ HOURS
MAKES: 12 SERVINGS

- **6 pounds pork baby back ribs**

BARBECUE SAUCE

- **3 cups ketchup**
- **2 bottles (11.2 ounces each) Guinness beer**
- **2 cups barbecue sauce**
- **⅔ cup honey**
- **1 small onion, chopped**
- **¼ cup Worcestershire sauce**
- **2 tablespoons Dijon mustard**
- **2 tablespoons chopped chipotle peppers in adobo sauce**
- **4 teaspoons ground chipotle pepper**
- **1 teaspoon salt**
- **1 teaspoon garlic powder**
- **½ teaspoon pepper**

1. Wrap ribs in large pieces of heavy-duty foil; seal edges of foil. Grill, covered, over indirect medium heat for 1 to 1½ hours or until tender.
2. In a large saucepan, combine sauce ingredients; bring to a boil. Reduce heat; simmer, uncovered, for about 45 minutes or until thickened, stirring occasionally.
3. Carefully remove ribs from foil. Place over direct heat; baste with some of the sauce. Grill, covered, over medium heat for about 30 minutes or until browned, turning once and basting occasionally with additional sauce. Serve with remaining sauce.

Pasta & Sun-Dried Tomato Salad

Orzo pasta can be served warm or cold, making it an ideal dish for casual picnics and cookouts.
—**DAWN WILLIAMS** SCOTTSBORO, AL

PREP: 20 MIN. • **COOK:** 15 MIN. • **MAKES:** 8 SERVINGS

- **1 can (49 ounces) reduced-sodium chicken broth**
- **1 package (16 ounces) orzo pasta**
- **¼ cup chopped oil-packed sun-dried tomatoes plus 2 teaspoons oil from the jar**
- **1 garlic clove, minced**
- **¾ teaspoon salt**
- **¼ teaspoon pepper**
- **⅓ cup shredded Parmesan cheese**
- **4 fresh basil leaves, thinly sliced**
- **Optional toppings: crumbled feta cheese and canned garbanzo beans**

1. In a large saucepan, bring broth to a boil. Stir in orzo; return to a boil. Cook for 8-10 minutes or until tender, stirring occasionally.

2. Drain orzo; transfer to a large bowl. (Discard broth or save for another use.) Stir in the tomatoes, oil from sun-dried tomatoes, garlic, salt and pepper; cool completely.

3. Add Parmesan cheese and basil; toss to combine. Cover and refrigerate until serving. Serve with toppings if desired.

Mushroom-Stuffed Cheeseburgers

You can stuff these burgers ahead of time so all you have to do the day of a get-together is slap 'em on the grill!
—**JOYCE GUTH** MOHNTON, PA

PREP: 30 MIN. • **GRILL:** 10 MIN. • **MAKES:** 8 SERVINGS

- **2 bacon strips, finely chopped**
- **2 cups chopped fresh mushrooms**
- **¼ cup chopped onion**
- **¼ cup chopped sweet red pepper**
- **¼ cup chopped green pepper**
- **2 pounds lean ground beef (90% lean)**
- **2 tablespoons steak sauce**
- **½ teaspoon seasoned salt**
- **4 slices provolone cheese, halved**
- **8 kaiser rolls, split**

1. In a large skillet, cook bacon over medium heat until crisp, stirring occasionally. Remove with a slotted spoon; drain on paper towels. Cook and stir mushrooms, onion and peppers in bacon drippings until tender. Using slotted spoon, remove to a small bowl; cool completely. Stir in bacon.

2. In a large bowl, combine beef, steak sauce and seasoned salt, mixing lightly but thoroughly. Shape into 16 thin patties. Top eight of the patties with cheese, folding over cheese to fit within ¾ inch of edge. Spread with mushroom mixture. Top with remaining patties, pressing edges to enclose filling.

3. Grill burgers, uncovered, over medium-high heat or broil 4 in. from heat 5-6 minutes on each side or until a thermometer inserted in meat portion reads 160°. Serve on rolls.

Lemon Vinaigrette Potato Salad

PICTURED ON PAGE 190

I developed this recipe for a friend who wanted a potato salad without mayonnaise. I have substituted fresh thyme for the basil. Any fresh herbs would be great!
—**MELANIE CLOYD** MULLICA HILL, NJ

PREP: 25 MIN. • **COOK:** 15 MIN. • **MAKES:** 12 SERVINGS

- **3 pounds red potatoes, cut into 1-inch cubes**
- **½ cup olive oil**
- **3 tablespoons lemon juice**
- **2 tablespoons minced fresh basil**
- **2 tablespoons minced fresh parsley**
- **1 tablespoon red wine vinegar**
- **1 teaspoon grated lemon peel**
- **¾ teaspoon salt**
- **½ teaspoon pepper**
- **1 small onion, finely chopped**

1. Place potatoes in a large saucepan and cover with water. Bring to a boil. Reduce heat; cover and simmer for 10-15 minutes or until tender. Meanwhile, in a small bowl, whisk the oil, lemon juice, herbs, vinegar, lemon peel, salt and pepper.

2. Drain potatoes. Place in a large bowl; add onion. Drizzle with vinaigrette; toss to coat. Serve warm or chill until serving.

Heirloom Tomatoes with Balsamic Vinaigrette

PICTURED ON PAGE 191

Sliced plum tomatoes and red onion are tossed with a homemade vinaigrette to create this summery salad. Fresh basil adds the finishing touch.

—ANN SOBOTKA GLENDALE, AZ

START TO FINISH: 10 MIN. • **MAKES:** 4 SERVINGS

- **6 medium plum or heirloom tomatoes, sliced**
- **½ cup sliced red onion**

- **3 tablespoons balsamic vinegar**
- **2 tablespoons olive oil**
- **½ teaspoon sugar**
- **⅛ teaspoon salt**
- **⅛ teaspoon garlic powder**
- **⅛ teaspoon pepper**
- **4 fresh basil leaves, snipped**

In a large bowl, gently combine tomatoes and onion. In a small bowl, whisk the vinegar, oil, sugar, salt, garlic powder and pepper. Pour over tomato mixture; toss gently to coat. Sprinkle with basil. Serve at room temperature with a slotted spoon.

Blackberry Beer Cocktail

This refreshing hard lemonade has a mild alcohol flavor; the beer adds just enough fizz to dance on your tongue as you sip. Sorry, adults only!

—GINGER SULLIVAN CUTLER BAY, FL

START TO FINISH: 10 MIN. • **MAKES:** 10 SERVINGS

- **4 bottles (12 ounces each) beer, chilled**
- **1 can (12 ounces) frozen raspberry lemonade concentrate, thawed**
- **¾ cup fresh or frozen blackberries, thawed**
- **½ cup vodka**
- **Ice cubes**
- **Lemon slices**

In a large pitcher combine the beer, lemonade concentrate, blackberries and vodka. Serve over ice and garnish with lemon slices.

Jalapeno Popper Spread

I've been told by fellow party-goers that this recipe tastes exactly like a jalapeno popper. I like that it can be made without much fuss.

—ARIANE MCALPINE
PENTICTON, BC

PREP: 10 MIN. • **BAKE:** 25 MIN.
MAKES: 16 SERVINGS

- **2 packages (8 ounces each) cream cheese, softened**
- **1 cup mayonnaise**
- **½ cup shredded Monterey Jack cheese**
- **¼ cup canned chopped green chilies**
- **¼ cup canned diced jalapeno peppers**
- **1 cup shredded Parmesan cheese**
- **½ cup panko (Japanese) bread crumbs**
- **Sweet red and yellow pepper pieces and corn chips**

In a large bowl, beat the first five ingredients until blended; spread into an ungreased 9-in. pie plate. Sprinkle with Parmesan cheese; top with bread crumbs. Bake at 400° for 25-30 minutes or until lightly browned. Serve with peppers and chips.

Peppered T-Bone Steaks with Salsa

We grill all year, and beef is so good cooked outdoors. The simple marinade makes these steaks very juicy. We enjoy them with tortillas and salsa.
—ROBIN HYDE LINCOLN, NE

PREP: 25 MIN. + MARINATING
GRILL: 15 MIN.
MAKES: 4 SERVINGS (3 CUPS SALSA)

- **1 cup red wine vinegar**
- **¼ cup lime juice**
- **¼ cup olive oil**
- **4 teaspoons chili powder**
- **2 garlic cloves, minced**
- **2 to 4 teaspoons crushed red pepper flakes**
- **2 teaspoons salt**
- **1 teaspoon pepper**
- **4 beef T-bone steaks (1 inch thick and 1 pound each)**

SALSA

- **2 large tomatoes, seeded and chopped**
- **2 medium ripe avocados, peeled and chopped**
- **4 green onions, thinly sliced**
- **2 tablespoons minced fresh cilantro**
- **2 tablespoons lime juice**
- **½ jalapeno pepper, seeded and finely chopped, optional**
- **2 garlic cloves, minced**
- **½ teaspoon salt**
- **½ teaspoon pepper**

1. In a small bowl, whisk the first eight ingredients until blended. Divide steaks between two large resealable plastic bags. Add 1/2 cup marinade to each; seal bags and turn to coat. Refrigerate steaks and remaining marinade 1 to 2 hours.

2. In another bowl, combine salsa ingredients. Refrigerate until serving.

3. Drain steaks, discarding marinade in bags. Grill, covered, over medium heat 6-8 minutes on each side or until meat reaches desired doneness (for medium-rare, a thermometer should read 145°; medium, 160°; well-done, 170°). Brush frequently with the reserved marinade during the last 5 minutes of cooking. Serve with salsa.

Grilled Mediterranean Eggplant & Tomato Salad

A friend of mine served a delicious grilled eggplant salad when she had me over for dinner, and I was so inspired that I went home and re-created it!

—JENN TIDWELL FAIR OAKS, CA

START TO FINISH: 30 MIN. • **MAKES:** 6 SERVINGS

- **1 medium eggplant, cut into ½-inch slices**
- **¼ cup olive oil, divided**
- **1½ teaspoons minced fresh thyme or ½ teaspoon dried thyme**
- **1½ teaspoons minced fresh oregano or ½ teaspoon dried oregano**
- **1 large onion, coarsely chopped**
- **½ pound sliced fresh mushrooms**
- **1 garlic clove, minced**
- **¼ teaspoon salt**
- **¼ teaspoon coarsely ground pepper**
- **⅓ cup dry red wine**
- **1½ cups cherry tomatoes, halved**
- **¼ cup minced fresh parsley**
- **2 tablespoons balsamic vinegar**
- **½ cup crumbled feta cheese**

1. Brush the eggplant with 2 tablespoons oil; sprinkle with thyme and oregano. Grill, covered, over medium heat 3-4 minutes on each side or until tender. When cool enough to handle, cut into bite-size pieces.

2. Meanwhile, in a large skillet, heat remaining oil over medium-high heat. Add onion and mushrooms; cook and stir 5-7 minutes or until tender. Add garlic, salt and pepper; cook for 1 minute longer. Add wine to pan; cook, stirring to loosen browned bits from pan. Bring to a boil; cook 2-3 minutes or until liquid is almost evaporated.

3. In a large bowl, combine eggplant, mushroom mixture, tomatoes, parsley and vinegar. Add cheese; toss to combine.

Mint Watermelon Salad

I invented this refreshing fruit salad one sultry afternoon while my friends were gathered around my pool. It was quick to prepare, and it disappeared from their plates even more quickly. Even the kids ate it up!

—ANTOINETTE DUBECK HUNTINGDON VALLEY, PA

START TO FINISH: 20 MIN. • **MAKES:** 8 SERVINGS

- **1 tablespoon lemon juice**
- **1 tablespoon olive oil**
- **2 teaspoons sugar**
- **6 cups cubed seedless watermelon**
- **2 tablespoons minced fresh mint**
- **Lemon wedges, optional**

In a small bowl, whisk the lemon juice, oil and sugar. In a large bowl, combine watermelon and mint. Drizzle with lemon juice mixture; toss to coat. Serve with lemon wedges if desired.

MELON MEASUREMENTS

The average large watermelon weighs about 20 pounds. A good rule of thumb is to expect about one cup of cubed fruit per pound of melon.

"Just one more pint." You might say it three or four times before your next berry-picking adventure comes to an end. With row after row of sweet, ripe gems just begging to be plucked, you'll wonder if you'll ever be able to stop. Just don't let a lack of recipes slow you down. With stratas, mojitos, salsas, tenderloins, pot stickers, tarts, and more, you're going to wish you had buckets of berries to prepare each one of these sensational dishes time and time again. So when it comes to stocking up on these sweet fruits, remember, the berrier the merrier!

Summer Harvest Tart (p. 202)

BERRY-PICKING **PARTY**

Summer Harvest Tart

PICTURED ON PAGE 201

One of my favorite bakeries makes this scrumptious tart that uses fall and summer fruit, so I created my own version. I like to serve it warm with whipped cream or ice cream and with a cup of coffee on late-summer evenings.

—**SARAH KNOBLOCK** HYDE PARK, IN

PREP: 45 MIN. • **BAKE:** 45 MIN. + COOLING • **MAKES:** 12 SERVINGS

- **⅔ cup butter, softened**
- **¼ cup sugar**
- **Dash salt**
- **2 tablespoons lightly beaten egg white**
- **½ teaspoon vanilla extract**
- **2 cups all-purpose flour**

FILLING

- **⅔ cup sugar**
- **⅓ cup all-purpose flour**
- **1 teaspoon ground cinnamon**
- **½ teaspoon ground nutmeg**
- **1 cup each fresh blackberries, blueberries and raspberries**
- **1 cup finely chopped peeled apple (about 1 medium)**
- **1 cup sliced peaches (about 2 small)**
- **2 teaspoons lemon juice**

TOPPING

- **⅓ cup butter, softened**
- **⅔ cup packed brown sugar**
- **¾ teaspoon ground cinnamon**
- **⅛ teaspoon ground nutmeg**
- **⅛ teaspoon ground cloves**
- **½ cup all-purpose flour**
- **½ cup old-fashioned oats**

1. Preheat oven to 350°. In a large bowl, cream butter, sugar and salt until light and fluffy. Beat in egg white and vanilla. Gradually beat in flour. Press onto bottom and up sides of an 11-in. fluted tart pan with removable bottom; place on a baking sheet.

2. Bake 25-30 minutes or until edges are light brown. Cool on a wire rack. Increase oven setting to 375°.

3. For filling, in a large bowl, mix sugar, flour, cinnamon and nutmeg. Add fruit and lemon juice; toss to combine.

4. For topping, in a small bowl, cream butter, brown sugar and spices until blended. Gradually beat in flour and oats.

5. Add filling to crust; sprinkle with topping. Bake 45-50 minutes or until top is golden brown and filling is bubbly. Cool on a wire rack. Serve warm or at room temperature.

Blackberry-Mango Crumble

My husband loves fresh-picked blackberries at the height of summer, and mango is a favorite combination with the berries in this crumble. A little lime adds just enough zing to balance the sweetness of the filling.

—**PATRICIA QUINN** OMAHA, NE

PREP: 20 MIN. • **BAKE:** 35 MIN. • **MAKES:** 8 SERVINGS

- **4 cups cubed peeled mangoes (about 4 medium)**
- **4 cups fresh blackberries**
- **1 tablespoon lime juice**
- **½ cup sugar**
- **¼ cup cornstarch**
- **¼ teaspoon salt**

TOPPING

- **½ cup quick-cooking oats**
- **¼ cup macadamia nuts, chopped**
- **¼ cup packed brown sugar**
- **2 tablespoons flaked coconut**
- **2 tablespoons all-purpose flour**
- **1 tablespoon grated lime peel**
- **Dash salt**
- **¼ cup cold butter, cubed**

1. Preheat oven to 375°. In a large bowl, toss mangoes and blackberries with lime juice. In a small bowl, mix sugar, cornstarch and salt; add to fruit and toss to coat. Transfer to a greased 11x7-in. baking dish.

2. In a small bowl, mix the first seven topping ingredients; cut in butter until crumbly. Sprinkle over fruit. Bake 35-40 minutes or until filling is bubbly and topping is golden brown. Serve warm.

Raspberry Mint Jam

I have so much mint growing in my yard that I add it to almost everything. What a revelation it was when it went in my raspberry jam—the mint really wakes up the raspberry flavor!
—LAURIE BOCK LYNDEN, WA

PREP: 20 MIN.
PROCESS: 10 MIN./BATCH + STANDING
MAKES: 8 HALF-PINTS

- **8 cups fresh raspberries**
- **6½ cups sugar**
- **½ teaspoon butter**
- **2 pouches (3 ounces each) liquid fruit pectin**
- **1 cup minced fresh mint**

1. In a Dutch oven, combine raspberries, sugar and butter. Bring to a full rolling boil over high heat, stirring constantly. Stir in pectin. Continue to boil 1 minute, stirring constantly. Remove from heat; skim off foam. Stir in mint.
2. Ladle hot mixture into hot half-pint jars, leaving ¼-in. headspace. Remove air bubbles and adjust headspace, if necessary, by adding hot mixture. Wipe the rims. Center lids on jars; screw on bands until fingertip tight.
3. Place jars into canner, ensuring that they are completely covered with water. Bring to a boil; process for 10 minutes. Remove jars and cool.
NOTE *The processing time listed is for altitudes of 1,000 feet or less. Add 1 minute to the processing time for each 1,000 feet of additional altitude.*

Pork Tenderloin with Three-Berry Salsa

My husband came home from a work meeting that had served pork with a blueberry salsa. He was amazed at how tasty it was, so I came up with my own rendition without seeing or tasting what he'd had. It took several tries, but this is the delicious result.
—ANGIE PHILLIPS TARZANA, CA

PREP: 30 MIN. + STANDING • **COOK:** 25 MIN. • **MAKES:** 6 SERVINGS

- **1¼ cups fresh or frozen blackberries (about 6 ounces), thawed and drained**
- **1¼ cups fresh or frozen raspberries (about 6 ounces), thawed and drained**
- **1 cup fresh or frozen blueberries (about 6 ounces), thawed**
- **1 medium sweet red pepper, finely chopped**
- **1 jalapeno pepper, seeded and minced**
- **½ medium red onion, finely chopped**
- **¼ cup lime juice**
- **3 tablespoons minced fresh cilantro**
- **¼ teaspoon salt**

PORK

- **2 pork tenderloins (¾ pound each), cut into ¾-inch slices**
- **1 teaspoon salt**
- **½ teaspoon pepper**
- **2 tablespoons olive oil, divided**
- **½ cup white wine or chicken broth**
- **2 shallots, thinly sliced**
- **½ cup chicken stock**

1. Place the first five ingredients in a bowl; toss lightly to combine. Reserve 1 cup berry mixture for sauce. For salsa, gently stir onion, lime juice, cilantro and salt into remaining mixture; let stand for 30 minutes.

2. Meanwhile, sprinkle pork with salt and pepper. In a large skillet, heat 1 tablespoon oil over medium-high heat. Add half of the pork and cook 2-4 minutes on each side or until a thermometer reads 145°. Remove from pan. Repeat with remaining pork and oil.

3. In same pan, add wine, shallots and reserved berry mixture, stirring to loosen browned bits from pan. Bring to a boil; cook 4-6 minutes or until liquid is reduced to 1 tablespoon. Stir in stock; cook 5 minutes longer or until shallots are tender, stirring occasionally. Return pork to pan; heat through. Serve with salsa.

Blackberry Brandy Sauce

Fresh blackberries, sugar and brandy make a rich-tasting sauce to serve over ice cream, cheesecake, pancakes, angel food cake ... the possibilities are endless, and it makes everything look gorgeous.
—**CRYSTAL BRUNS** ILIFF, CO

START TO FINISH: 25 MIN.
MAKES: 12 SERVINGS (¼ CUP EACH)

1 cup sugar
2 tablespoons cornstarch
¼ cup cold water
4 cups fresh or frozen blackberries, thawed
1 tablespoon brandy or ½ teaspoon vanilla extract
Vanilla ice cream, optional

In a large saucepan, mix sugar and cornstarch; stir in water. Add blackberries; bring to a boil. Reduce heat; simmer, uncovered, 10-12 minutes or until sauce is thickened, stirring occasionally. Remove from heat; stir in brandy. Cool slightly. If desired, serve with ice cream.

Strawberry Pot Stickers

My wife and daughter love this unusual dessert. Strawberries are my favorite fruit and marrying them with chocolate and cinnamon in this dim sum dish is a surprising treat for everyone.
—RICK BROWNE RIDGEFIELD, WA

PREP: 30 MIN. + COOLING
COOK: 10 MIN./BATCH
MAKES: 32 POT STICKERS (⅔ CUP SAUCE)

- **3 ounces milk chocolate, chopped**
- **¼ cup half-and-half cream**
- **1 teaspoon butter**
- **1 teaspoon vanilla extract**
- **¼ teaspoon ground cinnamon**

POT STICKERS

- **2 cups chopped fresh strawberries**
- **3 ounces milk chocolate, chopped**
- **1 tablespoon brown sugar**
- **¼ teaspoon ground cinnamon**
- **32 pot sticker or gyoza wrappers**
- **1 egg, lightly beaten**
- **2 tablespoons canola oil, divided**
- **½ cup water, divided**

1. Place chocolate in a small bowl. In a small saucepan, bring cream and butter just to a boil. Pour over chocolate; whisk until smooth. Stir in vanilla and cinnamon. Cool to room temperature, stirring occasionally.

2. For pot stickers, in a small bowl, toss strawberries and chopped chocolate with brown sugar and cinnamon. Place 1 tablespoon mixture in center of each gyoza wrapper. (Cover remaining wrappers with a damp paper towel until ready to use.)

3. Moisten wrapper edges with egg. Fold wrapper over filling; seal edges, pleating the front side several times to form a pleated pouch. Stand pot stickers on a work surface to flatten bottoms; curve slightly to form crescent shapes, if desired.

4. In a large skillet, heat 1 tablespoon oil over medium-high heat. Arrange half of the pot stickers, flat side down, in concentric circles in pan; cook 1-2 minutes or until bottoms are golden brown. Add 1/4 cup water; bring to a simmer. Cook, covered, 3-5 minutes or until water is almost absorbed and the wrappers are tender.

5. Cook, uncovered, 1 minute or until bottoms are crisp and water is completely evaporated. Repeat with remaining pot stickers. Serve with sauce.

Berry Brunch Strata

I wanted a simple way to use strawberries and blueberries in a breakfast recipe, so I created this strata. Because it's not an overly sweet recipe, I like to sprinkle it with sugar and serve it with sweetened whipped cream.

—DIANE DENNY JACKSONVILLE, FL

PREP: 20 MIN. + CHILLING • **BAKE:** 45 MIN. + STANDING • **MAKES:** 12 SERVINGS

- **1 prepared angel food cake (10 to 12 ounces), cut into 1-inch cubes**
- **1 package (8 ounces) cream cheese, softened**
- **1 tablespoon sugar**
- **1 teaspoon salt**
- **1 teaspoon ground cinnamon**
- **12 eggs**
- **1 cup half-and-half cream**
- **2 cups fresh strawberries, chopped**
- **2 cups fresh blueberries**
- **Coarse sugar**
- **Sweetened whipped cream, optional**

1. Place cake cubes in a greased 13x9-in. baking dish. In a large bowl, beat cream cheese, sugar, salt and cinnamon until blended. Gradually beat in eggs, beginning with one at a time. Stir in cream. Fold in berries. Pour over cake cubes. Refrigerate, covered, overnight.

2. Preheat oven to 350°. Remove strata from refrigerator while oven heats; sprinkle with coarse sugar.

3. Bake, uncovered, for 45-50 minutes or until a knife inserted near the center comes out clean. Cover loosely with foil if top browns too quickly. Let stand 10 minutes before cutting. If desired, serve it with a dollop of whipped cream.

Maple Blackberry Mojito

PICTURED AT LEFT

This refreshing cocktail is how you take advantage of prime berry season during the summer months. I've also used other types of fruit, including raspberries, kiwi and strawberries.

—DONNA NOEL GRAY, ME

START TO FINISH: 10 MIN. • **MAKES:** 1 SERVING

- **4 fresh or frozen blackberries, thawed**
- **5 fresh mint leaves**
- **1 tablespoon maple syrup**
- **1 lime wedge**
- **¼ cup club soda, chilled**
- **1½ ounces light rum**
- **½ to ¾ cup ice cubes**

In a glass, muddle the blackberries and mint with maple syrup. Squeeze lime wedge into the glass. Stir in club soda and rum. Strain into a chilled glass; serve with ice.

GET THE MOST OUT OF YOUR LIME

Zest limes before slicing them. You can freeze the zest in an airtight container or freezer bag for when you need it. Also, rolling the lime on the counter before you cut into it will help get the juices flowing.

Don't even try to tire out a group of giggling girls. Just be ready to keep their little hands busy with party-friendly food so adorable and delicious, they'll be gossiping about it for years to come. Let them help decorate their own Sleeping Bag Blondie (p. 215) or prepare for movie time by mixing up a batch of White Chocolate Party Mix (p. 212), which could also double as an easy party favor if tucked inside decorative takeout boxes or baggies. But no matter which recipes you decide to make, remember to keep the camera handy—these are the moments you'll want to always remember.

Strawberry-Peach Milk Shakes (p. 213)
White Chocolate Party Mix (p. 212)
Sleeping Bag Blondies (p. 215)

SLUMBER PARTY **FOR GIRLS**

Mini PB&J Cheesecakes

I got hooked on these mini cheesecakes when a friend made them. She let me steal her recipe, and now I'm sharing this tasty treat with you!
—**BETSY KING** DULUTH, MN

PREP: 35 MIN. • **BAKE:** 15 MIN. + COOLING • **MAKES:** 3½ DOZEN

- **1 cup creamy peanut butter**
- **½ cup sugar**
- **1 egg**

CHEESECAKE LAYER

- **1 package (8 ounces) cream cheese, softened**
- **½ cup sugar**
- **1 egg, lightly beaten**
- **1 teaspoon vanilla extract**
- **¼ cup strawberry jelly, warmed**

OPTIONAL DRIZZLE

- **½ cup confectioners' sugar**
- **2 to 3 tablespoons heavy whipping cream**

1. Preheat oven to 350°. In a small bowl, beat peanut butter and sugar until blended. Beat in egg. Press 2 teaspoons mixture into each of 42 paper-lined mini-muffin cups.

2. For cheesecake layer, in another bowl, beat cream cheese and sugar until smooth. Beat in egg and vanilla. Spoon a scant 2 teaspoons of cream cheese mixture into each cup. Drop the jelly by 1/4 teaspoonfuls over tops. Cut through the batter with a toothpick to swirl.

3. Bake 12-14 minutes or until centers are set. Cool completely on a wire rack.

4. If desired, mix confectioners' sugar and enough cream to reach desired consistency; drizzle over cheesecakes. Refrigerate until serving.

Taco Puff Pastries

You won't be able to stop eating these taco appetizers! And the recipe makes 80 servings, so you'll definitely be ready for guests to come over and chow down.
—**RUTH COFFLAND** FAIR OAKS, CA

PREP: 45 MIN. + COOLING • **BAKE:** 10 MIN./BATCH • **MAKES:** 80 APPETIZERS

- **2 pounds ground beef**
- **1 large onion, chopped**
- **4 garlic cloves, minced**
- **2 envelopes taco seasoning**
- **½ teaspoon pepper**
- **2 cans (8 ounces each) tomato sauce**
- **2 cans (4 ounces each) chopped green chilies**
- **2 packages (17.3 ounces each) frozen puff pastry, thawed**
- **2 egg whites**
- **1 tablespoon water**
- **½ cup grated Parmesan cheese**

1. Preheat oven to 400°. In a large skillet, cook beef, onion and garlic over medium heat 8-10 minutes or until beef is no longer pink, breaking up beef into crumbles; drain. Stir in taco seasoning, pepper, tomato sauce and chilies. Cool completely.

2. On a lightly floured surface, unfold one puff pastry sheet. Roll into a 15x12-in. rectangle; cut into twenty 3-in. squares. Spoon 1 rounded tablespoon beef mixture near the center of each square. Brush edges of pastry with water; fold pastry over filling, forming a triangle. Press edges with a fork to seal. Place on ungreased baking sheets. Repeat with remaining pastry and filling.

3. In a small bowl, whisk egg whites and water; brush over tops. Sprinkle with cheese. Bake 10-14 minutes or until golden brown. Serve warm.

Bean & Salsa Stuffed Pizza

Get the party started with this tantalizing pizza. It's everything you love about Mexican cuisine, all in convenient handheld slices!
—**ELIZABETH WRIGHT** LAS VEGAS, NV

START TO FINISH: 30 MIN.
MAKES: 6 SERVINGS

- **1 package (15 ounces) refrigerated pie pastry**
- **1 envelope taco seasoning, divided**
- **1 cup refried beans**
- **⅓ cup chopped onion**
- **1 can (15 ounces) black beans, rinsed and drained**
- **1 can (4 ounces) chopped green chilies, drained**
- **1 cup chunky salsa**
- **1 cup (4 ounces) shredded Mexican cheese blend, divided**
- **1 teaspoon canola oil**
- **Sour cream and additional salsa, optional**

1. Preheat oven to 400°. On a work surface, unroll one pastry sheet. Roll into a 12-in. circle. Transfer to an ungreased 12-in. pizza pan.

2. Reserve 1 tablespoon taco seasoning for topping. In a small bowl, mix refried beans and remaining taco seasoning; spread over pastry to within 1 in. of edge. Top with onion, black beans, chilies and salsa. Sprinkle with ¾ cup cheese.

3. Unroll remaining pastry sheet; roll into a 13-in. circle. Place over cheese. Trim, seal and flute edge. Cut slits in top. Brush top with oil; sprinkle with reserved taco seasoning.

4. Bake 15-17 minutes or until golden brown. Sprinkle with remaining cheese. Bake 3-5 minutes longer or until cheese is melted. If desired, serve with sour cream and additional salsa.

Baked Mozzarella Sticks

This is a fantastic, healthier substitute to deep-fried mozzarella sticks. I like to serve the sticks with spaghetti.
—JULIE PUDERBAUGH BERWICK, PA

START TO FINISH: 20 MIN. • **MAKES:** 16 APPETIZERS

- **2 tubes (8 ounces each) refrigerated crescent rolls**
- **8 pieces string cheese, cut crosswise in half**
- **1 cup marinara or spaghetti sauce, warmed**

1. Preheat oven to 375°. Unroll crescent dough and separate each tube of dough into eight triangles. Place one halved string cheese at the wide end of each triangle; roll up and seal edges.

2. Place 2 in. apart on a foil-lined baking sheet, point side down. Bake 10-12 minutes or until golden brown. Serve with marinara sauce.

White Chocolate Party Mix

PICTURED ON PAGE 208

Every time I prepare this crispy combination of cereal, popcorn, pretzels, nuts and candies, people rave about it. One bite and you'll see why.
—ROSE WENTZEL ST. LOUIS, MO

PREP: 10 MIN. + STANDING
COOK: 5 MIN. • **MAKES:** 9½ QUARTS

- **16 cups popped popcorn**
- **3 cups Frosted Cheerios**
- **1 package (10 ounces) fat-free pretzel sticks**
- **2 cups milk chocolate M&M's (about 12 ounces)**
- **1½ cups pecan halves**
- **1 package (8 ounces) milk chocolate English toffee bits or brickle toffee bits**
- **2 packages (10 to 12 ounces each) white baking chips**
- **2 tablespoons canola oil**

1. In a large bowl, combine the first six ingredients. In a microwave or heavy saucepan over low heat, melt baking chips with oil; stir until smooth.

2. Pour over popcorn mixture and toss to coat. Immediately spread onto two baking sheets; let stand until set, about 2 hours. Store in airtight containers.

HOW TO MAKE HEART-SHAPED STRAWBERRY GARNISHES

1. Wash and gently dry the berries.
2. Use a paring knife to cut a V-shaped notch at the top of each strawberry.

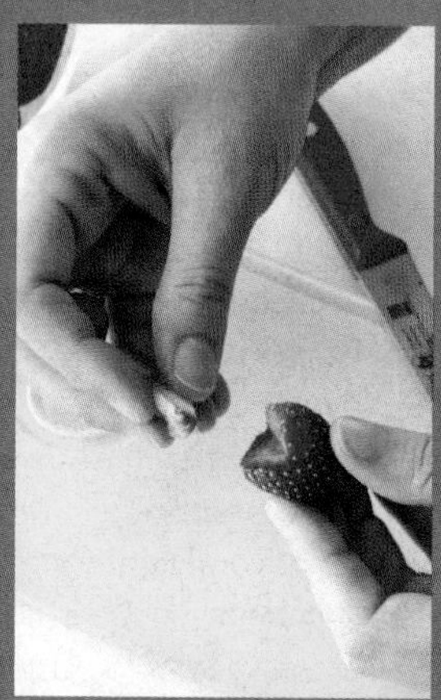

3. Slice each berry into ¼-inch hearts.

4. To use as a drink garnish, cut a short vertical slit at the bottom of each slice and arrange on glasses as desired.

Strawberry-Peach Milk Shakes

You'll need thick drinking straws for this refreshingly fruity shake.
—KAREN EDWARDS SANFORD, ME

START TO FINISH: 15 MIN.
MAKES: 4 SERVINGS

- **¼ cup milk**
- **3 tablespoons sugar**
- **2 cups halved fresh strawberries**
- **1¾ cups sliced peeled peaches (about 3 medium) or frozen unsweetened sliced peaches, thawed**
- **2 cups vanilla ice cream**

Place milk, sugar, strawberries and peaches in a blender; cover and process until fruit is pureed. Add ice cream; cover and process until blended. Serve immediately.

Magic-in-the-Middle Peanut Butter Cookies

I found this recipe on an advertisement years and years ago, and the cookies have been a family favorite ever since. I've won a few contests with them, and now my teenager is using the recipe and has won prizes at the 4-H fair!
—CHRISTY HARD STERLING, KS

PREP: 30 MIN. • **BAKE:** 10 MIN./BATCH • **MAKES:** 2½ DOZEN

- **½ cup butter, softened**
- **¼ cup creamy peanut butter**
- **½ cup sugar**
- **½ cup packed brown sugar**
- **1 egg**
- **1 teaspoon vanilla extract**
- **1½ cups all-purpose flour**
- **½ cup baking cocoa**
- **½ teaspoon baking soda**

FILLING

- **1 cup confectioners' sugar**
- **¾ cup creamy peanut butter**

1. Preheat oven to 375°. In a large bowl, cream butter, peanut butter and sugars until blended. Beat in egg and vanilla. In another bowl, whisk flour, cocoa and baking soda; gradually beat into creamed mixture.

2. For filling, in a small bowl, beat confectioners' sugar and peanut butter. Shape into 30 balls. Wrap tablespoons of chocolate dough around filling to cover completely. Place 2 in. apart on ungreased baking sheets. Flatten slightly with bottom of a glass dipped in sugar.

3. Bake 7-9 minutes or until set and slightly cracked. Cool on pans for 2 minutes. Remove to wire racks to cool. Store in airtight containers.

S'more Pops

My daughters and I came up with these treats when planning a candy-making party. They also make adorable hostess gifts, are perfect for potlucks and would sell out quickly at a bake sale.

—LISA HABOUSH GENEVA, IL

START TO FINISH: 20 MIN.
MAKES: 2 DOZEN

- **4 whole graham crackers, coarsely crushed**
- **24 lollipop sticks**
- **24 large marshmallows**
- **4 ounces milk chocolate candy coating, melted**

1. Place crushed crackers in a shallow bowl. Insert one lollipop stick into each marshmallow. Dip two-thirds of each marshmallow in melted candy coating; allow excess to drip off. Dip in cracker crumbs, covering about half of the chocolate.

2. Place on waxed paper; let stand until set. Store in an airtight container.

S'MORE SPRINKLES

Kids will have fun creating their own marshmallow pops using a variety of things to dip them in. In addition to graham cracker crumbs, try crushed cookies or candy coatings such as sprinkles or nonpareils.

Sleeping Bag Blondies

PICTURED ON PAGE 209

These tasty pecan bars can be dressed up for slumber parties, camping trips and Girl Scout events. We used mini vanilla wafers and marshmallows to make these adorable overnighters.

—SHARON BICKETT CHESTER, SC

PREP: 20 MIN. • **BAKE:** 35 MIN. + COOLING • **MAKES:** 16 BROWNIES

- **1 cup butter, softened**
- **1 cup sugar**
- **1 cup packed brown sugar**
- **2 eggs**
- **2 teaspoons vanilla extract**
- **2 cups self-rising flour**
- **2 cups chopped pecans, optional**
- **1½ cups white frosting**
- **Brown, yellow, green, orange, pink and blue gel food coloring**
- **8 large marshmallows**
- **16 miniature vanilla wafers**
- **Assorted sprinkles and mini honey bear-shaped crackers, optional**

1. Preheat oven to 325°. Line a 13x9-in. baking pan with foil, letting ends extend up sides; grease foil. In a large bowl, cream butter and sugars until light and fluffy. Beat in eggs and vanilla. Gradually beat in flour. If desired, stir in pecans.

2. Spread mixture into prepared pan. Bake 35-40 minutes or until a toothpick inserted in the center comes out clean. Cool on a wire rack.

3. Lifting with foil, remove brownie from pan. Trim ½ in. off edges. Cut remaining brownie lengthwise in half; cut each half crosswise into eight bars to make 16 sleeping bags.

4. Tint ¼ cup frosting brown and 2 tablespoons yellow; transfer to two resealable plastic bags. Cut a small hole in a corner of each bag and set aside. Divide remaining frosting among four bowls; tint green, orange, pink and blue. Spread each of the four frostings over four brownies, reserving a small amount of each frosting to attach wafers.

5. For pillows, cut marshmallows vertically in half; place on one end of brownies, cut side down. Attach vanilla wafers to pillows. Pipe faces and hair on wafers using brown and yellow frostings. If desired, decorate with the sprinkles and the teddy bear crackers.

NOTE *As a substitute for each cup of self-rising flour, place 1½ teaspoons baking powder and ½ teaspoon salt in a measuring cup. Add all-purpose flour to measure 1 cup.*

Queso Baked Nachos

I modified a nachos recipe I found, and my family loves it! It is now a regular at our dinner table.

—DENISE WHEELER NEWAYGO, MI

START TO FINISH: 25 MIN. • **MAKES:** 12 SERVINGS

- **1 pound ground beef**
- **1 enevelope taco seasoning**
- **¾ cup water**
- **1 package (13 ounces) tortilla chips**
- **1 cup refried beans**
- **1 jar (15½ ounces) salsa con queso dip**
- **2 plum tomatoes, chopped**
- **½ cup sour cream**
- **¼ cup minced fresh chives, optional**

1. In a large skillet, cook beef over medium heat 6-8 minutes or until no longer pink, breaking into crumbles; drain. Stir in taco seasoning and water. Bring to a boil. Reduce heat; simmer, uncovered, 3-5 minutes or until thickened, stirring occasionally.

2. In an ungreased 13x9-in. baking dish, layer a third of each of the following: tortilla chips, beans, meat mixture and queso dip. Repeat layers twice.

3. Bake, uncovered, 10-15 minutes or until heated through. Top with tomatoes, sour cream and, if desired, chives. Serve immediately.

Friends don't let friends have "just another birthday." The gesture of preparing a beautiful cake from scratch goes a long way in letting someone know you care. After all, the best gifts come in edible packages—and even better if that package is wrapped in sweet orange-spiked cream cheese frosting and garnished with a hint of thyme. Because these aren't your ordinary cakes—these are the cakes you make once a year to celebrate life, honor traditions and cherish unforgettable moments. So strap on your apron and get out the mixing bowl. You're about to make someone's birthday wish come true.

Three-Layered Carrot Cake (p. 222)

BIRTHDAY **CAKES**

Banana Pecan Cake with Coconut Frosting

One of my brothers always requested this banana cake for his birthday. When my mom entered the cake recipe in a county fair contest, she won the blue ribbon!
—EDNA HOFFMAN HEBRON, IN

PREP: 45 MIN. + CHILLING • **BAKE:** 25 MIN. + COOLING • **MAKES:** 12 SERVINGS

- **⅔ cup shortening**
- **1⅔ cups sugar**
- **2 eggs**
- **1½ cups mashed ripe bananas (about 3 medium)**
- **2½ cups cake flour**
- **1¼ teaspoons baking powder**
- **1 teaspoon salt**
- **½ teaspoon baking soda**
- **⅔ cup buttermilk**
- **⅔ cup chopped pecans**

FILLING

- **½ cup sugar**
- **2 tablespoons all-purpose flour**
- **¼ teaspoon salt**
- **½ cup heavy whipping cream**
- **2 tablespoons butter**
- **1 teaspoon vanilla extract**
- **½ cup chopped pecans**

FROSTING

- **6 tablespoons shortening**
- **6 tablespoons butter, softened**
- **¾ teaspoon vanilla extract**
- **½ teaspoon coconut extract**
- **3 cups confectioners' sugar**
- **3 to 5 tablespoons heavy whipping cream**

1. Preheat oven to 350°. Line bottoms of two greased 9-in. round baking pans with parchment paper; grease paper.
2. In a large bowl, cream shortening and sugar until light and fluffy. Add eggs, one at a time, beating well after each addition. Beat in bananas. (Mixture may appear curdled.) In another bowl, whisk flour, baking powder, salt and baking soda; add to creamed mixture alternately with milk, beating well after each addition. Fold in pecans.
3. Transfer batter to prepared pans. Bake 25-30 minutes or until a toothpick inserted in center comes out clean. Cool in pans 10 minutes before removing to wire racks; remove paper. Cool completely.
4. For filling, in a large saucepan, mix sugar, flour and salt. Whisk in cream. Cook and stir over medium heat until thickened and bubbly. Reduce heat to low; cook and stir 2 minutes longer. Remove from heat. Stir in butter and vanilla. Transfer to a small bowl. Press plastic wrap onto surface of mixture. Refrigerate until cold.
5. For frosting, in a large bowl, beat shortening, butter and extracts until blended. Beat in confectioners' sugar alternately with cream, adding enough cream to reach desired consistency; beat until smooth.
6. Stir pecans into chilled cream mixture. Place one cake layer on a serving plate; spread with filling. Top with remaining cake layer. Frost top and sides of cake. Refrigerate until serving.

MAKE A BETTER CAKE WITH THESE HELPFUL POINTERS

Most cakes call for creaming the fat and sugar together. Use an electric mixer for about 5 minutes or until the mixture is fluffy. Before you add your eggs, make sure they're at room temperature. This will give the batter better volume. When mixing wet batter with dry ingredients, remember to stop occasionally to scrape down the sides of the bowl. When baking, use aluminum pans with a dull rather than shiny or dark finish to get a tender, golden crust. If using glass baking dishes, reduce the oven temperature by 25°. Allow the cakes to cool in the pans for 10 minutes before removing and let them cool completely before frosting.

Chocolate-Cherry Brownie Cake

My grandmother taught me the tricks to making this cake, and I've added my own special touches. The melted chocolate keeps the icing from being too dry and gives it a texture similar to chocolate ice cream. I have more requests for the icing than I do anything else!

—SUSAN HAYES MASSAPEQUA, NY

PREP: 45 MIN.
BAKE: 1 HOUR + COOLING
MAKES: 12 SERVINGS

- **1¼ cups shortening**
- **2¾ cups sugar**
- **5 eggs**
- **4 ounces semisweet chocolate, melted and cooled**
- **1 teaspoon cherry extract**
- **1 teaspoon vanilla extract**
- **3 cups all-purpose flour**
- **½ teaspoon salt**
- **½ teaspoon baking powder**
- **1 cup heavy whipping cream**

CHOCOLATE CHERRIES

- **1 jar (10 ounces) maraschino cherries with stems**
- **4 ounces semisweet chocolate, chopped**
- **1 tablespoon shortening**

FROSTING

- **1 cup butter, softened**
- **2 ounces semisweet chocolate, melted and cooled**
- **1 teaspoon cherry extract**
- **1 teaspoon vanilla extract**
- **3¾ to 4 cups confectioners' sugar**

1. Preheat oven to 350°. Grease and flour a 10-in. fluted tube pan.

2. In a large bowl, cream shortening and sugar until light and fluffy. Add eggs, one at a time, beating well after each addition. Beat in melted chocolate and extracts. In another bowl, whisk flour, salt and baking powder; add to creamed mixture alternately with cream, beating well after each addition.

3. Transfer batter to prepared pan. Bake 60-70 minutes or until a toothpick inserted in center comes out with moist crumbs (do not overbake). Cool in pan for 10 minutes before removing to a wire rack to cool completely.

4. Drain cherries, reserving 3 tablespoons juice for frosting; pat cherries dry with paper towels. In a microwave, melt chocolate and shortening; stir until smooth. Dip cherries in chocolate mixture; allow excess to drip off. Place on waxed paper; let stand until set.

5. For frosting, in a large bowl, beat butter until creamy. Add melted chocolate and extracts. Beat in confectioners' sugar alternately with reserved cherry juice, adding enough confectioners' sugar to reach desired consistency; beat until smooth. Frost cake. Serve with chocolate cherries.

NOTE *To remove cakes easily, use solid shortening to grease plain and fluted tube pans.*

Chocolate & Grand Marnier Cake

I was running out of ideas on what to make for a friend for her upcoming 50th, so I made this cake and she was ecstatic. I knew that after dinner she enjoyed a glass of milk with an ounce of Grand Marnier mixed in, so what better way to surprise her than with this decadent birthday cake?

—LORRAINE CALAND SHUNIAH, ON

PREP: 50 MIN. + CHILLING • **BAKE:** 25 MIN. + COOLING • **MAKES:** 12 SERVINGS

½ cup butter, softened
1⅔ cups sugar
3 eggs
1 teaspoon vanilla extract
1¾ cups all-purpose flour
½ cup baking cocoa
1 teaspoon salt
1 teaspoon baking soda
½ teaspoon baking powder
1⅓ cups water

WHIPPED CREAM

2½ cups heavy whipping cream
⅓ cup confectioners' sugar

FILLING

1 envelope unflavored gelatin
¾ cup thawed frozen orange juice concentrate
¾ cup sugar
½ cup Grand Marnier, divided
3 tablespoons grated orange peel

1. Preheat oven to 350°. Line bottoms of two greased 8-in. round baking pans with parchment paper; grease paper.

2. In a large bowl, beat butter and sugar until crumbly. Add eggs, one at a time, beating well after each addition. Beat in vanilla. In another bowl, whisk flour, baking cocoa, salt, baking soda and baking powder; add to creamed mixture alternately with water, beating well after each addition.

3. Transfer batter to prepared pans. Bake 25-30 minutes or until a toothpick inserted in center comes out clean. Cool in pans 10 minutes before removing to wire racks; remove paper. Cool completely.

4. In a chilled large bowl, beat cream until it begins to thicken. Add confectioners' sugar; beat until soft peaks form. Refrigerate, covered, 1 hour or until very cold.

5. For filling, in a small saucepan, sprinkle gelatin over orange juice concentrate; let stand 1 minute. Stir in sugar. Heat and stir over low heat until gelatin is completely dissolved. Stir in ¼ cup Grand Marnier and orange peel. Let filling stand at room temperature just until spreadable, stirring occasionally. (If mixture becomes too firm, warm in microwave to soften, about 10-15 seconds.)

6. Meanwhile, using a long serrated knife, cut each cake horizontally in half. Brush layers with remaining Grand Marnier. Place one cake layer on a serving plate; spread with one-third of the filling. Repeat twice. Top with remaining cake layer.

7. To frost cake, cut a hole in tip of a pastry bag or in a corner of a food-safe plastic bag and insert #829 or other large star pastry tip. Gently stir whipped cream; spoon into bag and pipe onto top and sides of cake. Refrigerate at least 4 hours before serving.

CHOCOLATE & GRAND MARNIER GELATIN LAYERS

1. Sprinkle gelatin over the thawed orange juice. Make sure the gelatin doesn't have any clumps, or it won't properly dissolve. Allow to stand 1 minute before adding sugar and heating.

2. After stirring in Grand Marnier and orange peel, let it stand at room temperature just until spreadable. If the mixture sits too long, it will become too firm to work with.

White Chocolate Cake with Peaches

Topped with a to-die-for white chocolate frosting, this cake looks and tastes like a professional made it. I like to make it every summer when fresh peaches are at their peak.

—YVONNE STARLIN HERMITAGE, TN

PREP: 50 MIN. + CHILLING • **BAKE:** 25 MIN. + COOLING • **MAKES:** 16 SERVINGS

- **8 ounces white baking chocolate, chopped**
- **10 tablespoons unsalted butter, softened**
- **1⅓ cups sugar**
- **4 eggs**
- **1½ teaspoons vanilla extract**
- **2¼ cups cake flour**
- **2¼ teaspoons baking powder**
- **¼ teaspoon salt**
- **1¼ cups whole milk**

FROSTING

- **20 ounces white baking chocolate, chopped**
- **1¾ cups unsalted butter, cubed**
- **2 teaspoons vanilla extract**
- **2 cups confectioners' sugar**

ASSEMBLY

- **½ cup water**
- **¼ cup sugar**
- **4 cups sliced peeled fresh or frozen peaches, thawed (about 1 pound)**
- **¼ cup peach preserves, warmed**
- **1 cup finely chopped walnuts**

1. Preheat oven to 350°. Line bottoms of two greased 9-in. round baking pans with parchment paper; grease paper. In top of a double boiler or a metal bowl over hot water, melt white chocolate; stir until smooth. Remove from heat.

2. In a large bowl, cream butter and sugar until light and fluffy. Add eggs, one at a time, beating well after each addition. Beat in vanilla. In another bowl, whisk flour, baking powder and salt; add to creamed mixture alternately with milk, beating well after each addition. Stir in melted chocolate.

3. Transfer batter to prepared pans. Bake 25-30 minutes or until a toothpick inserted in the center comes out clean. Cool in pans for 10 minutes before removing to wire racks; remove paper. Cool completely.

4. For frosting, in top of a double boiler or a metal bowl over hot water, melt white chocolate; stir until smooth. Remove from heat; let stand to cool slightly but not set, about 15 minutes. In a large bowl, beat butter and vanilla until blended. Gradually beat in melted chocolate. Gradually add confectioners' sugar, beating until smooth. Refrigerate frosting for 45 minutes.

5. In a small saucepan, bring water and sugar to a boil over medium heat, stirring to dissolve sugar. Cool completely.

6. Using a long serrated knife, cut each cake horizontally in half. Place one cake layer on a serving plate; brush with some of the syrup. Beat chilled frosting 1-2 minutes or until light and creamy. Spread 1 cup frosting over cake; top with 1 cup of peaches. Repeat twice. Top with remaining cake layer. Frost top and sides of cake with the remaining frosting.

7. Arrange remaining peaches over top of cake; brush with preserves. Gently press walnuts into frosting on sides of cake. Store in refrigerator.

Three-Layered Carrot Cake

PICTURED ON PAGE 217

My mom loved carrots so much, she put them in various dishes at least five times a week when I was growing up. Her specialty was a homemade carrot cake that was requested for every special occasion. When I made this for her 70th birthday, she was so happy she cried.

—**PAULA MARCHESI** LENHARTSVILLE, PA

PREP: 1 HOUR + COOLING • **BAKE:** 20 MIN. + COOLING • **MAKES:** 16 SERVINGS

- **6 eggs, separated**
- **2¼ cups all-purpose flour**
- **1 teaspoon baking soda**
- **½ teaspoon salt**
- **⅔ cup orange juice**
- **⅓ cup sour cream**
- **1½ cups butter, softened**
- **1½ cups sugar**
- **½ cup packed brown sugar**
- **1 teaspoon grated orange peel**
- **1½ teaspoons minced fresh thyme, optional**
- **2 cups finely shredded carrots (about 4 medium)**
- **1 cup chopped pecans**

FROSTING

- **2 packages (8 ounces each) cream cheese, softened**
- **1 tablespoon grated orange peel**
- **1 tablespoon orange juice**
- **8 to 8¼ cups confectioners' sugar**

1. Place egg whites in a small bowl; let stand at room temperature 30 minutes. Preheat oven to 350°. Line bottoms of three greased 8-in.-square baking pans with parchment paper; grease paper.

2. In another bowl, whisk flour, baking soda and salt. In a small bowl, whisk orange juice and sour cream. In a large bowl, cream butter, sugars and orange peel until light and fluffy. Add egg yolks, one at a time, beating well after each addition. If desired, beat in thyme. Add flour mixture alternately with orange juice mixture, beating well after each addition.

3. With clean beaters, beat egg whites on medium speed until stiff peaks form. Fold into batter. Gently fold in shredded carrots and pecans.

4. Transfer to prepared pans. Bake 20-25 minutes or until a toothpick inserted in center comes out clean. Cool in pans for 10 minutes before removing to wire racks; remove paper. Cool completely.

5. For frosting, in a large bowl, beat the cream cheese, orange peel and juice until blended. Gradually beat in enough confectioners' sugar to reach the desired consistency.

6. Spread frosting between layers and over top and sides of cake. Refrigerate until serving.

TO DECORATE CAKE WITH CARROT RIBBONS...

Use a vegetable peeler to shave one large carrot into long ribbon-like strips. Reserve some of the longest strips for the sides of cake; roll up remaining strips to make curls for the bow. Arrange long and rolled-up strips on a paper towel-lined baking sheet; let dry 30-40 minutes before placing on cake. Decorate frosted cake with carrot ribbons just before serving. If desired, add fresh sprigs of thyme for added color.

Mocha Hazelnut Torte

I make this cake on special occasions and birthdays because it's so amazing in appearance and taste. The mild hazelnut and coffee flavor combination is impossible to resist and definitely adds to the overall deliciousness of the cake.

—**CHRISTINA POPE** SPEEDWAY, IN

PREP: 35 MIN.
BAKE: 25 MIN. + COOLING
MAKES: 16 SERVINGS

- **¾ cup butter, softened**
- **1¼ cups packed brown sugar**
- **1 cup sugar**
- **3 eggs**
- **3 ounces unsweetened chocolate, melted and cooled slightly**
- **2 teaspoons vanilla extract**
- **2¼ cups all-purpose flour**
- **1 tablespoon instant espresso powder**
- **1 teaspoon baking soda**
- **½ teaspoon baking powder**
- **¼ teaspoon salt**
- **1½ cups 2% milk**

FROSTING

- **1 cup butter, softened**
- **1 cup Nutella**
- **4 cups confectioners' sugar**
- **1 teaspoon vanilla extract**
- **3 to 4 tablespoons 2% milk**
- **½ cup chopped hazelnuts, toasted**

1. Preheat oven to 350°. Line bottoms of two greased 9-in. round baking pans with parchment paper; grease paper.

2. In a large bowl, cream butter and sugars until light and fluffy. Add eggs, one at a time, beating well after each addition. Beat in melted chocolate and vanilla. In another bowl, whisk flour, espresso powder, baking soda, baking powder and salt; add to creamed mixture alternately with milk, beating well after each addition.

3. Transfer batter to prepared pans. Bake 25-30 minutes or until a toothpick inserted in center comes out clean. Cool in pans 10 minutes before removing to wire racks; remove paper. Cool completely.

4. For frosting, in a large bowl, beat butter and Nutella until blended. Gradually beat in confectioners' sugar, vanilla and enough milk to reach the desired consistency.

5. Place one cake layer on a serving plate; spread with 1 cup frosting. Sprinkle with ¼ cup hazelnuts. Top with remaining cake layer. Frost top and sides with remaining frosting. Sprinkle with remaining hazelnuts.

NOTE *To toast nuts, spread in a 15x10x1-in. baking pan. Bake at 350° for 5-10 minutes or until lightly browned, stirring occasionally. Or, spread in a dry nonstick skillet and heat over low heat until lightly browned, stirring occasionally.*

Amaretto Cake with Buttercream Frosting

I came up with this recipe because I was craving something that tasted like wedding cake. The texture is similar to pound cake, which is exactly what I wanted. Everyone who tastes it LOVES it.
—MEGAN DUDASH YOUNGSVILLE, NC

PREP: 45 MIN.
BAKE: 30 MIN. + COOLING
MAKES: 16 SERVINGS

3½ cups all-purpose flour
1 teaspoon baking powder
½ cup sour cream
½ cup 2% milk
½ cup amaretto
1 cup butter, softened
½ cup shortening
3 cups sugar
6 eggs
2 teaspoons almond extract
1 teaspoon vanilla extract

BUTTERCREAM

1⅓ cups butter, softened
1 teaspoon vanilla extract
½ teaspoon salt
7½ to 8 cups confectioners' sugar
⅔ cup amaretto
Optional decorations: toasted sliced almonds, milk chocolate M&M's and melted chocolate

1. Preheat oven to 325°. Line bottoms of three greased 9-in. round baking pans with parchment paper; grease paper.

2. In a bowl, whisk flour and baking powder. In another bowl, whisk sour cream, milk and amaretto until blended. In a large bowl, cream butter, shortening and sugar until light and fluffy. Add eggs, one at a time, beating well after each addition. Beat in the extracts. Add flour mixture alternately with sour cream mixture, beating well after each addition.

3. Transfer batter to prepared pans. Bake 30-35 minutes or until a toothpick inserted in center comes out clean. Cool in pans 10 minutes before removing to wire racks; remove paper. Cool completely.

4. In a large bowl, beat butter, vanilla and salt until creamy. Beat in enough confectioners' sugar, alternately with amaretto, to reach desired consistency. Reserve 2⁄3 cup of frosting for the piping.

5. Place one cake layer on a serving plate; spread with 1⁄2 cup frosting. Top with remaining cake layer. Frost top and sides with remaining frosting.

6. Pipe reserved frosting around bottom edge of cake. If desired, decorate the cake with flowers, using almonds for petals and M&M's for the centers. Pipe designs on frosting with melted chocolate as desired.

NOTE *To toast nuts, spread in a 15x10x1-in. baking pan. Bake at 350° for 5-10 minutes or until lightly browned, stirring occasionally. Or, spread in a dry nonstick skillet and heat over low heat until lightly browned, stirring occasionally.*

German Black Forest Cake

As far as I know, this cake recipe can be traced back to my German great-grandma. When I got married, my mother gave me a copy, and I hope to someday pass it down to my children.
—STEPHANIE TRAVIS FALLON, NV

PREP: 45 MIN. + COOLING • **BAKE:** 30 MIN. + COOLING • **MAKES:** 12 SERVINGS

- **1 cup whole milk**
- **3 eggs**
- **½ cup canola oil**
- **3 teaspoons vanilla extract**
- **2 cups plus 2 tablespoons all-purpose flour**
- **2 cups sugar**
- **¾ cup baking cocoa**
- **1½ teaspoons baking powder**
- **¾ teaspoon baking soda**
- **¾ teaspoon salt**

FILLING

- **2 cans (14½ ounces each) pitted tart cherries**
- **1 cup sugar**
- **¼ cup cornstarch**
- **3 tablespoons cherry brandy or 2 teaspoons vanilla extract**

WHIPPED CREAM

- **3 cups heavy whipping cream**
- **⅓ cup confectioners' sugar**

1. Preheat oven to 350°. Line bottoms of two greased 9-in. round baking pans; grease paper.

2. In a large bowl, beat milk, eggs, oil and vanilla until well blended. In another bowl, whisk flour, sugar, cocoa, baking powder, baking soda and salt; gradually beat into milk mixture.

3. Transfer to prepared pans. Bake 30-35 minutes or until a toothpick inserted in center comes out clean. Cool in pans for 10 minutes before removing to wire racks; remove paper. Cool completely.

4. Meanwhile, for filling, drain cherries, reserving 1/2 cup juice. In a small saucepan, whisk sugar, cornstarch and reserved juice; add cherries. Cook and stir over low heat 10-12 minutes or until thickened and bubbly. Remove from heat; stir in brandy. Cool completely.

5. In a large bowl, beat cream until it begins to thicken. Add confectioners' sugar; beat until stiff peaks form.

6. Using a long serrated knife, cut each cake horizontally in half. Place one cake layer on a serving plate. Top with 1½ cups whipped cream. Spread 3/4 cup filling to within 1 in. of edge. Repeat twice. Top with remaining cake layer. Frost top and sides of cake with remaining whipped cream, reserving some to pipe decorations, if desired. Spoon remaining filling onto top of cake. Refrigerate until serving.

NOT TO BE CONFUSED WITH GERMAN CHOCOLATE

The heavily wooded Black Forest region of Germany may be the backdrop for many fairy tales, but it's also known for the production of sweet cherry brandy—called *Kirschwasser*. Because the German dessert above is traditionally made with this flavored liqueur, it was named Black Forest Cake. German Chocolate Cake, on the other hand, was named after the type of chocolate used in a recipe that appeared in the *Dallas Morning Star* in 1957. The cake recipe featured a rich coconut-pecan frosting and called for German chocolate, a type of baking chocolate developed by Sam German, an American.

An ode to the classics, hosting a vintage Halloween party is a playful way to enjoy the fun treats you looked forward to as a kid—the popcorn balls, the pumpkin ice cream, homemade caramel apples and candies. Celebrate an era when costumes were made with scissors and old sheets and Mom dressed in her annual witch costume to pass out candy. Cardboard black cats hung as decoration and pumpkins lit up the entryway.

This year, put your witchcraft to good use with a decoupage project (p. 235) that will dress up your party decor for the vintage occasion.

Witch's Snack Hats (p. 228)
Chocolate Candy Corn Cupcakes (p. 233)
Candy Corn & Peanut Popcorn Balls (p. 231)
Caramel Lollipops (p. 234)

VINTAGE **HALLOWEEN**

Witch's Snack Hats

PICTURED ON PAGE 226

These treats always go over well at parties, and they're guaranteed to be a hit at Halloween.
—**MARY ANN DELL** PHOENIXVILLE, PA

PREP: 50 MIN. + STANDING • **BAKE:** 10 MIN. + COOLING • **MAKES:** 16 SERVINGS

- **1 tube (16½ ounces) refrigerated sugar cookie dough**
- **¼ cup baking cocoa**
- **1 cup Corn Pops**
- **1 cup bite-sized Shredded Wheat**
- **1 cup square oat cereal**
- **½ cup dried cherries**
- **½ cup salted pumpkin seeds or pepitas, optional**
- **⅓ cup butter, cubed**
- **2 cups (12 ounces) semisweet chocolate chips, divided**
- **1⅓ cups confectioners' sugar**
- **1 tablespoon shortening**
- **16 ice cream sugar cones**
- **Orange and green sprinkles**

1. Preheat oven to 350°. Let cookie dough stand at room temperature for 5-10 minutes to soften. In a large bowl, beat cookie dough and cocoa until blended. Shape into 1½-in. balls; place 3 in. apart on ungreased baking sheets. Coat bottom of a glass with cooking spray. Press cookies with bottom of glass to flatten, recoating glass with cooking spray as needed.

2. Bake 10-12 minutes or until set. Cool completely on pans on wire racks.

3. In a large bowl, combine corn pops, Shredded Wheat, oat cereal, cherries and, if desired, pumpkin seeds. In a microwave, melt butter and ½ cup chocolate chips; stir until smooth. Pour over cereal mixture; toss to coat.

4. Place confectioners' sugar in a large resealable plastic bag; add cereal mixture. Close bag and shake to coat. Spread onto baking sheets to cool.

5. In a microwave, melt shortening and remaining chocolate chips; stir until smooth. Spread over sugar cones. Freeze until set, about 10 minutes. Fill each cone with 2 tablespoons cereal mixture.

6. Place a filled cone on each cookie; pipe melted chocolate around base of cones to adhere. Decorate as desired with sprinkles and remaining melted chocolate. Refrigerate until set, about 10 minutes. Serve with remaining cereal mixture.

Monster Munch

This sweet-salty snack is a favorite of mine because it can be adapted to any holiday, depending on the ingredients I decide to mix in.
—**PAM KENNEDY** LUBBOCK, TX

PREP: 15 MIN. + STANDING • **MAKES:** ABOUT 1½ POUNDS

- **12 ounces white candy coating, chopped**
- **Orange paste food coloring**
- **2 cups Golden Grahams**
- **1½ cups pretzel sticks**
- **¾ cup miniature marshmallows**
- **¾ cup milk chocolate M&M's**
- **2 tablespoons chocolate sprinkles**

1. In a large microwave-safe bowl, melt candy coating; stir until smooth. Tint with food coloring. Stir in cereal, pretzels, marshmallows and M&M's. Immediately spread onto a waxed paper-lined baking sheet; top with sprinkles.

2. Let stand 1 hour or until set. Break into pieces. Store in an airtight container.

Caramel Apple Donut Muffins

Welcome autumn and Halloween into your kitchen with these muffins. The recipe will remind you of cinnamon-sugar cake donuts.
—JULIE RUBLE CHARLOTTE, NC

PREP: 50 MIN. • **BAKE:** 15 MIN.
MAKES: 4 DOZEN
(SCANT 1 CUP SAUCE)

- **1½ cups all-purpose flour**
- **¾ cup sugar**
- **2 teaspoons baking powder**
- **¼ teaspoon salt**
- **¼ teaspoon ground nutmeg**
- **1 egg**
- **¾ cup 2% milk**
- **¼ cup canola oil**
- **1 teaspoon vanilla extract**
- **1 medium apple, peeled and finely chopped (about 1 cup)**

CARAMEL SAUCE

- **¾ cup sugar**
- **2 tablespoons water**
- **½ cup heavy whipping cream, warmed**
- **2 tablespoons creme fraiche or sour cream**
- **¼ teaspoon vanilla extract**
- **⅛ teaspoon salt**

COATING

- **⅓ cup sugar**
- **1 tablespoon ground cinnamon**
- **3 tablespoons butter, melted**

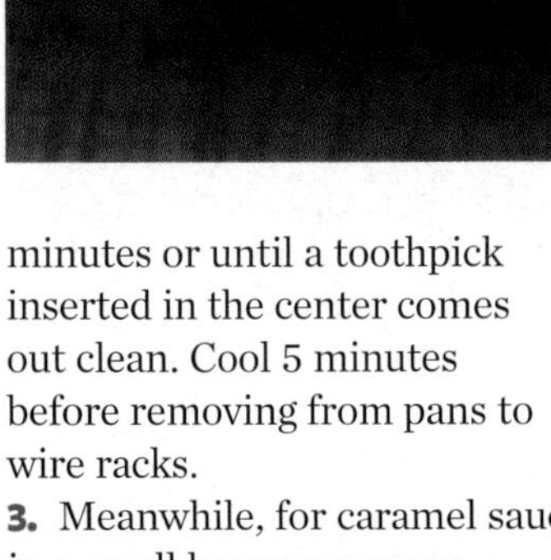

1. Preheat oven to 350°. In a large bowl, whisk flour, sugar, baking powder, salt and nutmeg. In another bowl, whisk egg, milk, oil and vanilla until blended. Add to flour mixture; stir just until moistened. Fold in apple.

2. Fill greased mini-muffin cups three-fourths full. Bake 15-17 minutes or until a toothpick inserted in the center comes out clean. Cool 5 minutes before removing from pans to wire racks.

3. Meanwhile, for caramel sauce, in a small heavy saucepan, combine sugar and water; stir gently to moisten all the sugar. Cook over medium heat, gently swirling pan occasionally, until syrup turns a medium amber color, about 8-10 minutes.

4. Remove from heat; gradually stir in warm cream. Transfer to a small bowl; place bowl in an ice-water bath, stirring frequently until cooled, about 5 minutes. Remove bowl from ice water. Whisk in creme fraiche, vanilla and salt.

5. For coating, combine sugar and cinnamon. Dip tops of warm muffins in butter, then coat in cinnamon-sugar. Serve muffins with caramel sauce.

Halloween Black Cat Cookies

I show my students how to make these cookies every Halloween. They usually want to eat them all on the spot!
—**TRICIA BIBB** HARTSELLE, AL

PREP: 25 MIN. • **BAKE:** 10 MIN./BATCH • **MAKES:** 2½ DOZEN

- **1 cup chunky peanut butter**
- **2 eggs**
- **⅓ cup water**
- **1 package chocolate cake mix (regular size)**
- **Sugar**
- **90 M&M's minis (about 2 tablespoons)**
- **60 pieces black licorice (¾ inch)**

1. Preheat oven to 375°. In a large bowl, beat peanut butter, eggs and water until blended. Gradually beat in cake mix.

2. Shape into 1½-in. balls; place 2 in. apart on greased baking sheets. Flatten with a glass dipped in sugar. Pinch top of cookie to form ears.

3. Bake 10-12 minutes or until set and bottoms are lightly browned. Remove from oven; immediately press on M&M's for eyes and noses. Insert licorice for whiskers. Remove to wire racks to cool.

Tarantula Treats

We host a Halloween party every year where guests are treated to "terrifying" edible tarantulas. In only a few minutes, you can have perfectly spooky treats for a crowd.
—**CHARLES INSLER** SILVER SPRING, MD

PREP: 45 MIN. • **MAKES:** 20 SERVINGS

- **6 cups Cocoa Krispies**
- **1 package (10 ounces) large marshmallows**
- **3 tablespoons butter**
- **Black shoestring licorice**
- **Green decorating gel**
- **Candy corn**

1. Place Cocoa Krispies in a large bowl. In a large saucepan, combine marshmallows and butter. Cook and stir over medium-low heat until melted. Pour over Cocoa Krispies; mix well. Cool slightly.

2. With greased hands, shape by ¼ cupfuls into 20 balls and by tablespoonfuls into 20 more balls. Attach two different-sized balls to make spider bodies.

3. With a bamboo skewer or toothpick, poke four holes on each side of spider bodies for inserting legs. Cut licorice into 2-inch pieces; insert into each hole. Draw eyes on head with gel. Cut white portion off candy corn for fangs; attach with gel. Serve the same day for best texture or store in airtight containers.

Candy Corn & Peanut Popcorn Balls

PICTURED ON PAGE 227

My daughter and I enjoy baking and cooking together, and this recipe is one she can help make and then share at school.

—KIM SHIREMAN SEARCY, AR

PREP: 15 MIN.
COOK: 5 MIN. + STANDING
MAKES: 1 DOZEN

- 3 **packages (3.3 ounces each) butter-flavored microwave popcorn**
- 1 **package (18½ ounces) candy corn**
- 1 **jar (16 ounces) dry roasted peanuts, coarsely chopped**
- 1 **package (10½ ounces) miniature marshmallows**
- ½ **cup butter, cubed**
- 2 **tablespoons canola oil**
- 1 **teaspoon vanilla extract**

1. Cook popcorn according to package directions; place in a large bowl. Add candy corn and peanuts; mix well.

2. In a large saucepan, combine marshmallows, butter and oil. Cook and stir over medium-low heat until melted. Stir in vanilla. Pour over popcorn mixture; mix well. Cool slightly.

3. With greased hands, shape mixture into 12 popcorn balls, about 2⅓ cups each. Place on waxed paper; let stand until set.

Autumn Tree Cake

You can decorate this special cake any way you like for Halloween or the colorful fall months.
—MARIE PARKER MILWAUKEE, WI

PREP: 40 MIN.
BAKE: 20 MIN. + COOLING
MAKES: 12 SERVINGS

- **1 package butter recipe golden cake mix (regular size)**
- **1 cup orange juice**
- **⅓ cup butter, softened**
- **3 eggs**

FROSTING

- **6 cups confectioners' sugar**
- **⅔ cup butter, softened**
- **Orange food coloring, optional**
- **5 to 6 tablespoons orange juice**
- **½ cup crushed chocolate wafers (about 8 wafers)**
- **1 cup (6 ounces) semisweet chocolate chips**
- **1 tablespoon shortening**
- **Assorted candy and chocolate leaves**

1. Preheat oven to 350°. Line bottoms of two greased 9-in. round baking pans with parchment paper; grease paper. In a large bowl, combine cake mix, orange juice, butter and eggs; beat on low speed for 30 seconds. Beat on medium 2 minutes. Transfer to prepared pan. Bake 20-25 minutes or until a toothpick inserted in center comes out clean. Cool in the pans for 10 minutes before removing to wire racks; remove paper. Cool completely.

2. For frosting, in a large bowl, beat confectioners' sugar, butter, food coloring if desired, and enough orange juice to achieve desired consistency. Spread frosting between layers and over top and sides of cake. Lightly press wafer crumbs onto sides of cake.

3. In a microwave-safe bowl, melt chocolate and shortening; stir until smooth. Transfer to a pastry bag or a food-safe plastic bag; cut a small hole in the tip of bag. Pipe a tree on top of cake. Decorate as desired with candy and chocolate leaves.

Pumpkin Milk Shakes

My son loved this festive milkshake growing up—it's nicely spiced and tastes like pumpkin pie. I like cutting off both ends of a licorice twist and serving it as a straw.
—JOAN HALLFORD NORTH RICHLAND HILLS, TX

START TO FINISH: 10 MIN. • **MAKES:** 6 SERVINGS

- **1 cup orange juice**
- **4 cups vanilla ice cream**
- **1 cup canned pumpkin**
- **½ cup packed brown sugar**
- **1 teaspoon ground cinnamon**
- **½ teaspoon ground ginger**
- **½ teaspoon ground nutmeg**
- **Black licorice twists, optional**

In batches, place the first seven ingredients in a blender. Cover and process 20-30 seconds or until smooth. Serve immediately with licorice stirrers if desired.

Chocolate Candy Corn Cupcakes

PICTURED ON PAGE 227

My oldest son asks me to make these cupcakes every year for his class Halloween party. I always get compliments about how tasty and cute these treats are.
—NICOLE CLAYTON PRESCOTT, AZ

PREP: 25 MIN. • **BAKE:** 20 MIN. + COOLING • **MAKES:** 2 DOZEN

- **1 package fudge marble cake mix (regular size)**
- **1 cup (8 ounces) sour cream**
- **2 eggs**
- **½ cup 2% milk**
- **⅓ cup canola oil**
- **Orange paste food coloring**
- **1 carton (8 ounces) frozen whipped topping, thawed**
- **Chocolate candy corn**

1. Line 24 muffin cups with paper liners.
2. In a large bowl, combine the first five ingredients; beat on low speed for 30 seconds. Beat on medium for 2 minutes. Transfer half of batter to a small bowl; tint with food coloring. To the other half of batter, mix in contents of cocoa packet.
3. Divide chocolate batter among prepared cups. Carefully top with orange batter; do not swirl. Bake and cool as package directs. Top cupcakes with whipped topping and candy corn. Refrigerate leftovers.

TWO-TONED TREATS

This colorful method of layering different colors of cake batter into muffin cups can be used to make festive treats for all occasions. Instead of using fudge marble cake, you can use yellow or white cake mix. Divide the batter in half, then color each one with the food coloring of your choice; layer and bake as directed in the Chocolate Candy Corn Cupcakes recipe.

Caramel Lollipops

PICTURED ON PAGE 227

These pops offer a fun and unique way to enjoy the sweet, toasty flavor of homemade caramel.

—KATHRYN CONRAD MILWAUKEE, WI

PREP: 15 MIN. • **COOK:** 20 MIN. • **MAKES:** 1½ DOZEN

- **1 cup sugar**
- **¼ cup water**
- **¼ cup light corn syrup**
- **½ teaspoon lemon juice**
- **¼ cup butter, cubed**
- **1 teaspoon vanilla extract**
- **18 lollipop sticks**
- **Dark or white chocolate chips, melted**

1. Line two baking sheets with foil; coat with cooking spray. In a large heavy saucepan, combine sugar, water, corn syrup and lemon juice. Bring to a boil over medium heat, about 5 minutes. Using a pastry brush dipped in water, wash down the side of the pan to eliminate sugar crystals.

2. Carefully stir in butter, one piece at a time. Cook until a candy thermometer reads 310° (hard-crack stage), stirring occasionally.

3. Remove from heat; stir in vanilla. Cool until slightly thickened, about 2-3 minutes. Coat a metal measuring tablespoon with cooking spray; drop caramel by tablespoonfuls onto prepared pans. (Reheat mixture over low heat if necessary). Immediately press a lollipop stick into the center of each.

4. Cool completely on prepared pans. Decorate as desired with melted chocolate. Refrigerate until set, about 10 minutes. Store between pieces of waxed paper in an airtight container.

NOTE *We recommend that you test your candy thermometer before each use by bringing water to a boil; the thermometer should read 212°. Adjust your recipe temperature up or down based on your test.*

Vintage Halloween Decoupage Trays

PICTURED AT RIGHT

For serving or decorating, these custom party trays double as wall hangings for creating a vintage Halloween scene.

MATERIALS

- **Decoupage glue (We used Mod Podge gloss finish.)**
- **Choice of wooden trays**
- **Fine grade sand paper and cloth**
- **Scrapbook papers or card stock to fit tray interior**
- **12-in. long tearing ruler or regular ruler (optional)**
- **Choice of acrylic paint**
- **Sponge brushes**
- **Paper plates**
- **Clear drying polyurethane sealer (optional)**

DIRECTIONS

1. Sand the trays and wipe off with clean cloth to remove dust. Then use a sponge brush to basecoat the trays in your choice of acrylic paint color. Apply as many coats as needed letting dry between each coat.

2. Cut a piece or pieces of paper or card stock to fit the interior of the tray. You can use one large piece or several overlapping pieces with varied patterns.

3. Lay the paper or card stock face down on a paper plate. Use a sponge brush to coat the back with decoupage glue. Use a dry sponge brush to press it down on the interior of the tray aligning it with the edges and removing any excess glue as you go. For multiple pieces, begin at one end of the tray and overlap pieces, gluing down one at a time until the tray interior is covered.

4. For a sealer, coat tray with a thick layer of decoupage glue and let dry. (For a waterproof sealer, use clear drying polyurethane instead.)

Vintage Halloween Decoupage Pumpkins

Oh my gourd! You don't have to gut a pumpkin to set the stage for your Halloween party. Check out how easy it is to patch your own with fun patterns and designs.

MATERIALS

- **Decoupage glue (We used Mod Podge gloss finish.)**
- **Choice of artificial pumpkin**
- **2-3 sheets each of 3 different patterned 12-in. square scrapbook papers**
- **Black or dark brown inkpad**
- **12-in. long tearing ruler or regular ruler**
- **Black or dark brown acrylic paint**
- **Sponge brushes**
- **Paper plates**
- **Clear drying polyurethane sealer (optional)**

DIRECTIONS

1. Using the tearing or regular ruler, tear 1½ to 2-in. wide strips of patterned paper.

2. Use the inkpad to rub along the edges of each strip giving the paper an aged look. Let ink dry. If needed, cut strips shorter to fit the side length of the pumpkin. Also cut a curve along one end of each strip to fit the edge of the stem.

3. Lay a strip of paper face down on a paper plate. Use a sponge brush to coat the back with decoupage glue. Beginning at the stem, adhere the strip along the edge of the pumpkin. Use a dry sponge brush to press it down as you go forming it to the curves and removing any excess glue. There may be wrinkles.

4. Repeat Step 3 overlapping strips as you go around the pumpkin. Continue until the entire pumpkin is covered and let it dry.

5. For a sealer, coat the pumpkin with a thick layer of decoupage glue and let dry. (For a waterproof sealer, use clear drying polyurethane instead.)

6. If desired, use a sponge brush to paint the stem of the pumpkin black or dark brown and let dry.

After the final furniture configuration has been settled on and the boxes have been (mostly) unpacked, it's time to break in the kitchen, meet the new neighbors and show off your digs to friends and family.

With this comforting buffet of potluck favorites, you're ready to put the stress of moving behind you and throw an inviting housewarming party that will make everyone feel at home.

HOUSEWARMING **PARTY**

Crab Rangoon Tartlets

PICTURED ON PAGE 237

Serve up this crab classic without all the hassle! These savory bites are prepared without the frying and usual mess. Plus, they don't take long to make if company drops over unexpectedly.

—DONNA MARIE RYAN
TOPSFIELD, MA

START TO FINISH: 25 MIN.
MAKES: 2½ DOZEN

- **1 carton (8 ounces) whipped cream cheese**
- **3 tablespoons sour cream onion dip**
- **⅔ cup fresh crabmeat**
- **2 packages (1.9 ounces each) frozen miniature phyllo tart shells**
- **Sweet-and-sour sauce, optional**

1. Preheat oven to 400°. In a small bowl, beat cream cheese and onion dip until blended; stir in crab. Arrange tart shells on an ungreased baking sheet. Fill with crab mixture.

2. Bake 11-13 minutes or until golden brown and heated through. If desired, serve with sweet-and-sour sauce.

Caramel Apple Cider Float

Who doesn't love the flavor of caramel, apples and vanilla ice cream together? If I'm feeling fancy, I drizzle caramel syrup around the inside of my glass before adding the apple cider and ginger ale. It's such a quick treat to serve guests.

—CINDY REAMS PHILIPSBURG, PA

START TO FINISH: 10 MIN. • **MAKES:** 2 SERVINGS

- **1 cup chilled apple cider or unsweetened apple juice**
- **1 cup chilled ginger ale or lemon-lime soda**
- **1 cup vanilla ice cream**
- **2 tablespoons caramel sundae syrup**

Divide cider and ginger ale between two glasses. Top with ice cream; drizzle with caramel syrup.

Hot Mushroom Spread

I've made this creamy, hearty mushroom appetizer for years—it's a party favorite every time. You can serve it with crostini or crackers, and it's also good to spread over flatbread.

—BARBARA PLETZKE HERNDON, VA

START TO FINISH: 25 MIN. • **MAKES:** 1½ CUPS

- **2 tablespoons butter**
- **½ pound sliced fresh mushrooms, chopped**
- **1 shallot, finely chopped**
- **1 garlic clove, minced**
- **1 package (8 ounces) cream cheese, softened**
- **4 teaspoons minced fresh oregano or 1 teaspoon dried oregano**
- **2 teaspoons Worcestershire sauce**
- **1½ teaspoons lemon juice**
- **¼ teaspoon salt**
- **¼ teaspoon pepper**
- **French bread baguette slices, toasted if desired**

1. In a large skillet, heat butter over medium-high heat. Add mushrooms and shallot; cook and stir 3-4 minutes or until tender. Add garlic; cook 1 minute longer.

2. Reduce heat to low; stir in cream cheese, oregano, Worcestershire sauce, lemon juice, salt and pepper until blended and heated through. Serve with baguette slices.

Spiced Green Tea

Cozy up with a mug of this unique blend of green tea, fruit juices and spice.

—SANDY MCKENZIE BRAHAM, MN

START TO FINISH: 25 MIN. • **MAKES:** 12 SERVINGS (1 CUP EACH)

- **5 cups water**
- **5 individual green tea bags**
- **½ cup sugar**
- **¼ teaspoon pumpkin pie spice**
- **5 cups unsweetened apple juice**
- **2 cups cranberry juice**
- **⅓ cup lemon juice**

1. In a Dutch oven, bring water to a boil; remove from heat. Add tea bags; steep, covered, 6-8 minutes according to taste.

2. Discard tea bags. Stir in sugar and pie spice until sugar is dissolved. Stir in remaining ingredients. Serve warm or chill and serve cold over ice.

STEEPING TEA

When steeping tea, it's important to note the time. Letting the tea steep for too long will produce a bitter taste. If you prefer a stronger flavor, simply add more tea, not more minutes. In general, green tea does not need to steep as long as black, oolong or herbal teas.

Bacon-Wrapped Chicken Nuggets

Chicken nuggets, bacon and teriyaki...what more could you ask for in an appetizer? Everyone who tries them asks for a copy of the recipe.
—JULIE MERRIMAN SEATTLE, WA

PREP: 45 MIN. + MARINATING • **BAKE:** 25 MIN. • **MAKES:** 4 DOZEN

- **1 cup unsweetened pineapple juice**
- **⅔ cup reduced-sodium soy sauce**
- **⅔ cup honey**
- **4 green onions, thinly sliced**
- **⅓ cup Worcestershire sauce**
- **2 tablespoons white vinegar**
- **2 tablespoons olive oil**
- **2 to 3 garlic cloves, minced**
- **2 to 3 teaspoons minced fresh gingerroot**
- **2 pounds boneless skinless chicken breasts, cut into 1-inch cubes**
- **1 pound bacon strips**
- **½ cup packed brown sugar**

1. Preheat oven to 350°. In a bowl, whisk the first nine ingredients until blended. Reserve 1½ cups mixture for sauce; cover and refrigerate. Place chicken in a large resealable plastic bag. Add remaining pineapple juice mixture; seal bag and turn to coat. Refrigerate for 1-2 hours.

2. Cut bacon strips crosswise in thirds. In a large skillet, cook bacon over medium heat until partially cooked but not crisp. Remove to paper towels to drain.

3. Drain chicken, discarding marinade. Wrap a bacon piece around each chicken cube; secure with a toothpick. Place on racks in 15x10x1-in. baking pans. Sprinkle brown sugar over tops.

4. Bake 25-30 minutes or until bacon is crisp and chicken is no longer pink. Meanwhile, in a small saucepan, bring reserved pineapple juice mixture to a boil; cook 8-10 minutes or until liquid is reduced to 1 cup. Serve nuggets with sauce.

MARINATING TIME

The savory-sweet marinade used in the Bacon-Wrapped Chicken Nuggets imparts incredible flavor to the chicken, but be careful not to let it marinate beyond the recommended time. Enzymes in the pineapple juice, called proteases, break down protein in meat. If the chicken is left too long in the pineapple mixutre, it will start to get mushy.

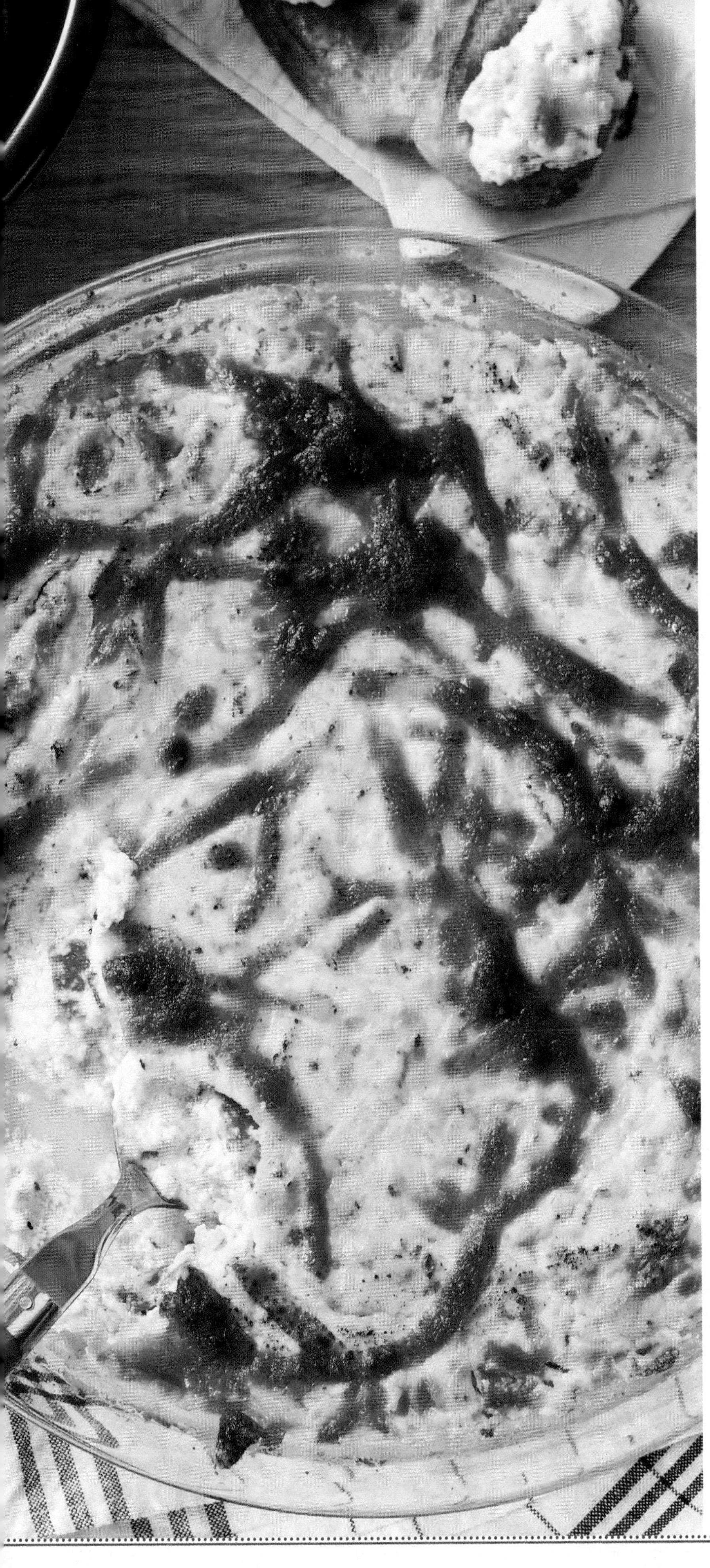

White Pizza Dip

I first served this dip during a Super Bowl party, and boy, did it disappear fast! It's a great addition to a snack table because it can be made ahead of time and refrigerated until you're ready to pop it in the oven.
—MOLLY SEIDEL EDGEWOOD, NM

PREP: 10 MIN. • **BAKE:** 35 MIN.
MAKES: 12 SERVINGS (¼ CUP EACH)

- **2 cups (16 ounces) sour cream**
- **1 cup whole-milk ricotta cheese**
- **1 cup (4 ounces) shredded part-skim mozzarella cheese, divided**
- **¼ cup chopped pepperoni**
- **1 envelope Lipton savory herb with garlic soup mix**
- **French bread baguette slices, toasted**

1. Preheat oven to 350°. In a small bowl, mix the sour cream, ricotta cheese, ¾ cup mozzarella cheese, pepperoni and soup mix until blended. Spread into a greased 9-in. pie plate. Sprinkle with remaining mozzarella cheese.
2. Bake, uncovered, for 35-40 minutes or until bubbly. Serve with baguette slices.

Roasted Garlic White Bean Dip

My version of classic hummus features white kidney or cannellini beans with lemon and garlic. Use it as a dip or a topping for bruschetta.
—**SHIRLEY SHIRLEY** ADA, OK

PREP: 50 MIN. + CHILLING • **MAKES:** 2¼ CUPS

- **1 whole garlic bulb**
- **1 teaspoon plus 3 tablespoons olive oil, divided**
- **2 cans (15 ounces each) white kidney or cannellini beans, rinsed and drained**
- **1 to 1½ teaspoons grated lemon peel**
- **2 tablespoons lemon juice**
- **1½ teaspoons Italian seasoning**
- **¾ teaspoon salt**
- **Assorted fresh vegetables**

1. Preheat oven to 425°. Remove papery outer skin from garlic bulb but do not peel or separate the cloves. Cut off top of garlic bulb, exposing individual cloves. Brush with 1 teaspoon oil. Wrap bulb in foil. Bake 30-35 minutes or until cloves are soft. Unwrap and cool 10 minutes.

2. In a food processor, combine beans, lemon peel, lemon juice, Italian seasoning, salt and remaining oil. Squeeze garlic from skins into food processor. Process until smooth. Refrigerate, covered, until cold. Serve with assorted vegetables.

Mulled Pomegranate Sipper

PICTURED ON PAGE 236

This warm, comforting cider fills the entire house with a wonderful aroma as it bubbles in the slow cooker. And guests are never disappointed when they start sipping!
—**LISA RENSHAW** KANSAS CITY, MO

PREP: 10 MIN. • **COOK:** 1 HOUR • **MAKES:** 16 SERVINGS (¾ CUP EACH)

- **1 bottle (64 ounces) cranberry-apple juice**
- **2 cups unsweetened apple juice**
- **1 cup pomegranate juice**
- **⅔ cup honey**
- **½ cup orange juice**
- **3 cinnamon sticks (3 inches)**
- **10 whole cloves**
- **2 tablespoons grated orange peel**

In a 5-qt. slow cooker, combine the first five ingredients. Place cinnamon sticks, cloves and orange peel on a double thickness of cheesecloth. Gather up corners of cloth to enclose seasonings; tie securely with string. Add to slow cooker. Cover, covered, on low 1-2 hours or until heated through. Discard spice bag.

Cranberry-Pecan Brie Cups

These appetizer cups are convenient for entertaining since you can make them ahead of time and refrigerate until you're ready to pop them in the oven. Serve them hot or at room temperature—your choice.

—TRISHA KRUSE EAGLE, ID

PREP: 25 MIN. • **BAKE:** 10 MIN.
MAKES: 2 DOZEN

24 wonton wrappers
Cooking spray
1 cup whole-berry cranberry sauce
¼ cup orange marmalade
¼ cup honey
2 tablespoons brandy
½ teaspoon ground ginger
½ teaspoon apple pie spice
½ pound Brie cheese (rind removed), cut into 24 pieces
½ cup chopped pecans

1. Preheat oven to 350°. Press wonton wrappers into miniature muffin cups coated with cooking spray. Spritz wrappers with cooking spray. Bake 6-8 minutes or until edges begin to brown.

2. Meanwhile, in a small saucepan, combine cranberry sauce, marmalade, honey, brandy and spices; heat through over medium heat, stirring frequently. Remove from heat.

3. Divide cheese among wonton cups; top with cranberry mixture. Sprinkle with pecans. Bake 8-10 minutes or until heated through and the wonton wrappers are golden brown.

Meatless Mushroom & Black Bean Chili

This bold-flavored chili is so stuffed with beans and spices that I bet no one notices the missing meat. I like to serve it with either crackers, tortilla chips, corn bread or grilled cheese sandwiches.

—FREDERICK HILLIARD
CHARLESTON, WV

PREP: 25 MIN. • **COOK:** 20 MIN.
MAKES: 8 SERVINGS (2¾ QUARTS)

- **2 tablespoons olive oil**
- **1 pound portobello mushrooms, coarsely chopped**
- **2 medium onions, chopped**
- **½ cup chopped sweet red pepper**
- **½ cup chopped green pepper**
- **3 tablespoons brown sugar**
- **2 tablespoons chili powder**
- **2 garlic cloves, minced**
- **1½ teaspoons ground cumin**
- **1 can (6 ounces) tomato paste**
- **2 cans (15 ounces each) black beans, rinsed and drained**
- **2 cans (14½ ounces each) diced tomatoes, undrained**
- **3 cups mushroom or vegetable broth**
- **¼ cup lime juice**
- **2 tablespoons minced fresh cilantro**
- **1 tablespoon minced chipotle peppers in adobo sauce**
- **1 teaspoon dried thyme**
- **1 teaspoon dried basil**
- **½ teaspoon salt**
- **½ teaspoon pepper**
- **Optional toppings: shredded Monterey Jack cheese, sour cream and chopped green onions**

1. In a Dutch oven, heat oil over medium-high heat. Add mushrooms, onions, red and green peppers, brown sugar, chili powder, garlic and cumin; cook and stir until vegetables are tender. Add tomato paste; cook and stir 3-4 minutes or until slightly caramelized.

2. Stir in beans, tomatoes, broth, lime juice, cilantro, chipotle peppers and seasonings. Bring to a boil. Reduce heat; simmer, uncovered, 8-10 minutes or until slightly thickened, stirring occasionally. Serve with toppings as desired.

Pulled Chicken Sandwiches

PICTURED ON PAGE 236

I was raised as a Southern girl with a love of barbecue built into my DNA. This slow-cooker recipe allows me to enjoy the flavors I grew up eating.
—HEIDI MULHOLLAND CUMMING, GA

PREP: 20 MIN. • **COOK:** 4 HOURS • **MAKES:** 6 SERVINGS

- **1 medium onion, finely chopped**
- **1 can (6 ounces) tomato paste**
- **¼ cup reduced-sodium chicken broth**
- **2 tablespoons brown sugar**
- **1 tablespoon cider vinegar**
- **1 tablespoon yellow mustard**
- **1 tablespoon Worcestershire sauce**
- **2 garlic cloves, minced**
- **2 teaspoons chili powder**
- **¾ teaspoon salt**
- **⅛ teaspoon cayenne pepper**
- **1½ pounds boneless skinless chicken breasts**
- **6 whole wheat hamburger buns, split**

1. In a small bowl, mix the first eleven ingredients. Place chicken in a 3-qt. slow cooker. Pour sauce over top.

2. Cook, covered, on low for 4-5 hours or until chicken is tender. Remove chicken; cool slightly. Shred meat with two forks. Return meat to slow cooker; heat through. Serve in the buns.

FREEZE LEFTOVERS

To freeze leftovers, allow chicken mixture to cool in freezer containers before placing in the freezer. To use, partially thaw in refrigerator overnight. Heat through in a saucepan, stirring occasionally and adding a little broth if necessary.

Garlic & Onion Cashews

PICTURED ON PAGE 236

You'll be set for either a quick snack or an easy hostess gift when you whip up this recipe.
—ANNDREA BAILEY HUNTINGTON BEACH, CA

PREP: 15 MIN. + COOLING • **MAKES:** 3 CUPS

- **4 teaspoons onion salt**
- **2 teaspoons sugar**
- **¾ teaspoon garlic powder**
- **2 tablespoons olive oil**
- **3 cups salted cashews**
- **2 teaspoons lemon juice**
- **4 teaspoons dried parsley flakes**

1. Mix onion salt, sugar and garlic powder. In a large skillet, heat oil over medium heat. Add cashews, seasoning mixture and lemon juice; cook and stir for 4-7 minutes or until the cashews are toasted.

2. Stir in parsley. Drain on paper towels; cool completely. Store in an airtight container.

GENERAL **RECIPE INDEX**

This index lists every recipe by food category and major ingredient.

CONDIMENTS

COOKIES & BARS

CORNISH GAME HENS

CRANBERRIES

DESSERTS

EGGS

FISH & SEAFOOD

FRUIT *(also see specific kinds)*

OATS

OLIVES

ORANGE

PASTA & NOODLES

PEPPERMINT

PEPPERS & CHILIES

PIES & TARTS

PORK

(also see Bacon; Sausage & Pepperoni)

POTATOES *(also see Sweet Potatoes)*

PUMPKIN

QUICK BREADS, COFFEE CAKES & MUFFINS

ALPHABETICAL **RECIPE INDEX**

Refer to this index for a complete alphabetical listing of all recipes in this book.

T

W

Z

SHARE YOUR **MOST-LOVED RECIPES**

Do you have a special recipe that has become part of your family's holiday tradition? Are homemade gifts and crafts included in your celebrations? We want to hear from you. To submit a recipe or craft for editorial consideration, visit **tasteofhome.com/submit.**